WORKING TOGETHER WITH
HANDICAPPED CHILDREN

HUMAN HORIZONS SERIES

WORKING TOGETHER WITH HANDICAPPED CHILDREN

Guidelines for Parents and Professionals

Edited by
MARGARET GRIFFITHS
and
PHILIPPA RUSSELL

A CONDOR BOOK
SOUVENIR PRESS (E & A) LTD

Foreword

By Dr Ronald Davie, Ph.D., F.B.Ps.S.,
Director, National Children's Bureau

As the reader will quickly see, the authorship of this book is shared by fourteen writers, who span eight different disciplines – nine if you count being the parent of a handicapped child. This multiplicity of authorship and expertise is not of itself necessarily a matter for commendation, but it is an indication of the many facets of the topic which have been considered at some depth. Fortunately, the reader can be assured that depth has not been allowed to bring obscurity and, although no attempt has been made to impose a common style on the authors, one gets a clear sense of continuity and coherence throughout the book. This is largely due to Dr Margaret Griffiths' contribution, for not only did she personally invite the co-operation of many of the authors but she also made by far the largest single contribution to both the writing and the editing. Mrs Philippa Russell, who shared the editing with Dr Griffiths, is herself the parent of a handicapped young person and was able to bring this valuable perspective, among many others, to the task.

The book – or perhaps I should say the first conception of the book – emerged from discussions in the Voluntary Council for Handicapped Children and the National Children's Bureau, to which both editors and several of the authors belong. For a number of reasons, however, the book required to be re-thought and re-structured, in consultation with a number of new authors and, of course, the Council members. The book stands out from many others in the field because of its combination of positive characteristics: it is authoritative yet readable, objective yet caring. All the individual contributors share those characteristics and the whole, being more than the sum of its parts, is in my view a most valuable addition to the literature on handicapped children.

Finally, I should like to take this opportunity to acknowledge the extremely valuable contribution of the many members of the Voluntary Council and of the Bureau who helped with support and advice along the way from the original conception through to the finished book; and also to thank the Disabilities Study Unit most warmly for a grant which primed the pump at just the right time.

Contents

Preface

During the past decade a change of attitude has taken place, both in individuals and organisations, towards the care of handicapped children. It is increasingly realised that, however good the facilities supplied by statutory or voluntary services, the brunt of the caring falls upon the parents. This perspective is reflected in the involvement of parents in the management of most schools, the respect paid to the views of parents on the education of their handicapped children and the mushrooming of schemes to help and, if necessary, train parents to help their children.

It has not always been easy for professionals to accept parents as full partners in decision-making and in implementing programmes to help the child; nor is it always easy for parents to find time during a busy day to undertake the extra activities that this new role thrusts upon them.

This book makes an attempt to examine the principles which must underlie successful support for an individual child, concentrating upon those children with special needs due to some minor or major impairment of brain functioning. The nature, cause and effect of the common handicaps are considered, and the needs for specialist and non-specialist care are outlined. No attempt is made to give 'recipes', but an extensive bibliography is included to guide readers to sources of fuller information.

We make no apology for considering different types of handicap under separate headings, because we find in practice that no professional or specialist discipline can give all the answers to one child's problems. For this reason, the authorship represents a wide range of disciplines. We all need to play our part, and we hope that we have made it clear that, in analysing a child's difficulties and skills in certain fields, we can then synthesise our findings to formulate a plan to help the 'whole child' and his family.

Many people have helped in gathering information and material for this book. In particular, we should like to thank Sarah Denvir for the drawings illustrating motor development that appear in Chapters 1 and 5. These were taken from slides, some of which appear in the tape/slide series *Developmental Screening* produced by the Graves Medical Audio-Visual Library, and also in *Teaching Aids at Low Cost* (Department of Tropical Paediatrics, Institute of Child Health, London) by permission. Sarah also prepared the diagrams to illustrate Chapter 4. The plates in Chapter 5 were taken by A. J. Coote of Dudley Health Authority, and those in Chapter 6 are reproduced by permission of the Royal National Institute for the Blind. For the diagram in Chapter 11 we are indebted to the Rev D. T. M. Nott. Lastly, we should like to thank Heinemann Medical Books for permission to quote from 'Parents' Problems' by J. Bavin, which appeared in *Handling the Young Cerebral Palsied Child at Home*, edited by N. R. Finnie (1974).

Margaret Griffiths
Philippa Russell

List of Contributors

Mary Clegg — Superintendent Paediatric Physiotherapist, Dudley Health District.

Tony Cline — Principal Educational Psychologist, School Psychological Service, Inner London Education Authority.

Ruth Day — Consultant Paediatrician (Developmental Medicine and Neurological Handicap), Royal Hospital for Sick Children, Glasgow.

Margaret Edwards — Lecturer, Institute of Neurology, London University.

Elizabeth Grantham — Associate Specialist in Developmental Paediatrics, Peterborough Child Development Unit.

Margaret Griffiths — Consultant Paediatrician (Retired). Hon. Research Fellow, Institute of Child Health, Birmingham University.

Sister John — Education Psychologist Consultant, St Vincent School for Visually Handicapped, Liverpool, and Royal National Institute for the Blind, London.

Sheila McDougall — Senior Clinical Medical Officer, North Birmingham Health District.

David Mellor — Consultant Paediatric Neurologist, City and University Hospitals, Nottingham.

Tony Paddon	Senior Specialist Educational Psychologist, School Psychological Service, Inner London Education Authority.
Margaret Radcliffe	Teacher, Fraser of Allander Unit, Royal Hospital for Sick Children, Glasgow.
Philippa Russell	Senior Officer, Voluntary Council for Handicapped Children, National Children's Bureau, London, parent of a handicapped child.
Alan Sherliker	Head of Visiting Teacher Service for Children with Special Educational Needs, City of Birmingham Education Department.
David Wilson	Consultant Psychiatrist in Mental Handicap, Gloucester Health District.

1 Setting the Scene

By Margaret Griffiths

In 1970 the first edition of *Living with Handicap* was published by the National Children's Bureau, edited by Younghusband and formulated by a large and distinguished working party. This publication drew attention to the problems faced by families with a handicapped child and suggested some of the ways these could be alleviated. At that time, emphasis in this and other publications tended to be upon the needs of the family to receive an improved level of professional help.

More recently, parents and professionals have come to see the parents as central figures in the care of the child. The role of any parent is never easy. Most of us are untrained when we take it on, and even if we have received some professional training in one of the disciplines concerned with children, we still have to learn from each individual child; our caring consists of a life-long dialogue between two disparate individuals. Because, as parents, we have an intense emotional involvement with our children, we are often not able to 'see the wood for trees' and we cannot always take an objective view of our problems; it is often very helpful to have an outsider analyse them for us and help us to find the solution.

If this is so for our relationship with our ordinary children, how true it must be when they are handicapped. To help them properly it is essential that the parents – who are closest to the child, with an intimate knowledge of him as a person and strong motivation towards helping his progress – and the professionals – who have the experience of supporting many children with specific handicapping conditions – should not only work together but should also have a common understanding of the problems and a concerted and co-ordinated approach to the solutions.

The aim of this book is to clarify some of the factors at the core of the problems causing handicap and to identify principles which will bring practical support to all those concerned with caring for the child. By working together in this way, the life of a family with a handicapped child can become truly rewarding, and the child himself will be enabled to contribute according to his abilities.

HANDICAP

Handicap has been variously defined as: 'a considerable interference with the ability to live a normal life' (Rutter *et al*, 1970); 'a disability which . . . adversely affects normal growth, development or adjustment to life' (Court, 1976); 'a disability (which) puts him at a disadvantage in his particular environmental circumstances' (Drillien and Drummond, 1977). The definition given by the World Health Organization (1980) goes into more detail and is as follows: 'In the context of health experience, a handicap is a disadvantage for a given individual, resulting from an impairment or disability, that limits or prevents the fulfilment of a role that is normal (depending on age, sex and social and cultural factors) for that individual.'

Younghusband and her colleagues (1970) introduced the concept of a gradation between defect (impairment), disability and handicap, and this concept is developed by Court (1976) and the WHO (1980). Defect is seen as 'some imperfection, impairment or disorder of the body, intellect or personality' (Court, 1976), repeated by the WHO as 'loss or abnormality of psychological, physiological or anatomical structure or function'. Disability is looked upon as the result of an impairment which does not necessarily affect the individual's normal life (Court, 1976). This gradation, linking defect with disability and disability with handicap, is important because parents and professionals can work together to limit the progression from defect to disability to handicap, and can sometimes reverse the trend to become handicap to disability to defect.

Fraser (1980) puts forward an interesting concept of handicap in which he describes three factors: A, related to impairment and rooted in structural and functional impairment; B, related to the organisation of the physical and social world; C, secondary, arising from attitudes to the disabled in the social world. Impairment and disability are therefore seen as attributes of the child; handicap is seen partly in his relationship with his social world.

In this book we shall consider many of the impairments which may be related to handicap, and we shall endeavour to outline principles which can be used to combat a child's disability and minimise his handicap. We have chosen to consider mainly impairment of brain function (defined by Drillien and Drummond, 1977 and 1983, as NDD, 'neuro-developmental disorder'), as the resulting disabilities are those which particularly affect the child's educational needs. We shall also be looking at the most important part of his social world, his family and, later, his school. In this way, we shall emphasise throughout how parents and professionals can work together.

Finally, we shall reiterate time and again the importance of the individual characteristics and needs of each child and family. In offering advice to parents and professionals, we shall attempt to adhere to Cunningham's (1975) dictum to present 'principles' (which we hope can be universal) and to encourage parents and professionals together to choose the 'recipes' which best suit the child and his circumstances.

Working Together with Handicapped Children therefore sets out to alleviate the effects of the handicap so that the burden on the life of the child and his or her family is minimised as far as possible. The verb 'to work' was chosen deliberately, since life will not be easy, either for the child or the family, but work itself can always be rewarding if it is carried out in company and leads to definable goals. Parent/professional intervention is often compared to teamwork in games or an orchestra, emphasising the group of collaborators working closely together. This is helpful in describing close co-operation and mutual support but is too overwhelming an analogy for the care of a child. We need to think more of Mum's role in the kitchen, where many ingredients go into a recipe but where too many cooks will spoil it! Although many professionals will contribute to the child's and family's welfare, the number of individuals directly involved with the cook at any one time must be kept to a minimum, and the person directly involved must always be compatible and acceptable.

The degree to which a defect is considered a handicap or a

disability may be influenced both by the family and the environment. Attitudes, positive or negative, on the part of the child, the parents and the professionals, affect the outcome.

CAUSES OF IMPAIRED BRAIN DEVELOPMENT

Consideration of some of the more important causes of impaired brain development underlines the difficulties in finding suitable words or phrases to define a wide category of defects and problems.

1 The cause of impaired brain development may be determined at conception, either by an abnormality in the chromosomes (as in Down's Syndrome) or by the absence of a single gene bearing an enzyme which is essential to normal brain function. The presence of a chromosomal abnormality means that every cell in the body is affected, and therefore that both growth and function may be abnormal in many aspects. This is shown in the characteristic facial appearance of such syndromes as Down's and in the fact that sometimes other organs, such as the heart, are affected; it is, however, the impaired development of the brain which causes the significant handicap. In the case of single gene disorders where there is a missing enzyme, such children may be quite normal at birth (the mother supplies the enzyme through the placenta) and the handicap may only develop later as the effect of impaired brain development becomes manifest; when the nature of the missing enzyme is known it may be possible by medical means to prevent its effects on the brain (as in phenylketonuria), and eventually biochemical research may discover ways of replacing the missing enzyme.

2 Some hazard during pregnancy may interfere with brain development: This may be an infection which is able to cross the placental barrier (as in German measles); forms of chemical poisoning (eg. alcohol, drugs of various kinds); or physical causes such as nuclear radiation. Metabolic disorders in the mother, including phenylketonuria or unstable diabetes may also affect the developing brain of the foetus. Starvation of the mother at this stage very rarely affects the infant's brain, as the nutritive elements available to the foetus are adequately balanced; if the mother's nutrition is severely impaired it is

more likely that that baby will be miscarried or stillborn. Some of the children 'damaged' or 'injured' pre-natally may be obviously sick at birth, some may be very small with very small heads, but others may not show the effects until later.

3   One of the major birth hazards is a premature delivery. However, if the baby has developed normally until that time and is nursed in a Special Care Baby Unit where there are skilled and experienced staff dealing with premature babies, the development should continue normally. Some babies are premature because of some kind of 'insult' and, if this is the case, these babies may already be 'damaged'. Such babies also frequently have considerable problems during the first two or three weeks of life: they are more likely to have convulsions or become jaundiced, and sometimes their later handicap may be ascribed to problems after birth which may have initiated in pregnancy. Babies who have experienced a pregnancy of normal length may suffer problems at birth; these may have been foreseen and hopefully the mother would have been admitted to hospital for special care before the baby was born; others may be totally unforeseen, and this is one of the major reasons for advising hospital delivery in all cases. Adequate antenatal care should enable the obstetrician to be forewarned of trouble; when a mother has not had proper care during her pregnancy, one can expect an increased possibility of a 'brain-damaged' child.

4   Sometimes a child who was normal at birth and has progressed normally for weeks, months or even years, may be subjected to adverse factors which can lead to 'brain damage'. Such conditions are: accidents of various kinds, infections affecting the brain or its membranes, medical conditions which may lead to haemorrhage within the skull or to sudden respiratory or cardiac arrest, rare biochemical disorders or reactions to preventive or curative agents. Socio-cultural factors in a normal child may lead to some delay in general development but do not cause impaired brain development. If, however, an organic condition is present, adverse socio-cultural environments reinforce the handicap.

When damage occurs in an older child, the effects produced begin to resemble the conditions that are found in adults.

Already the brain has a store of memories – visual, auditory, kinaesthetic and emotional; impairment of brain function at this stage may interfere with storage of new impressions and with the use of old ones.

The severity and the manifestation of the impairment of brain function varies according to its cause, and therefore children with impaired brain development present with many different problems. In those children in whom the damage is chromosomal, or in whom the 'insult' happens early in development, it is more likely that there will be a fairly global impairment of brain development, leading to mental handicap of some severity. In other situations, where the brain is damaged later, after the functions of the various parts of the brain have been established, the 'damage' caused may be purely local and the child may have evidence of spasticity, visual or auditory handicap or learning difficulties, without any serious mental handicap. On the other hand, some mentally handicapped children may have associated handicaps such as spasticity, visual or auditory problems, epilepsy and behaviour disturbances.

ENCOURAGEMENT OF DEVELOPMENTAL PROGRESS

In our observation of normal children, whether as parents, teachers or other professionals, we can but agree that all children are different; and the closer we are to the child and the more continuous our contact, so the variations become more noticeable. Nevertheless, particularly during the first two years of life, we are able to define an underlying pattern of development, and as the child grows older and acquires more sophisticated skills, we are still able to construct a framework within which we expect his capabilities to develop.

In this we are aided by knowledge of the way in which the brain develops, recently summarised by Dickerson (1981). Research has shown that there are certain brain growth spurts, at which times the brain is particularly vulnerable. In the human brain the first spurt occurs from about 10–18 weeks of pregnancy, when the specialised brain cells are formed and migrate to their allotted positions in the geography of the developing brain. Cell growth continues thereafter at a slower rate until the age of two to three years, and this second spurt is largely concerned with the developments of supporting cells and connections.

When we begin to suspect that there is a degree of impaired brain development, we need to know how its various forms can interfere with a child's general development and how we can help him to use his strengths to overcome, to some extent, his weaknesses. This poses a forthright challenge both to the professionals involved and to the parents, yet it is only by true partnership between them that the child can be satisfactorily helped. The professionals' contribution comes from training, skill and experience of the varied effects of a handicap in many children; the parents offer an intimate knowledge of their own child and a devotion to his welfare that no professional can equal. These differing assets need to be fused into a vital weapon for the child's and family's advantage.

NORMAL DEVELOPMENTAL PROGRESS

A child's development depends upon interaction with his environment. Each child is differently endowed with the seeds of his own potential and is encouraged or inhibited by the environment in which he lives. During the first few months, the child acquires control of his own body, and because this is dependent on the rapid maturation of the brain, the patterns of development at this stage are similar in all normal children irrespective of culture, race, or period. Cognitive and conceptual ability develops early, but cannot be adequately expressed until the child can use his tools of mobility, speech, language and manipulation. From the outset a loving, encouraging, secure environment will encourage progress and the converse will inhibit it. Progress depends upon a steady, simultaneous, consistent development in all fields of skill, and delay or deviance in any one aspect is likely to affect the whole. Children's normal developmental progress is described by a number of writers (eg. Sheridan, 1973), and some aspects are illustrated in Fig 1 and Figs 6–9.

During the first two years of life the child changes from a small creature dependent on adults, particularly the mother, for all his needs, to an independent personality able to impose himself upon his surroundings. This ability need not wait for co-ordinated movements or sophisticated sounds; within his

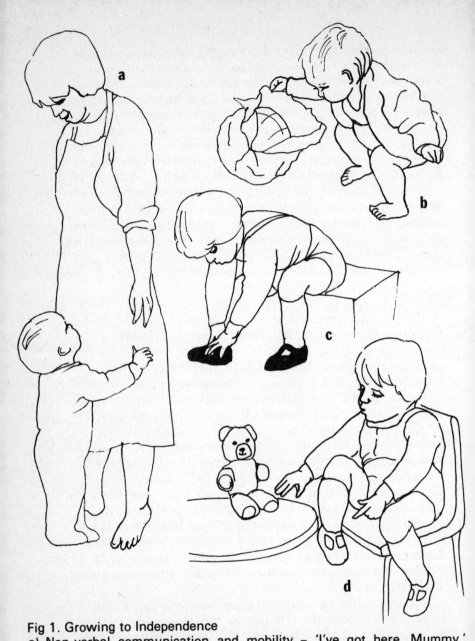

Fig 1. Growing to Independence
a) Non-verbal communication and mobility – 'I've got here, Mummy.'
b) Balance, manipulation, vision and curiosity. 'What's in my parcel?'
c) Social independence, using hands, vision and balance. 'I'll try to get this shoe on.' (See also Fig 9c.)   d) Increasing vocabulary and knowing some parts of our body. 'These are our toes.'

first few weeks of life he will attract attention by crying, by smiling or by looking, without the need of words. The ready responses of people in his surroundings then encourage further development of social approaches and an increasing control of the ways of expressing them. During the first six months of life, the signals he gives are simple ones; he cries his need for food, for comfort and for nearness to people; his responses are quietness, a smile and sometimes a chuckle. From six months to a year he can move by rolling, crawling or shuffling, he can play with his toys, discard them and demand their return, and begin to manifest definite likes and dislikes. Throughout, his acquisition of new skills depends in some degree on the responses of the people he lives with, which are in their turn encouraged by his own progress.

Half-way through his second year, he is mobile, able to move about and to explore his environment; as shown in Figs 1a–d, he is able to make his wants and desires known, first by gesture and appropriate noise, and later by words; he can use his hands to investigate how things are made, to feed himself, to help to dress himself, and to grab what he wants; he has a will of his own. From the age of two he begins to mix with his peers, to improve his social skills, to assemble and to construct instead of taking to pieces, to express himself in words and painting, song and drama, and thence to go on to formal education.

DELAYED DEVELOPMENTAL PROGRESS
Impaired brain function may interfere with development in a variety of ways: it may prevent the child from seeing, or hearing, or moving; it may limit his understanding; it may affect his ability to make relationships with others or to communicate by speech and gesture; it may make it difficult or impossible for him to acquire the important social skills of feeding, dressing and continence; it may lead to specific learning difficulties. In addition, any of these problems will affect his environment by making it much more difficult for people (including his parents, siblings, teachers and peers) to respond to his needs. The encouragement, support and reinforcement of progress so essential to development will be lacking, and both the child and family will suffer bewilderment and frustration if they do not receive early and adequate help.

As a result of this very wide variation in the effects of handicap in children with impaired brain function, it is clearly impossible to conceive any method of treatment which can be applicable to all handicapped children. We shall therefore attempt to outline principles and guidelines for those situations in which handicapped children and their families have problems common to all (Chapter 3) and those in which specific skills and expertise are needed to help them. (Chapters 4–11)

QUESTIONS TO BE ANSWERED

1   *WHY is the child handicapped?*
In technical terms this entails making a *diagnosis*, ie. defining the cause of his disability. In some cases, eg. in Down's Syndrome or in a child who has suffered an accident or an infection, this may be comparatively simple, in others it is more difficult; in some it is impossible with our present knowledge. Why, then, undertake what may be a laborious and, occasionally, painful procedure? The advantages are threefold: a) in some children specific medical or surgical treatment, or the provision of aids, may remove, correct or remediate the disability and enable the child to live a normal life; b) once the cause is known, knowledge of the usual effects of the condition upon a child's development facilitates prediction for the child's future and planning for his support; c) the parents, affected child and wider family can be informed of any risk of repetition in future pregnancies.

In spite of advances in medicine over the past decades, which have resulted in far greater knowledge of the causes of handicap, there remain many conditions in which these are still unknown. It may be necessary in many cases for the professionals, doctors in particular, to say, 'I do not know why', and in such a situation for parents to retain confidence in their advisers, to accept the verdict, and to hope (and help, if occasion arises) for explanations in the future.

2   *HOW does the condition limit his progress?*
This can be established by *assessment*, ie. by investigating a child's abilities and disabilities so that he can make the most of himself as a person.

Ordinary children are involved in this process every day, and indeed they contribute a great deal to it. They find out for themselves, they show by their reactions what they like doing and what they are capable of; they ask for help when they need it, and adult involvement, even in small children, is often that of observing and enabling rather than leading and forcing. Later in the school years it may be necessary to quantify a child's ability by tests and examinations, so that the advice, education and training that is offered is realistically geared to what he can accomplish in childhood and adolescence.

When a child does not seem to be keeping up with his peers, or when he shows abnormalities in his developmental progress or his behaviour, it becomes necessary to evaluate in greater detail his abilities and disabilities in all fields. As in the case of the ordinary child this needs to be a continuing process, undertaken by a number of professionals who are experienced in the problems posed by a specific disorder and are able if necessary to advise the family in its management. Each person involved needs to evaluate the child's present state of development in a particular field; to advise ways in which a defined problem can be tackled; to monitor the child's progress in that one field; to modify the help being given as the child develops. The professional disciplines which should be available in any assessment team are detailed in Chapter 2. The skills which may be needed by an individual child are varied, and the way in which they are used is described in more detail in chapters dealing with specific handicaps.

The major criterion for optimum progress is the effective functioning of parents and professionals as a team. For this rapid communication, frequent contact, readiness to co-operate and an understanding and acceptance of the role of other helpers is essential; joint thinking, joint planning and joint action are essential both for comprehensive assessment and effective management.

3   *WHAT can be done to encourage his development?*
Concurrently with the assessment, a *programme of management* is devised by the same team in consultation with the parents. Programmes for helping the child both at home and at school, drawn up at the time of assessment, will be followed.

These should not entail lengthy sessions of 'treatment' but should be aimed at activities for daily living within the home or playgroup situation, devised with that particular child in mind.

Working with handicap is always difficult because it involves such a complexity of individual needs in the children and their families, and hence it requires considerable expertise in the multidisciplinary team (of which not all members will be needed for any particular child). In carrying out therapeutic programmes, one of the aims should be that as few individuals as possible should be allocated to the family; of these, the person most acceptable to the parents should be designated leader and spokesman.

In the following chapters of this book, the specific needs of individual children will be discussed and a number of treatments, methods, approaches and philosophies will be mentioned. If attention were confined purely to present methods of treatment, and present successful units, such a publication would be out of date before it was printed. It is essential to realise that new ideas, treatments, management and sharing of the burden will be continually developed and need to be encouraged. However, what will not change is the individuality of children and the strain on their families; in reviewing the reasons for one or other type of management, it is essential to bear in mind the advantages or disadvantages of any approach with regard to the child's needs and the resources available in his environment. It is essential to remember that, while it is possible to generalise family needs – which may be very similar, irrespective of the nature of the child's handicap – it is important to be specific about the help provided to an individual child. Hence, much of this book will deal with principles, both with regard to general family problems and to specific difficulties related to individual handicaps and individual children. New treatment procedures need to be evaluated on the principles expressed in more detail in subsequent chapters.

GUIDELINES

1 *Help needed by all families*
The emotional impact of a handicapped child upon the whole

family is similar whatever the handicap. The contribution made by professionals to this most important factor is crucial; much of the disillusionment of parents and their often justified criticism that '*they* don't understand' or '*they* don't listen' is related to professionals' inadequate training in relationships and family dynamics. Problems also arise when the help offered is not sufficiently organised, so that the home suffers from either a 'feast' or a 'famine', and the family is either deluged with contradictory advice from many different sources or receives no help at all. Much of this can be prevented by providing a comprehensive team assessment service (Chapter 2), and by arranging for one of its members to be the home therapist or home visitor.

When an older child has a disability, such as a specific learning difficulty or an uncomplicated physical condition, and it is clear that with adequate help his disability need not become a handicap, it may be clear from the outset that a formal, comprehensive assessment is unnecessary. For a younger child with delayed development, support in the home is often a life-line; several schemes are described in later chapters and in the Appendix (see Pugh, 1981). Such generalist schemes appear to be most successful in children who are mildly mentally handicapped or disadvantaged (Reader, 1984) and there is evidence (Barna *et al*, 1980) that children who have a visual handicap or cerebral palsy may show only limited progress.

2   *Specific help for individual children*
Accounts of the theoretical basis and practical approach to the management of various specific conditions will be dealt with in other chapters. To enable objective decisions to be made, incorporating the views of professional workers involved and the wishes and needs of the parents, patience, understanding and the goodwill of all who take part are required. The composition and leadership of an appropriate team may change during the child's development but the goal should always be the child's best interest and support to the family.

Whereas the generalist schemes usually involve the provision of home advisers without specialist professional skills, in those children with a specific disability a trained professional is usually essential; this may be a teacher of the hearing impaired or the visually handicapped, a therapist (speech, physio- or occupational), or a nurse working under the direction of a psychologist. It is always advisable that there should be back-up support from a child development centre, wherever based.

3 *Availability of services*
It is very often not possible to find a perfect solution to a problem. The course decided upon will need to take into account not only the child's difficulties and the parents' wishes, but also the facilities available. For young children, help must be taken into the home, and it is at this stage, when the child's needs are being 'teased out' by the assessment team, that the professional who will work most closely with the family must be carefully selected. Often the parents, mother in particular, make this choice for themselves, and are soon on first-name terms with the health visitor, community nurse, nursery nurse, social worker, therapist (whether occupational, physio- or speech) or the nursery teacher. Outside the home, as the child grows older he and the family will gain immeasurably if he is able to mix with other children. Starting with a playgroup, through nursery school, all school grades and on to further education (especially important for handicapped young people) the team of professionals will change, but the principle of one key worker, often spontaneously selected by the parents, should still apply.

In the education of children with 'special educational needs', the Warnock committee (DES, 1978) stressed the importance of multidisciplinary assessment, parental involvement in decision-making, integration as much as possible into the ordinary educational and social world and early intervention to ensure that all children should be able to realise their potential. Many of their recommendations have been embodied in the 1981 Education Act (including the concept of a key worker), and, if the spirit of the Act is observed, parent/professional co-operation will be an important educational component in the upbringing of all children who have special educational needs.

Sometimes the local services for ordinary children may offer the ideal or 'next best' facilities for the handicapped child. At other times, requisite professional skills may be located so far from the home that residential placement may need to be considered; short-term residential provision is particularly helpful for some severely physically handicapped or disturbed children. Voluntary societies, whether local or national, often have a large part to play in providing specialised services.

Whatever the general economic situation, financial constraints will always loom large. Good will, hard work, adaptability and professional competence need not be rationed and, used imaginatively, should be enough to provide solutions to most problems. Our aim should be to provide a free, co-ordinated service to *all* children who suffer from any form of handicap, that will enable each one to achieve his potential.

References

BARNA, S., BIDDER, R. T., GRAY, O. P., CLEMENTS, J. and GARDNER, S. (1980). 'The progress of developmentally delayed preschool children in a home training scheme', *Child: care, health and development*, **6**, 157–164.

COURT, D. (1976). *Fit for the Future*, Report of the Committee on Child Health Services, Vol I. London: HMSO.

CUNNINGHAM, C. (1975). 'Parents as therapists and educators' in *Behaviour Modification with the Severely Retarded – Study Group 8* (pp 175–193), KIERNAN, C. C. and WOODFORD, F. P. (eds). Amsterdam: Associated Scientific Publishers.

DEPARTMENT OF EDUCATION AND SCIENCE (1978). *Special Educational Needs*, Report of Committee of Enquiry into the Education of Children and Young People (The Warnock Report). London: HMSO.

DICKERSON, J. W. T. (1981). 'Nutrition, brain growth and development' in *Maturation and Development* (pp 110–130), CONNOLLY, K. J. and PRECHTL, H. F. R. (eds). London: Heinemann Medical Books; Philadelphia: Lippincott.

DRILLIEN, C. and DRUMMOND, M. (1977). *Neurodevelopmental Problems in Early Childhood*. Oxford: Blackwell.

DRILLIEN, C. and DRUMMOND, M. (1983). *Development Screening and the Child with Special Needs*. London: Heinemann Medical Books; Philadelphia: Lippincott.

FRASER, B. (1980). 'The meaning of handicap in children', *Child: care, health and development*, **6**, 83–91.

PUGH, G. (ed) (1981). *Parents as Partners*. London: National Children's Bureau.

READER, L. (1984). 'Preschool intervention programmes', *Child: care, health and development*, **10**, 237–251.

RUTTER, M., TIZARD, J. and WHITMORE, K., (eds) (1970). *Education, Health and Behaviour*. London: Longman.

SHERIDAN, M. D. (1973). *Children's Developmental Progress from Birth to Five Years, The Stycar Sequences*. Windsor: NFER.

WORLD HEALTH ORGANISATION. *International Classification of Impairments, Disabilities and Handicap*. Geneva: WHO.

YOUNGHUSBAND, E., BIRCHALL, D., DAVIE, R. and PRINGLE, M. L. K. (1970). *Living with Handicap*. London: National Children's Bureau.

2 Assessment

By Margaret Griffiths

In the context of child development the word assessment can be grievously misunderstood. To many parents, it represents a solemn entrance examination to the world of normality. It may appear to them that, if their child 'fails', he will be denied access to the delights, the challenges, the disappointments and achievements of his peers. When parents have these feelings, they experience an extra burden and another barrier in their fight to help their child who has a disability.

Some professionals may fall into the trap of believing that their own contribution, even at a single session, has an overriding importance in evaluating the child's abilities, and in these circumstances may find it difficult to give due weight to the opinions of colleagues in other fields, or to the parents' views.

Fortunately, neither of these concepts need express the true state of affairs. Unfortunately, they are still found in some paediatric and educational units and, where this is the case, inevitably reinforce the pressures on the parents and their fear of children 'failing the tests'.

It is important, therefore, to find a definition of the assessment procedure, in terms that will avoid these pitfalls. A simple early definition still appears to be appropriate. This states, 'Assessment may therefore be defined as a "summing up, based on adequate information, of the abilities and needs of an individual child"' (Griffiths, 1962). The following chapters will outline very briefly the great variety of problems which may affect children who have some form of 'brain damage', or impairment of brain function.

In the past, and sometimes even at the present time, parents have had to spend time trailing their child from one clinic to another to get an opinion about a single aspect of his or her disability, until finally, after long and sometimes tardy correspondence, some general solution may emerge. The provision of assessment services in one centre means that the experts come to the child and parents. By this means, adequate information can be obtained and collated in a way that is enjoyable for the child, supportive to the parents and helpful to the professionals.

It is useful, therefore, to consider the criteria to be established and the composition of the team that will be needed to carry out the observations and to implement the supportive plan.

CRITERIA FOR ASSESSMENT

The aim should be to provide a unit which combines a relaxed, friendly atmosphere with full professional services; offering a meeting place where child, family and professionals can feel at home, share the facilities and pool ideas. The criteria necessary can be classified as follows:

1 *Attitudes and Ambience*

The unit should be centred on the needs of the child and family. The décor and furnishings should be attractive to children and welcoming to their parents. Waiting areas should provide play facilities, suitable toilet accommodation and room for parents to get together and chat. Whether in the building or on the telephone, staff of all grades must be welcoming and helpful. (These may seem very minor details, but they can make a big difference to feelings and relationships.)

2 *Location*

There are three possible locations. Each has its own advantages and disadvantages.

a)   A hospital site will be adjacent to the more sophisticated diagnostic facilities, X-ray departments, laboratories, audio-visual electrodiagnostic techniques, etc., facilitating the use of these whenever they are required. Staff can also have easy access to colleagues and libraries. The disadvantages are that some parents dislike anything to do with hospitals, having memories of their early anxieties about the child. On the other hand, finding a really supportive unit within the hospital may restore their confidence and allay fears and hesitations over a further pregnancy.

b)   An educational site has the advantage of ready access to teachers and other children and enables an easy transition from specialist nursery to school. However, children attending for assessment may go on to different schools, and the disadvantage of an educational setting lies in its distance from a hospital and the diagnostic facilities needed for some children in the early years.

c)   An independent site is usually run by a voluntary body and has the advantage of being free in the parents' eyes of any taint of officialdom. However, it suffers the disadvantage of lack of technical facilities.

Whichever location is finally decided upon, it is essential that there should be contact between unit staff and the local services for children – health services in hospital and community; educational services in home, ordinary and special schools; and voluntary services in the neighbourhood, toy library, play groups, etc. The unit should also be easily accessible to all families living within the administrative area.

3 *Facilities Available*
Within the unit, in addition to suitable social and waiting areas, there should be certain general technical facilities available for all children.

a)   A large nursery area for play, both free and structured.

b)   Suitable smaller rooms adapted for simple hearing and vision testing, for speech therapy and for individual sessions with psychologist or teacher.

c)   Accommodation for physiotherapy and occupational therapy.

d)   Offices for staff including secretaries, a staff room, and at least one room for medical examinations and consultation.

e)   Observation facilities for other members of staff and for parents may be provided in various ways. CCTVR* is probably

---

* Closed Circuit Television Recording.

the least intrusive, and has the advantage of providing a permanent record for use at case conferences and reviews of progress (Griffiths, 1974). One-way windows offer useful alternatives for interested visitors.

4 *Diagnosis*

In emphasising the importance of what the child can do and in looking for a way to help him in his difficulties, it is easy to lose sight of the importance of searching for the cause of his handicap. Diagnosis (definition of the nature and cause of the disability) should always be an important part of the assessment procedure. There is quite rightly a revolt against 'labelling' a child, and it is unfortunate that this has given rise in some circles to the idea that diagnosis is purely a theoretical concept, of interest only to some professionals. It can be of the greatest practical value in planning a supportive programme, for three main reasons: a) because it will alert the professionals to the possible presence of other disabilities; b) because it will be a guide to the future outlook and to likely progress; c) because it will enable the parents to receive informed advice about the cause of their child's condition and the likelihood of its recurrence in other members of the family.

Most parents prefer to know as much as possible about their child's problem and, indeed, a firm diagnosis probably leads to greater confidence between them and their professional advisers. It is often very hard for such confidence to be established when the professionals have to admit that no cause can be found for a child's condition.

5 *Programme Planning*

a) Assessment procedures should always lead to an agreed, but flexible, plan for support to the child and family. The parents should always be involved in decision making, and they should be helped to understand the implications of all the problems discovered and the skills the child has mastered.

b) Case conferences and progress reviews, when frank discussion can take place, accomplish far more than detailed reports and lengthy correspondence, although this does not preclude the necessity for keeping careful records and the issue of a report agreed by the team. Complete unanimity is not always possible, but a joint programme can always be produced by consensus.

c) One result of the planning should be to designate a member of the team as key-worker (or home visitor or home therapist). The person's professional background and seniority will be decided according to the child's needs, but the overriding consideration will be the development of a friendly and supportive relationship with the child and his family.

THE MULTIDISCIPLINARY TEAM

In organising effective assessment for a child and support for him and his family, we are immediately presented with a paradox. Emphasis is made in almost every chapter on the importance of a multidisciplinary team to identify the child's abilities and needs in a number of fields; at the same time it is essential to avoid giving a family contradictory advice or overwhelming them with too many helpers. However, 'team work' need not necessarily imply a chorus of verbal or mass of written instructions, nor a regular stream of visitors to the home.

It must be obvious that no one individual or profession can hope to have the skills required to help children who have the variety of disabilities that may be caused by impaired brain function, nor can there be a universal programme to help all such children. Practical individual help must always be offered as part of an assessment procedure, as the child's responses can be a helpful guide both to his abilities and his needs. The composition of the team will vary from child to child and, when with growth and development his needs are seen to change, so may the designated key worker. Such variations require great flexibility in approach and close co-operation in all team members.

It is convenient, therefore, to consider three aspects of team function, entailing different compositions, and these are set out in Table 1. At first sight this may seem a formidable list of professionals, and may reinforce parents' ideas of the entrance examination formula. In practice, without the availability of each and every one, some children could not be helped.

Table 1. Composition of Multidisciplinary Team.
(*It is assumed that parents will be an integral part of each group*).

GROUP A*	GROUP B*	GROUP C*
Core of professionals based at Central Unit	*Professionals related to home, child & family*	*Specialists needed for specific handicaps*
audiometrician/or audiology technician	community nurse	dentist
nursery nurses	family doctor	physicians
nursery teacher	health visitor	ophthalmologist
orthoptist	home therapist	orthopaedic surgeon
physicians: paediatrician or community paediatrician	home visitor	otorhinolaryngologist
psychologist	key worker°	psychiatrist
receptionist	social worker	psychologists
secretary		specialist teachers for
social worker		hearing impaired
therapists		learning difficulties
occupational		mental handicap
physical		physical handicap
speech		visual handicap
		technical specialists
		audiotechnician
		optician
		orthoptist
		orthotist
		therapists
		occupational
		physical
		speech

° if not already included
* in alphabetical order

Group A.   In a well run unit these members of staff may almost seem to the child as part of the furniture and should not appear threatening to the parents. A friendly and efficient receptionist smoothes the way at the first visit and at future attendances becomes a well known face and a firm friend. The nursery nurses and teacher are there to see that children are happily and suitably occupied. The therapists, psychologists, orthoptist and audiometrician may first be introduced to child and parent in the play situation before an individual interview which can appear to be a continuation of play. The social worker is at hand to help and advise parents over social and financial problems, and to discuss welfare benefits for families with a handicapped child. One of the doctors will see the family at the first visit unless they have already met; they will be available for discussions with individual members of the staff and for guidance on procedures. Some children will need regular prolonged attendance in the nursery group and may in this situation attend without their parents, although occasional parental help, as in ordinary playgroups, should be encouraged.

For some children, an early visit may make it plain that a specific disability will require further specialist help, eg. more careful ophthalmic examination, referral for help with a hearing impairment and so on. Action should be taken immediately a specific problem is encountered. Tests of vision and hearing should be carried out in every child, whatever their suspected disability.

Group B. These professionals cannot spend much time in an assessment unit, but they may be full-time as far as a family is concerned. The family doctor and health visitor will know the family well, although they may not have had much first-hand knowledge of the handicap affecting the child; they are, however, important members of the team supporting the family and will need close links with the central unit. The community nurse (for mental handicap), the home therapist, home visitor, or key worker are alternative persons for offering the week-to-week individual support needed for development and daily living, and will be mentioned in the context of the child's needs. They will need to have very close association with the work of the central unit team, and are of particular importance in helping those children who are not yet ready to take part in nursery activities.

Group C. These are professionals whose specialist skills will be needed for a limited number of children with specific disabilities. The special education teachers may visit the children at home or advise the nursery teacher in the unit about a child's special needs, and they are likely to follow up the children when they start at school. The specialist physicians (and surgeons) will be invited to undertake sessions at the unit where they can see the child and talk to the parents in a setting in which the latter are comfortable and relaxed. The psychologists and therapists may already be members of the core team described as Group A. The technical specialists may or may not be able to bring their equipment to the unit and the child may have to be seen at a special unit from which appliances are supplied.

THE AIM OF ASSESSMENT

So far this chapter has considered criteria for action and the composition of the multidisciplinary team. These are objectives to help a child attain a realistically defined potential. In the early years the task of parents and professionals is to encourage the child's sensory input and use of his motor skills to enable him to communicate, to express emotion, to learn social awareness and habits, and to attain as much independence as possible. Consideration can then be given to find the best educational placement for him as an individual.

It is now accepted in paediatric and educational circles that no child can be deemed 'ineducable', and that all children should have access to the type of education that suits their needs. It follows that no professionals can say to the parents that 'nothing can be done'. Some activities may be difficult, but progress should always be sought and expected. Guidelines should be prepared as to ways in which the child and family can be helped, and to measures which will be used for specific difficulties.

Following this, the most suitable type of school can be defined. In the United Kingdom, following the Court (1976) and Warnock (1978) reports, the Education Act (1981) introduced legislation pertaining to children with special educational needs. Decisions on the educational placement for an individual child are to be based on a 'statement' of the child's needs and attainments in the educational, medical and psychological fields, together with the parents' views. Clearly, the need for multidisciplinary assessment and support is envisaged in the concept of a multidisciplinary statement, and the findings as regards a child's abilities and needs will be collated and compiled by an appropriate professional and studied by the parents. If they should disagree with the findings or the recommendations for educational placement they can appeal (Russell, 1984). When decisions are taken by people conscious of the paramount interests of the child, there should be no difficulty about mutual acceptance.

The question of integration into ordinary school versus admission to a special school must be settled by agreement during the review conference. Often the perfect solution is unavailable; the balance of conflicting advantages and disadvantages in the local situation must then be taken into account. Residential placement may sometimes be considered.

References

COURT, D. (1976). *Fit for the Future*, Report of the Committee on Child Health Services, Vol. I. London: HMSO.

DEPARTMENT OF EDUCATION AND SCIENCE (1978). *Special Educational Needs,*, Report of Committee of Enquiry into the Education of Children and Young People (The Warnock Report). London: HMSO.

DRILLIEN, C. and DRUMMOND, M. (1977). *Neurodevelopmental Problems in Early Childhood.* Oxford: Blackwell.

GRIFFITHS, M. I. (1962). 'Assessment – the Team Approach', *Spastics Quarterly*, **11**, 31–33.

GRIFFITHS, M. I. (1974). 'The use of CCTVR in the assessment of children with handicaps', *Medical and Biological Illustration*, **24**, 28–31.

RUSSELL, P. (1984). *The Wheelchair Child*, second edition. London: Souvenir Press.

3 Parents as Partners

By Elizabeth Grantham and Philippa Russell

The Development of Family Relationships

Under normal circumstances, the first person with whom a baby makes a relationship is his own mother. We hope that she has the chance to 'fall in love' with her own baby, but we realise that 'maternal instinct' will not necessarily 'flow' automatically at the first sight of the baby.

There are many factors that influence the special mother-child relationship, and this 'bonding' may not come easily, even if the wanted child is a beautiful, normal baby. Some mothers may have very mixed feelings about motherhood. They may not have been well mothered themselves and may have had unhappy experiences which have led to feelings of maternal deprivation.

They may not have a realistic mental image of a 'good mother' on which to model themselves. Many of today's mothers have never seen, nor have they handled, a new-born baby until their own is placed in their arms. Their expectations of how a baby (or a toddler) behaves are quite inaccurate. All these things apply to both normal and to handicapped babies.

Much work is being done on how the events surrounding a baby's birth influence the establishment of the mother/child relationship. Unfortunately, many brain-damaged children have traumatic birth histories which can make the initial bonding difficult. These babies may have to be nursed away from their mothers, perhaps in special care baby units where they spend a long time isolated in incubators, and cannot be handled or cuddled.

The worry that 'something is not quite right' can stop the growth of bonding. Some mothers have said that they deliberately suppressed their feelings for the baby because the doctors said that there might be something wrong, or because there was a fear that the baby might not survive.

Once the relationship is established, it grows as the mother and child interact together. It is a reciprocal relationship, the mother and the child each drawing responses from the other.

For example, the baby looks intently into his mother's eyes, then, at six weeks, smiles, thus rewarding his mother for her attention. Mother's delight at the baby's smile rewards the baby for his response and so each rewards the other. This interplay between mother and child (father and child as well) continues right through the normal maturation process of development, the mother's response and the type of mothering that she provides changing as the child matures and gives her different cues.

The social interchange between them grows from the intent look, to the coos and gurgles, and then the twisting of the baby's limbs in an effort to respond to the mother's verbal stimulation. The motor development shows a rapid sequence: pushing up in the prone position to watch mother; rolling over; sitting; the delight in exploring his hands, his feet, space around him; touching his mother's face and hair; later the acquisition of mobility, the chance to explore a wider area of space but always keeping within the 'magic circle' of mother's influence, and always glancing back to check from her expression and her attitude that all is well.

After a year, he knows his own body and the immediate space around it; he is mobile and off to explore the world. But then comes the realisation that mother may not be just where he left her – she also can move, and move away from him. So comes the stage of clinging and not letting the caring figure out of his sight. Some say that the greatest fear a baby has is of being abandoned, because that means he will not survive (Bowlby, 1979). In conjunction with this stage of clinging, there often comes the stage of establishing his own identity, the stage of toddler conflict. Mother may sit him on the pot, but she can't squeeze it out of him! He can say 'no', he can run away from her, he can be naughty. He can also be nice to her. He can take the initiative, he can 'woo' her. A fistful of crumpled flower heads placed in her lap with a beaming smile; an invitation to share the delight of some tactile experience, such as a puddle, or a patch of mud.

Then at around three years of age, one hopes, he emerges

from his phase of conflict with a sense of his own identity, of his own position. He is a boy, not a girl, he lives in a certain house, he has a certain family. He is now ready to go beyond the family circle, perhaps to join a group for a few hours a day; ready to learn to play, first alongside other children and then with other children, until by five and six he has a happy circle of friends of his own peer group and is passing from the stage of 'Mummy knows best' to that of 'Teacher knows best'.

After the latent years of the seven-to-twelve year-old comes the stage of teenager conflict where once again he is forming his own personality, his own role in life. He learns to take responsibility for his decisions and to realise that mistakes that he has made are his own fault and cannot be blamed on something or somebody else. This is the time when the parents have to let go; they must stand back and realise that their baby is now growing into a mature and responsible adult.

The Effect of Handicap on the Bonding Process
With a child who has some form of handicap or special needs, many of these responses and stages are delayed or may never take place. A child with visual problems may not smile in response to mother's face and, as she does not understand why, she may feel rejected. A child with hearing problems will not be interested when she talks to him. He will not respond when his name is called and, again, if the parents do not understand why, they may feel that the child is rejecting them. Moreover, difficulty in any one area is likely to spill across into other areas of function. A child with motor problems is late in finding out about himself, how to move himself, what shape he is; he is late in exploring the space around him, his mobility may be restricted so that he cannot run away and he cannot be naughty. A child with communication problems may find it increasingly frustrating to be unable to communicate his needs or express his anger. Visual problems alone can create locomotive difficulties. Difficulties in hearing will delay comprehension of social behaviour that is expected from him. Difficulties in movement will delay comprehension of how the world works. Behaviour problems similar to those encountered in ordinary children are thus likely to be exacerbated in handicapped children. Indeed, some children have so many

areas of malfunction that, even if they have normal intellectual potential, it is difficult for them to acquire the experience with which to develop that potential or the means to express their feelings other than through their behaviour.

The normal child learns about the world by play within a relaxed, secure setting. If a mother is having fun with her child and enjoys him as a person in his own right, then by spontaneous play and being sensitive to the cues he gives her she will be doing the right thing to help him. So often it is the child who tells the mother what she must do to help him learn. This means that the mother must feel confident in her own value as a person, and confident that she knows how to handle the child. She comes to realise that she is the one who knows most about her child – she is his expert. It is this kind of expertise that parents need to acquire with regard to their handicapped child.

The Effect of Handicap on the Development of Family Relationships

If the mother and father have been told that their child is not the normal baby they were expecting, the normal baby to cuddle and have fun with, but a child who has difficulties and special needs, then they may lose their confidence in their ability to enjoy him and also in themselves as parents, as people. Their feelings towards this child may be different from their feelings towards other siblings.

To be told that your child is not the hoped for normal baby but is, or may become, a handicapped child, is a shattering shock and the parents may take a long time to go through the stages of reaction to this traumatic event. Sometimes it is obvious at birth that all is not well; there may be physical abnormality such as a deformed limb or limbs, a spina bifida child, a Down's child. Sometimes the child is ill, he may have some medical condition, he will perhaps be separated from the parents, he may be in an incubator or on a ventilator. During this time there will be a period of anxiety, of doubt about the outcome. Unfortunately the doubt about the subsequent normal development can last for months, and a definite diagnosis that all is well – or that something is wrong – may have to wait until the child is six to nine months old or even older. During this time the natural bonding process between mother and child is being disturbed, which is why some doctors are reluctant to say anything until they are quite certain that this child does have problems.

Sometimes he may have seemed normal at birth, but the parents gradually become aware that the child is not developing as expected, he is not functioning as a child of his age, being reared in that environment, should be functioning. At first they may be reluctant to seek advice in case their fears are confirmed. Sometimes there is the agonising situation when a normal child, developing quite normally, is damaged by accident or illness. However it comes about, the actual confirmation that their child is handicapped will be a shock. The first reaction is often *disbelief*: 'This happens to other people'; 'Not to us'; 'It can't be true'. The parents at this stage need to be able to ask the same question again and again, to talk to knowledgeable people, to be quite certain that there is no doubt about the diagnosis. They may ask generally for information to try to grasp the implications of the diagnosis, but this does not indicate that they are seeing far ahead to what their child may or may not be able to do, it is an indication that they are trying to understand what it is the doctors are saying to them.

They often feel *anger*, they feel it is someone's fault. The medical care was not good enough, they were given the wrong medicines or it is due to the in-laws' genes. Then comes the *grief*, the mourning for the normal child they had expected, the feelings of sadness, the feelings of inadequacy and/or failure.

In the mourning stage, the parents are accepting that the expected normal child has gone and in his place is a child who is 'different'. If their child is 'different', then they, too, are 'different', and because they are different they may want to withdraw from the outside community and they may enter the second stage of *isolation* (Drotar *et al*, 1975). This stage can be self-perpetuated: the more they withdraw the more isolated they become. At this stage, too, professional help may not be welcomed. They do not want to meet the parents of other handicapped children, they may not want to meet parents of normal children or to see normal children – in fact they may not want to meet anyone outside the immediate family circle. They need time to come to terms with the new situation, so this is not usually the moment to start therapeutic programmes nor to introduce them to special provisions for their child, be it a statutory or voluntary one (such as a mother and toddler group, a playgroup or a home visiting scheme). It is the time for a true, trusted friend to come and have cups of coffee and to listen and just be there.

In time, hopefully, they will pass through this stage. Some mothers say, 'I suddenly felt that I couldn't just sit there and look at him, I had to do something!' This third stage, of 'do something', can be to find care for their child outside the home while the parents return to their previous lifestyle. It may be, and more often is, a stage of *hyperactivity*, when the whole family life revolves around 'handicap'. This is the stage when parents seek other opinions, other treatments, when they join or start up groups, clubs, special provision for their child. Much valuable work is done by parents in this stage, but their efforts are not only helping their child, they are also helping themselves. It can happen that the handicapped child becomes the focus of the family and that in meeting his needs, the needs of other members of the family are overlooked, siblings can become deprived, marital relationships may be neglected. Any therapist working with the family must be aware of this hyperactivity and aim gently to help the family through this phase and into the final stage of *acceptance*, when the needs of all the family are considered: the needs of the siblings and the needs of the parents, one to each other, and their needs as individuals in their own right. Some mothers may have begun to feel that their only reason for their existence is to look after this child. They may have separated themselves from the rest of the family. Then the separation of mother and child, by putting the child into some provision outside the home, can be more traumatic for the mother than for the child. So before provision is arranged it is wise to enquire about mother's lifestyle, her hobbies, her interests apart from her handicapped child.

Once the needs of the whole family can be balanced, then the family can operate as a normal family. Maybe a normal family with a problem, but a great many normal families have problems such as redundancy, in-laws, illness, moving, etc. A normal family is the best background any child can have, be it a normal child, be it a handicapped child. Even if the handicapped child's needs are met by using care agencies outside the home, the family still provides a safe base to which the child can return in times of trouble. It is therefore in the best interest of this child to make sure that the family can function as normally as possible; any therapeutic programme that is devised which does not consider the family as a whole, though it may in the short term benefit the child, in the long term may have an adverse effect.

In order that the family may be helped to function as a 'family', the father's role and reactions must be considered. Babies are born to *two* parents, and there is growing evidence that many fathers have additional difficulties in adapting to a child with disability. Some fathers equate the birth of a damaged child with their own inadequacies as men. They may find it difficult to express feelings of ambivalence or powerlessness to relatives and colleagues. Professional demands to support the mother may merely exacerbate the grief and denial felt, but seldom expressed, by the father. If a father is excluded (often accidentally because of work or family commitments) from professional discussions about how the child may be helped, he may become distanced both from the child and the development of his own fathering role. The normal phases of grief already described may happen at different rates in the two parents, so that the father may not be at the same stage as the mother who has more day-to-day contact with their child. For instance, she may have reached the 'wanting to do something' stage when he is still in a mourning phase, and such differences may lead to conflict within the marriage. Research clearly indicates the often unequal division of parental care of a child with a handicap and the impact on the marriage of such 'unshared care' (Burden, 1979 and 1980). Both parents need sympathetic counselling and support, even if one or both may be pursuing apparently contradictory and professionally unvalidated solutions to a child's problems.

As well as coping with their own reactions, the parents also have to contend with the reaction of relatives and neighbours. Relatives may not believe the diagnosis. Granny will say, 'Oh

give him time, he will grow out of it, you were just like that.'
Relatives do not always see the professionals; they may not
understand and, because of this lack of understanding, they
may not be supportive at the time when their support is most
needed. They may give conflicting advice which further
undermines the parents' confidence. Neighbours can also
unwittingly cause distress to the parents by their altered
behaviour. They may be embarrassed and not know what to
say, and so deliberately avoid meeting the parents. This can
reinforce feelings of isolation. One of the things parents value,
when their child goes to the local mother-and-toddler group or
playgroup, is that they are accepted as parents by other
parents. This boosts their confidence in themselves as ordinary,
normal people.

To sum up, the arrival of a handicapped child may affect the
family relationship in three ways. Firstly, the family themselves
have to come to terms with the diagnosis, they may have to
work through a sequence of reactions. Secondly, they have to
cope with the altered behaviour of relatives and friends and,
finally, the child himself may not evoke caring responses from
the parent nor give rewarding responses in return.

WHAT CAN BE DONE TO HELP?

Partnership in Early Intervention Programmes

1 *Understanding the Child's Handicap*
Parents may need considerable help in accepting their child's
handicap. Denial is common and recent research suggests that,
a year after birth, many parents have not in fact fully accepted
their child's disability. There is some evidence that parents of
lower intellectual groups find mental handicap less disturbing
than those who find their own value systems challenged. The
prevalence of denial is born out by Wolfensberger and Kurtz
(1984) who found that only 42 per cent of a sample of parents of
a child with mental handicap actually admitted to their child
being mentally retarded – though they did admit to language
delay and other problems.

Goddard and Rubissow (1977) found that it is tricky
beginning work with families who have not yet acknowledged
that there is a problem. Parent readiness (with counselling and

access to support services as required) is essential for effective partnership.

2   Time and Opportunity
All parents need some time and opportunity to talk through their feelings before being asked to participate in a programme. Firstly, parents must be clear about the level of undertaking. Secondly, they must be aware that they must participate positively in order to continue (although exclusion is rare). Thirdly, early success encourages ongoing participation.

3   Skills
Parents need to be given skills to help them solve their own problems. Over-dependence on therapists or home visitors is always a threat and never productive. Some parents, however, go the other way and reject home-based intervention programmes, because they wish their child to have expert treatment. Therapists and home visitors (as in the Honeylands Home Visiting Scheme) have a responsibility to demonstrate that no service is exclusive and that home-based learning is not a cheap substitute for help which would be more appropriately provided elsewhere. Parents who have received further education may be better able to learn from lectures or reading materials, whilst those without may need more demonstration and discussions. However, the level of parental education has no relationship to the long-term results for the child.

4   Support from other Professions
The growth of domiciliary services (peripatetic teacher for the deaf, health visitor, social worker, home liaison teacher, etc.) can be confusing and daunting. Professional partnership is critical to ensure that agreement is reached as to who is most suitable and acceptable to the mother and who has most to offer at the time in visiting the home.

5   The Role of Voluntary Organisations
An important source of help, support and friendship for parents with handicapped children lies in parents' groups and voluntary organisations. Having a handicapped child may make one lonely. Many mothers (and fathers) find it difficult to

make friends with other parents. They may feel depressed and isolated. Small self-help groups may be run by voluntary organisations with local or national affiliations; or by local parents; or in association with health or education services using health visitors or other professionals. Many voluntary organisations run direct services such as discussion groups, toy libraries, holiday play schemes or home visiting services. Almost all act as signposts to other local services. Partnership between parents is encouraged by the 1981 Education Act (which for the first time requires health authorities to inform the parents of children with special needs about any voluntary organisation which might offer them help). Partnership between parents is a professional resource – and an enrichment of everyday life not only for the handicapped child, but for family and siblings. However, such partnership will only flourish if there is active encouragement from professionals on the potential of parents' and voluntary groups and accurate information on their whereabouts.

6   Planned Success

Planned success is an important factor for many families; there must be rewards for the parents as well as the child. A happy mother enjoying the programme will be spontaneously rewarding her child. A depressed, apathetic mother may not promote rewarding responses from the child. Recent work suggests that depression and non-reaction of the mother will change the behaviour pattern of the infant who becomes disengaged and negative in effect (Cohn and Tronick, 1983). However, parents need to be helped to see that, whereas the relative ease of many early stages of a home intervention programme may subsequently be followed by problems and a period of 'no growth', this does not indicate failure. Planned success needs to take into account not only immediate contingency activities but also long-term objectives.

7   Training or Education?

Sometimes the purpose of the activity is not clear. Should parents teach their children? Training is primarily concerned with the mastery of skills and does not necessarily require the user to question the rationale of the training. The distinction, as Cliff Cunningham (1975) notes, is that education is aimed at the needs of the learner, not those of the parent or attendant. Parents may need help both in giving choice and exploration to a handicapped child and helping that child acquire skills which are socially acceptable. There is no doubt that parents need training in order to work more effectively with children who may present professionals with quandaries and unanswered questions when considering problem solving and longer term development. Indeed, as the Warnock Report noted (Department of Education and Science, 1978), parents must be key people in ensuring that professional intervention is truly effective, and shared goals and an understanding of the strategies for meeting them must now be an integral part of professional support.

8   *Who Else can Work with the Child?*

The new growth in early intervention programmes appears to be in working with the care givers, in day nurseries, with residential care staff, etc. Indeed, one of the questions that has to be asked of early intervention is, should parents be allowed to opt out? The level of involvement may vary according to other family needs and there are certain dangers in expecting parents to be over-attentive to the handicapped child, so tending to neglect the other children and the spouse. The desirability of treating a child away from the family in order to alleviate stress, or to attend other facilities such as a Child Development Centre or playgroup, enhances and is enhanced by parental participation in a home-based learning scheme. Levels of activity and goals may be adapted to match personal needs and timetables, always assuming that good communication between home and centre ensures that these will be compatible.

Effect of Parental Support on the Developing Infant – what advantages do we look for?

1   Early home visiting programmes tend to judge success by improvement in morale and general satisfaction of the mother (Burden, 1980).

2   What difference does it make to the children? Early home visiting programmes have long suggested that early intervention

of a specific nature enhances mobility (Finnie, 1974) and communication and also encourages those cognitive and social skills which are brought out by most education programmes (Cunningham and Jeffree, 1975; Revill and Blunden, 1980). These children do appear to do better in school. The earlier the intervention, the less the loss after the start of school.

3 Merely observing regular assessment seems to give parents ideas and to encourage more purposeful interaction. Modelling can be a powerful training device for parents of mentally handicapped children; some specific difficulties may need more direct help, with training. Many writers, including Brinkworth (1975), Coriat (1968), Cunningham (1975) and others, have demonstrated a significant difference in ability of children of those parents enrolled in educational programmes from the child's birth onwards, and those left alone to 'spontaneous evolution'.

4 How much is enough? Some children with specific difficulties, such as a severe motor or visual handicap, may need regular visits at least once a week, but the Hester Adrian Research Centre's Parent Involvement Project (Cunningham and Jeffree, 1975) found that children visited twice-weekly did not differ greatly from those visited every six weeks. However, the parents of the latter would have liked more frequent visits. Parents seem to learn as much from the informal end of the visit as from the more structured earlier part, and the overall support by a known and trusted professional is therefore as important as a structured developmental programme.

Principles not Recipes
Home-based learning programmes, which are described in the Appendix, offer parents the opportunity to understand the principles behind any intervention rather than offering, like a car care manual, rigid recipes for tightening belts and guaranteeing better performance. As Elizabeth Newson (1976) has often said, parents are experts on their own child. They have a rich and unique knowledge of how that child functions and of his abilities and disabilities. But they may not know how to organise that knowledge in a way which is directly relevant to helping the child. Indeed, that knowledge, without the help of a professional, may actually hinder parents in helping the

child, since it may appear depressing, confusing and hopeless. A detailed assessment of the child will identify both the problems the child has and also the areas where there are no problems.

Many parents feel very anxious about assessment. They seek labels, hoping that a label will bring diagnosis and treatment. They are worried about the child's long-term future, as well as the problems of the present. Professional attitudes to assessment are important, since they need to stress the positive as well as the negative side of a particular child's development. It is often not possible to give an accurate diagnosis, nor to predict the future with certainty. Parents will naturally ask why a child is not functioning as he should. What caused the problems? What can be done to produce good results in the future? Not knowing can be very hard for professionals and parents. If the professional has a good relationship with the parents, and shares their confidence, it should be possible to give an honest 'I don't know why'. Where there is a partnership and mutual respect, the 'don't know' will be accepted as part of a commitment to go on trying and working with child and family in the future. The unknown is always frightening, and many parents have emphasised that they would prefer the truth. But information imparted must be accurate, for wrong information or wrong diagnosis (or failure to ensure that the parents have really understood what is being said to them) may create tremendous disappointment and unhappiness in the future. 'Knowing that a child has, for instance, minimal brain damage, without knowing the nature of his environment will not tell us how he will develop.' (Schaffer, 1977).

For an early intervention scheme to be effective certain criteria need to be looked for:

a)   It must utilise what the parents already know. They need to build on their knowledge of themselves, their own child, their family surroundings and their hopes and fears for the child's future. If parents are not fully aware of the implication of their child's disability and, indeed, if they deny the existence of any problems, an early intervention programme is likely to have minimal success. One concern about any home teaching initiative is that it may, by implication, teach parents that by altering their behaviour they can alter the child's behaviour; it is then only a small step for parents to say that the problem was theirs in the first place and, importantly, to believe that they have failed in not making their child 'normal' (Yule, 1976).

Many parents are incapable of working systematically with their children until they have been able to resolve their own problems and depression (Pugh, 1981). Thus an early task of a home visitor or a home therapist may be to work with the parents in resolving their difficulties; in identifying major problem areas (which lie in self-care skills, play, behaviour and other specific areas, as well as in broader developmental terms) and acting as an honest broker.

b)   It must involve a caring and trained home visitor who is able to link back to a wider network of professionals. The partnership with the home visitor or educator is seen as an integral part of the success – not least because it can act as a change agent in relationships to professionals (like teachers and psychologists) later encountered in the child's life. The programmes teach success to mothers who often feel dismal failures on every level. Their active contribution in enhancing their child's linguistic and cognitive development, as well as their motor and social skills, can be seen as their success. Some mothers are unaware that young children need to be taught certain skills: that they frequently lack skills in play and are unable to create spontaneous play or learning situations without demonstration.

c)   It is a personal service inasmuch as it can take place in a venue chosen by the parents. Successes and failures need not be prematurely displayed before a wide range of professionals who could be perceived as judging the parents.

d)   The parents can select priorities for them in their lives. Educational goals in the terms of formal learning may be less important (and indeed unattainable) unless the parents have first overcome practical problems like difficult behaviour, non-attainment of social skills or poor motor control.

e)   The actual level of parental involvement can be matched to individual family dynamics. In a real world the mother of pre-school children, living in poor housing and depressed by marital problems, is unlikely to participate as actively as a young couple with few other commitments, time, a good home environment and an enthusiastic attitude to working with their child. In their own home, parents do not need to compare themselves surreptitiously with each other. The home visitor can also act as an 'honest broker' for other professional colleagues and encourage maximum take-up of services.

f) Meeting other parents. There are occasions where parents may find it helpful to have the chance to talk with other parents (when they are ready for it). A mother may say, 'I felt sorry for myself until I saw the problem she had to cope with,' not knowing that the other mother was saying exactly the same thing about her. If a constant group gathers regularly, whether at a therapy session or at a nursery group, real friendships can be formed. These friendships, and discussions with other mothers rather than with so-called experts, can be non-threatening and a source of commonsense information. They may provide not only support, but also a forum where fears and feelings can be discussed and worries about the future aired.

Early home visiting schemes are rapidly growing in number, in distribution and in diversity. It is for this reason that none of the present programmes has been described in detail in this chapter, but all are given in some detail in the Appendix. Their very diversity makes it easier to choose a scheme that is applicable to health and educational backgrounds in various parts of the country; in some cases professional teams may even wish to adapt one or other scheme to suit their own environment. We have therefore attempted to set out what seemed to us to be the major criteria for this type of service, and it is important also to utter a caveat as to the dangers of rigid adherence to any one scheme.

The last few years have seen increasing criticism – or questioning – about home-based learning schemes and their application. Many criticisms reflect, probably correctly, the earlier, relatively ill-considered and rigid applications of some approaches; none can exist in a vacuum. A specific task-orientated curriculum must be put in the broader context of parents' other needs and must be backed by general supportive services. No programmes can be seen as providing a universal 'cookbook' for improving the performance of a handicapped child and offering instant teaching skills to the parents. The individual nature of a child's difficulties needs to be stressed over and over again and emphasis placed on the fact that the parents are being helped to encourage development in their one special child. The skills they learn may not always be applicable to parents of other children, even if they have similar handicaps.

Shopping for New Treatment Programmes

Sometimes parents may feel that the local services provided, which may or may not fit the criteria we have suggested, are not fulfilling their child's needs and they may look around for other ways of helping their child which are not provided free by either the statutory or voluntary services. If they do decide to do this, professionals may find themselves in a difficult and ambiguous position. Initial hostility or criticism is likely to ensure that contact with that family is broken. However, the professional has a duty to the child – and many families desperately need the advice they reject. Unfortunately, many of the more controversial approaches to handicap are expensive both in time, labour and finance. If money is raised by local rotary clubs, pubs or social clubs, the family may for the first time feel important. Not only are they the object of local solidarity and good will, but their handicapped child appears an asset and not a deficit. The mother, in particular, may feel excited by local press interest and perhaps by active participation from volunteers. Since many parents of handicapped children greatly fear rejection of their child by friends and neighbours, such optimistic treatment may well initially produce new self-confidence and acceptance for the child. In the early days, parents may have hopes and expectations which the professionals consider unrealistic. For example, many parents express the wish for a cure, or the longing to wake up one morning to find that their experiences were just a nightmare. Unfortunately, some treatment programmes which promise cure (and hence can demand tremendous involvement from friends and neighbours) do not necessarily justify their claims. Local interest and volunteer participation in labour-intensive therapy programmes are dependent upon improvement being maintained. Local schools which supply large numbers of volunteers for a few months (perhaps as part of a time-limited community service programme), cannot guarantee such support in the holidays. Volunteers may equally become bored if there is no emotional feedback for them. Long-term programmes of rigid patterning or exercises, or adherence to rigid diets for supposed allergy-linked deficits, are unlikely to offer the interaction and satisfaction they need. Equally, parents may become embarrassed because neighbours and friends, having given time and money, look for results for their investment.

In such situations, the family is trapped. If they do not proceed with a programme which may totally disrupt normal family life for negligible rewards, they have in effect wasted money and time. On the other hand, proceeding with a programme which is non-productive and unrewarding is also stressful. In the end, the family itself may break under the stress: the child may be admitted to residential care and much effort wasted. A background cause of such a spiral of difficulty is undoubtedly the time which some parents take to accept that a child has a handicap and that they themselves need help. If acknowledgement of the reality comes slowly, parents may actually have slipped out of routine contact with caring professionals. Unless assistance and support is persistently offered, such parents may present an efficient front whilst concealing many difficulties. Parents may feel a real dilemma in accepting help and, as noted in their reports on Honeylands' progress, Green and Evans (1982 and 1984) were able to highlight some of these problems of relationships and the reasons given by parents for using or rejecting the services offered.

Family support does not only mean facilitating the parent's skills in caring for a handicapped child. It should also mean family relief. Studies by the Family Fund (1979 and 1984) and other agencies clearly indicate the financial, emotional and physical strain of caring for a handicapped child. Parents need time to develop their own interests, enjoy their other children, meet other family needs. As one parent succinctly put it, 'remember, parents and handicapped children are PEOPLE, not machines.' It is easy to over-emphasise the parents' caring role to the extent that the parent may feel diminished as a person. Currently there is little funding for 'relief services' for families with handicapped children. But experimentation in using voluntary/statutory provision and short-term fostering schemes offers guidelines for the future. Volunteers are also becoming increasingly interested and skilled in the care of the handicapped, and can supplement some of the gaps in local services.

However, the crux of the matter is the availability of support when it is required. Most family crises cannot be anticipated two months in advance – but many families can only obtain respite care on this forward-planning basis. Parents with children at Honeylands, where 24-hour care is available on demand, emphasise how such a service can tip the balance between the family staying together or breaking down under the strain. The cost of permanent residential care is enormous, both in terms of personal and financial resources, and should never be necessary for young children. If long-term substitute care is needed, fostering should always be the aim.

THE FUTURE

As parents become adjusted to the fact that their child has problems, they will begin to consider the future, fathers sometimes sooner than mothers. The future for children who have been 'damaged' has perhaps an even wider continuum than for 'normal' children. Some of these children will always be children. They will need sheltered care all their lives; their developmental goals are to learn, as far as they can, self-help skills, methods of communication or hobbies to avoid boredom. They will not need to make big decisions, they will not need to take responsibility for their own lives.

At the other extreme are those children who are intellectually able but have physical or sensory disabilities; with modern technology many still lead creative and significant lives, taking full responsibility for their own decisions and actions. These children need to go through the normal stages of emotional development, establishing their own identity, learning to take responsibility not only for their own lives but perhaps, in the course of their work, for decisions about the lives of other people. In addition to this development they have to cope with the problems caused by their particular disabilities. For these children life is more challenging than for normal children.

They therefore have a special need for a good relationship with their mother, with their father, with their family, a chance of peer-group interaction both with normal children and children who have problems. These children will need to go through the stages of toddler conflict, of teenage conflict. It is normal for children in their late teens to leave the parental home and this also applies to all handicapped children, and especially to this group. The parents will need support in order that they can let their children go. Perhaps it is harder for parents to 'let go' of a handicapped child than of a child who does not have any special problems. Therefore these parents will need to be strong, mature people, able to absorb the aggression and conflicts that so often happen during the turbulent teenage stage when a young adult finds his own individuality.

In order to encourage the child to develop his personality to his maximum potential, the claims of the various therapists looking after him may come into conflict. For example, giving the toddler-stage child the chance to be naughty, giving him the means of mobility whereby he can run away from mother, get into mischief. This may mean providing him with some piece of equipment to encourage his mobility, but using this equipment may not meet with the physiotherapist's approval and he may thereby develop undesirable motor patterns.

Time spent in an unstructured way with a peer group might be more beneficial than a therapy session. The learning of aggressive words might help in emotional development, even if this resulted in parental disapproval. As the years go by the areas of malfunction may change, the needs of the child may change. So it is desirable to have a review, or perhaps reassessment, at intervals. In time the parents will gain the confidence and expertise to balance the child's needs, their needs and the suggestions of the various therapists, always remembering that programmes made have to be a balance of shelter and challenge tailored individually for each child. For some handicapped children, future happiness lies in conforming. They need a slightly more authoritarian, perhaps old-fashioned type of upbringing, when they are not expected to question but rather to conform. But on the other hand, the mentally able child with physical disabilities desperately needs the ability to question. This stage of development needs to go one stage further, simply because he has so many problems to cope with: the problems associated with his disability, plus the problems of growing up which will include not only the physical problems of moving around, but the emotional problems of having a stigma. Because he has these additional burdens, it is very necessary that he should have a secure emotional upbringing which is also challenging. He needs parents who are strong enough to be able to stand aside and watch him make mistakes and learn from them. It is only by questioning, adapting, improvising that he is going to be able to use modern technology and lead a full life.

References

BOWLBY, J. (1979). *The Making and Breaking of Affectional Bonds.* London: Tavistock Publications.

BRINKWORTH, R. (1975). 'The unfinished child: early treatment and training for the infant with Down's syndrome', *Royal Society of Health*, **2**, 73.

BURDEN, R. L. (1979). 'Intervention programmes with families of handicapped children', *Bulletin of the British Psychological Society*, **32**, 137–141.

BURDEN, R. L. (1980). 'Measuring the effects of stress on the mothers of handicapped infants', *Child: care, health and development*, **6**, 111–125.

CARLYLE, J. (1980). 'A paediatric home therapy programme for developmental progress in severely handicapped infants', *Child: care, health and development*, **6**, 339–350.

COHN, J. F. and TRONICK, E. (1983). 'Three months old infant reaction to simulated maternal depression', *Child Development*, **54**, 185–193.

CORIAT, L., THESLENCO, L. and WAKSMAN, J. (1968). 'The effects of psychomotor stimulation on the IQ of young children with trisomy 21', in RICHARDS, B. W. (ed). *Proceedings of the 1st Conference of the International Association for the Scientific Study of Mental Deficiency*, Montpellier, 1967. Reigate: Michael Jackson Publishing Co Ltd.

CUNNINGHAM, C. (1975). 'Parents as therapists and educators', in *Behaviour Modification with the Severely Retarded – Study Group 8* (pp 175–193), KIERNAN, C. and WOODFORD, F. P. (eds). Amsterdam: Associated Scientific Publishers.

CUNNINGHAM, C. and JEFFREE, D. M. (1975). 'The organisation and structure of workshops for parents of mentally handicapped children', *Bulletin of the British Psychological Society*, **28**, 405–411.

CUNNINGHAM, C. and SLOPER, P. (1978). *Helping Your Handicapped Baby*. London: Souvenir Press.

DEPARTMENT OF EDUCATION AND SCIENCE (1978). *Special Educational Needs*, Report of Committee of Enquiry into the Education of Children and Young People (The Warnock Report). London: HMSO.

DROTAR, D., BASKIEWIEZA, I. N., KENNELL, J. and KLAUS, M. (1975). 'The adaptation of parents to the birth of an infant with congenital malformation. A hypothetical model', *Pediatrics,* **56**, 710–717.

FINNIE, N. R. *Handling the Young Cerebral Palsied Child at Home*. London: Heinemann Medical Books.

GODDARD, J. and RUBISSOW, J. (1977). 'Meeting the needs of handicapped children and their families. The evolution of Honeylands: A family support unit, Exeter', *Child: care, health and development*, **3**, 261–273.

GREEN, J. M. and EVANS, R. K. (1982). 'Honeylands' role in the pre-school years. I. Developing a relationship', *Child: care, health and development*, **8**, 21–38.

GREEN, J. M. and EVANS, R.K. (1984). 'Honeylands' role in the pre-school years. II. Patterns of use. III. Factors inhibiting use', *Child: care, health and development*, **10**, 81–89.

NEWSON, E. (1976). 'Parents as a resource in diagnosis and assessment', in *Early Management of Handicapping Disorders*, OPPÉ, T. E. and WOODFORD, E. P. (eds). IRMMH Reviews of Research and Practice. Amsterdam: Associated Scientific Publishers.

PUGH, G. (ed) (1981). *Parents as Partners*. London: National Children's Bureau.

REVILL, S. and BLUNDEN, R. (1980). *A Manual for Implementing a Portage Home Training Service for Developmentally Handicapped Pre-School Children*. Windsor: NFER.

SCHAFFER, R. (1977) *Mothering*. London: Fontana/Open Books.

WOLFENSBERGER, W. and KURTZ, R. A. (1974). 'The Youth of Retardation – related diagnostic and descriptive labels by parents of retarded children', *Journal of Special Education*, 131–142.

YULE, W. (1976). 'Teaching psychological principles to non-psychologists; training parents in child management', *Journal of the Association of Educational Psychologists*, **10**, 5–16.

4 How the Brain Works

By David Mellor

WHAT THE BRAIN LOOKS LIKE

The brain of an adult is slightly smaller than a soccer ball, weighs approximately 3 lb (1½ kg) and has a pinkish-yellow colour. The two cerebral hemispheres with the basal nuclei and thalamus make up by far the biggest part of the brain (Fig 2). The brainstem connects the cerebral hemispheres to the spinal cord. The cerebellum is attached to the brainstem and lies behind and below the rest of the brain. Certain parts of the brain contain collections of nerve cells which appear darker than their surroundings and are called grey matter. Grey matter forms the outermost layer or cortex of the cerebral hemispheres and the cerebellum and deeper collections in the brain which are called nuclei. The white matter in between is composed of nerve cell processes known as axons which carry messages to other nerve cells in the brain and spinal cord.

Brainstem

The brainstem contains nuclei, some of which control movements of the eyes, face, tongue, jaw and palate, some of which function as relay stations for sensations coming from the face and mouth and hearing from the ears, and others which act as 'vital centres' controlling breathing, blood pressure and heart beat. The white matter of the brainstem contains major thoroughfares for messages passing down from the brain to the spinal cord controlling movements of the body, and for messages passing up to the brain from the spinal cord with information about the body.

Cerebellum

The cerebellum is attached by two stalks to the middle of the brainstem. It receives information from all the muscles and joints in the body and from that part of the inner ear which

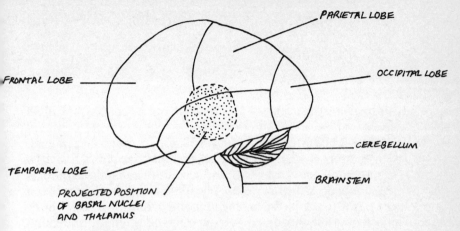

PARIETAL LOBE

OCCIPITAL LOBE

FRONTAL LOBE

CEREBELLUM

BRAINSTEM

TEMPORAL LOBE

PROJECTED POSITION
OF BASAL NUCLEI
AND THALAMUS

Fig 2. Diagram of the left side of the brain.

registers balance. After processing this information the cerebellum is responsible for balance reactions and for making
sure that movements of the eyes, mouth, body and limbs are
smooth and co-ordinated.

Basal Nuclei and Thalamus
The caudate (comma-shaped) and lentiform (lens-shaped)
nuclei are the biggest of the basal nuclei and are situated deep
in the white matter of the cerebral hemispheres. They govern
the involuntary changes in muscle tone necessary for the
maintenance and alteration of head, body and limb posture.
   The thalamus is a mass of nerve cells lying at the junction of
the brainstem and cerebral hemispheres. It acts as the major
relay station for the pathways conducting vision, hearing and
sensation from the head, body and limbs to the cerebral cortex.

Cerebral Hemispheres
Each cerebral hemisphere can be divided into frontal, temporal,
parietal and occipital lobes (Fig 2). Voluntary movements of
one side of the body are initiated in the cortex of the frontal
lobe on the opposite side. Speech is generated in a special area
of the left frontal lobe known as Broca's area. The temporal
lobes play a very important part in memory and learning.
Hearing also is registered in both temporal lobes but the left

temporal lobe contains a special centre for the understanding of language and is known as Wernicke's area. Body sensations such as touch are analysed in the parietal lobes and vision in the occipital lobes.

Ventricles and Cerebrospinal Fluid

Deep inside the brain are four inter-communicating fluid-filled spaces called ventricles (Fig 3). Each lateral ventricle (left and right) is in the middle of the corresponding cerebral hemisphere. Both communicate with the third ventricle which is at the junction of the brainstem and cerebral hemiheres and is surrounded by the thalamus. The fourth ventricle lies between the brainstem and the cerebellum and communicates with the third ventricle through a narrow channel called the aqueduct. Cerebrospinal fluid (CSF) is produced continuously in all four ventricles and flows through the system, escaping from the fourth ventricle to bathe the outer surfaces of the cerebral hemispheres and spinal cord. The CSF eventually drains into veins in the membranes surrounding the brain.

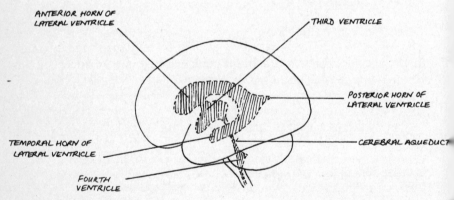

Fig 3. Diagram of the left side of the brain showing the projected positions of the ventricles.

Under the Microscope

The brain, like other organs in the body, is made up of many cells. The nerve cells that do the brain's unique work are called neurones but there are other cells which support and feed the neurones. A child's or an adult's brain contains approximately

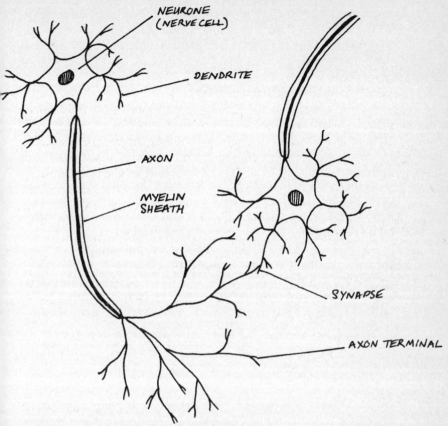

Fig 4. Two neurones showing a synapse between an axon terminal of one and a dendrite of the other.

100,000,000,000 (one hundred thousand million) neurones. Each neurone has many finger-like processes called dendrites (Fig 4) which receive messages from other neurones. Each neurone is capable of sending messages along the single filament which leaves the nerve cell and is called the axon. Axons may be shorter than one millimetre or as long as one metre, and have a pale fatty coat called a myelin sheath which is responsible for the colour of white matter. Each axon eventually divides and makes synapses (connections) with the dendrites of other neurones. It is estimated that an adult's brain contains 100,000,000,000,000 (one hundred million million) synapses so that on average every neurone receives messages from, and passes messages to, a total of one thousand other neurones.

HOW THE BRAIN IS FORMED

The foetus starts life as a single cell formed by the fusion of the mother's egg cell with one of the father's sperm cells. This cell multiplies rapidly and by two weeks a ridge of cells called the neural plate has formed along the length of the foetus from which the whole of the nervous system will develop. At three weeks the neural plate becomes folded over to form the neural tube which has a single central ventricle. The lower part of this tube will become the spinal cord and the brain will develop from the upper part. At four weeks, swellings appear in the upper end of the neural tube which will eventually become the cerebral hemispheres, the brainstem and the cerebellum. Immature neurones first develop near the central ventricle at five weeks and migrate outwards to form the basal nuclei and the grey matter cortex of the cerebral hemispheres and cerebellum. By twenty-five weeks the adult number of cerebral neurones has been achieved and production ceases for ever.

Although there is now a full complement of neurones, their complex connections have yet to develop. During the last fifteen weeks of pregnancy the neurones develop axons and dendrites which grow out and make preordained connections (synapses) with the dendrites and axons of other neurones. The mechanism whereby axons come to synapse with the 'right' dendrites is little understood, but it is thought to be under the control of the genetic code. Growth of axons and dendrites and synapse formation is not complete at birth but continues for at least the first two to five years of life. Myelinisation of the axons has only just begun at the time of birth and is also gradually completed during the same period.

WHAT THE BRAIN DOES

Basically the brain processes, integrates, interprets and stores information coming from the body (touch, body position, pain, etc.), the eyes (vision) and the ears (sound and speech). It organises, generates and controls body posture and movements including speaking. It is also the seat of learning, thinking, behaviour and emotional responses.

Seeing

An image is produced of the outside world on the sensitive layer (retina) at the back of each eye. This information is passed along the optic nerves and tracts to the occipital lobes of the cerebral hemispheres. The occipital cortex processes and interprets this visual information. Some visual information such as reading cannot be fully interpreted in the occipital cortex and has to be passed on to other parts of the brain for further processing.

Hearing

Sounds and speech arriving at the ears are changed into nerve impulses by the middle and inner parts of the ears. This information passes along the auditory nerves to the brainstem and then up to the temporal lobes of the cerebral hemispheres. The auditory part of the temporal cortex processes and interprets this information. The specialised part of the left temporal cortex known as Wernicke's area is responsible for interpreting the language content of the incoming information. It receives partially processed information from the auditory cortex (spoken language – speech) and from the visual cortex (written language – reading).

Movement, Co-ordination and Posture

Conscious voluntary movements of the limbs, body or head are organised and put into effect by neurones in the frontal cortex of each cerebral hemisphere. The left frontal cortex is responsible for movements of the right side of the body and vice versa. Messages from the neurones pass down their axons which terminate either in the brainstem (for movements of the eyes, face, tongue and palate) or the spinal cord (for movements of the limbs and body). Nerves arising from the brainstem or spinal cord pass on the messages to the individual muscles concerned with that particular movement.

Voluntary movements would be unco-ordinated if it were not for the action of the cerebellum. This part of the brain receives information from the 'balance' (vestibular) part of the inner ears and from the muscles and joints themselves. It then uses this information to co-ordinate and 'smooth' the voluntary movements generated in the frontal cortex.

As well as taking part in voluntary movements, all muscles in the body are in a state of varying 'tone' which is governed largely by messages arising in the basal nuclei. Changes in the distribution of muscle tone are brought about by the basal nuclei without involving conscious thought and are responsible for the maintenance and alteration of normal bodily posture.

Speaking
A specialised part of the left frontal cortex known as Broca's area is responsible for changing thought into language. If the language generated is to be spoken, messages pass to the part of the frontal cortex which governs voluntary movements of the tongue, lips, palate and larynx. Axons from these neurones in the frontal cortex terminate in the brainstem from which nerves pass on the message to the individual muscles concerned with the production of the particular speech sounds.

Thinking and Learning
Thinking is one of the highest functions of the brain and cannot be localised to one particular part. However, it is possible to state that thinking and problem solving are as much dependent on connections between different parts of the cerebral cortex as they are on efficient functioning of the individual areas.

Similar comments can be made about learning, but there are two extra points to note. Firstly, learning is very much influenced by environmental factors such as opportunity for, and quality of, learning experiences. Secondly, memory plays an important role in the learning processes and both temporal lobes and their connections are known to be closely involved in memory storage and recall, particularly in the short term.

Behaviour and Emotions
Behavioural patterns and emotional reactions, whether learned or inborn, are clearly functions of the brain but they cannot be

precisely localised. However, it is known that parts of the frontal and temporal lobes, the thalamus and their inter-connections are particularly involved in behavioural and emotional responses.

HOW THE BRAIN CAN BE DAMAGED

The definition of brain damage in this chapter has purposely been made very wide. It includes those conditions which influence the very early formation of the nervous system and lead to its faulty development, as well as those which damage the more fully developed nervous system around the time of birth or later.

Although much is known about the causes of brain damage, no definite cause can be found in a number of children who are diagnosed as having mental handicap or cerebral palsy in early childhood. The frequency of finding a cause depends on many variables, including how much reliable information is available about the pregnancy, delivery, new-born period, early infancy and family history and the results of investigations performed on the child and sometimes the parents. Few pregnancies or deliveries are free of all possible complications, but most result in a normal baby. When an infant is found to be handicapped, it is very easy to blame some complication of pregnancy or delivery or some untoward event after birth. Often it is a matter of fine judgement as to whether such a 'cause' can be accepted or whether it has to be taken as 'not proven'.

Genetic and Chromosomal Causes

Genetic faults are responsible for a number of relatively rare disorders which are associated with handicap. Some are dominantly inherited, such as tuberous sclerosis, and can affect members of several generations of a family. Others are recessively inherited, such as phenylketonuria (PKU), and can only affect a proportion of the children of one family.

Abnormalities of the chromosomes are another fairly rare cause of handicap. There may be a deficiency or an excess of chromosomal material. The commonest chromosomal disorder is Down's Syndrome in which there are three instead of the usual two chromosomes number 21 in each cell. This leads to faulty development of the nervous system and mental handicap.

Brain Infections

Bacteria can cause infection of the membranes surrounding the brain producing a meningitis. With modern antibiotic treatment, meningitis does not usually produce brain damage, unless the treatment is delayed. Meningitis in new-born babies, or due to certain bacteria such as the tubercle bacillus, may be more serious.

Viruses can infect the brain and cause encephalitis which may result in brain damage. Encephalitis may complicate measles, chicken pox, German measles and many other virus infections during childhood. Two virus infections are known to be able to pass from the mother to the baby during pregnancy and produce an encephalitis before birth. One is German measles and the other is called cytomegalovirus. It is now possible to prevent this happening in the case of German measles by ensuring that all young teenage girls and young women are immunised against the disease before the child bearing period, unless they are already immune.

Vaccine Damage

Much publicity has been given recently to the possibility of brain damage following immunisation procedures. It is accepted that one in approximately every three hundred thousand children has a neurological reaction after small pox vaccination which may damage the brain. Fortunately, small pox is now eradicated and routine vaccination is no longer justified. The position with whooping cough and measles immunisations is less clear, but many authorities believe that they can be followed by a neurological reaction and brain damage in a very small minority. Immunisation against diphtheria, tetanus, polio and German measles is generally considered safe in this respect.

Head Injuries

Many mothers fear that a fall or abdominal injury during pregnancy might cause the baby to suffer brain damage, but this is most unusual because the baby's head is cushioned by the surrounding fluid. Injury to the baby's head can occur during a difficult birth if there is a disproportion between the mother's pelvis and the baby's head, if the birth is precipitate, if there is a difficult forceps delivery or if there is an unusual presentation. However, such injuries are extremely rare with modern obstetric practice. Non-accidental head injury 'battered baby' is sadly not uncommon in infancy and may leave permanent brain damage in survivors. Road traffic accidents are the most frequent cause of severe head injuries in older children.

Poisons
Although few drugs have been shown to be able to cause brain damage to the baby when given to an expectant mother, the thalidomide experience suggests that no drugs should be taken during pregnancy unless absolutely necessary. Excessive smoking and alcohol in pregnancy are known to be dangerous for the baby and should also be avoided. Jaundice is common in new-born babies and is caused by a yellow pigment called bilirubin in the blood stream. Usually the jaundice settles without treatment and without causing any damage. If the jaundice is severe, treatment by means of phototherapy or exchange transfusion will prevent brain damage occurring. Before these treatments were available, very severe jaundice was responsible for brain damage in a number of babies and survivors often showed athetoid cerebral palsy and deafness.

Too much salt in a baby's blood can cause brain damage. Severe gastro-enteritis is the usual cause but making up bottle feeds too strong and not offering water in the form of fruit juices between milk feeds in hot weather can also be responsible. Lead poisoning is uncommon in the UK because paints for household use no longer contain lead, domestic waterpipes are now commonly made of copper or plastic and it is now illegal for children's toys to be made of lead. Severe lead poisoning in childhood can cause brain damage. Milder degrees of lead poisoning, which may be discovered by measuring the amount of lead in the blood, probably do not damage the brain but the evidence is conflicting.

Oxygen Lack
During pregnancy and birth the baby is supplied with oxygen by his mother through the placenta and umbilical cord. This supply of oxygen can be jeopardised by a threatened miscarriage,

placental insufficiency, toxaemia or premature separation of the placenta during pregnancy. During delivery the supply of oxygen to the baby may be impaired if there is prolapse of the umbilical cord, placenta praevia or breech presentation. Modern obstetrics has made tremendous progress in detecting and managing such complications during pregnancy and delivery, with a corresponding reduction in the incidence of brain damage.

Premature new-born babies often have breathing difficulties, either because of lung immaturity or poor control of breathing. In either case oxygen lack and brain damage may occur.

In older children, drowning, suffocation in house fires, severe pneumonia, very prolonged epileptic fits or cardiac arrest during operations are rare causes of oxygen lack and potential brain damage.

Sugar Lack

The brain utilises sugar for energy requirements and can be damaged if the supply of sugar in the blood is inadequate. Babies born to diabetic mothers and babies that have grown poorly before birth are at risk of developing a low blood sugar soon after birth but this can be prevented if diagnosed early.

Brain Haemorrhage

Premature babies have delicate blood vessels in their brains, which can rupture producing a haemorrhage into the ventricles. When this happens some babies die, some survive with brain damage but a number apparently recover fully. Brain haemorrhages in older children are usually associated with head injury.

Hydrocephalus

When a baby is born with some obstruction to the flow of CSF within the head, the fluid accumulates inside the ventricles which become distended and compress the surrounding brain. Hydrocephalus may be associated with spina bifida or occur on its own. Nowadays it is possible to treat hydrocephalus surgically with a shunt operation which bypasses the obstruction and prevents the progressive brain compression.

Thyroid lack

The brain requires normal amounts of thyroid hormone in its blood supply if it is to develop normally during the latter part of pregnancy and early childhood. Some of the mother's thyroid hormone can cross the placenta but if the baby's thyroid is deficient a severe lack of thyroid hormone commences after birth. This leads to increasing failure of growth and development of the brain. Many hospitals now routinely do a blood test on all new-born babies to check for thyroid deficiency. If the test is positive, early treatment usually prevents brain damage occurring.

Malnutrition

It is generally accepted that a good balanced diet (especially meat, fish, eggs, milk, fresh fruit and vegetables) is important for a pregnant mother, but the evidence for this statement is hard to find. Most babies born to mothers who have had a very poor diet during pregnancy will be quite normal, perhaps because the placenta acts to give the foetus a special priority for nutrients. This has been the experience even amongst women who had babies in the gruelling conditions of a concentration camp during the last war. However, evidence has been produced recently which associates spina bifida with poor maternal diet in some cases and vitamin supplements have been shown to reduce the risk of recurrence in mothers who have already had one spina bifida baby.

A poorly functioning placenta may not provide for the nutritional needs of the foetus even though the mother's diet has been perfectly adequate throughout the pregnancy. The baby fails to grow properly and is very underweight at birth. Because brain growth and development is dependent on foetal nutrition, brain damage is more common in children who have been born 'light for dates'. Nowadays it is possible to measure the rate of a baby's growth before birth by means of ultrasound scans, and the adequacy of the placenta's function can be checked with a blood or urine test carried out on the mother. Poor foetal growth or reduced placental function which does not respond to treatment would be an indication for early delivery to minimise the risk of brain damage.

Early infantile malnutrition can produce brain damage in

some animals but it probably has to be very severe to do so in human infants. African children who have survived the gross malnutrition known as Kwashiorkor may subsequently show learning disorders. There is no evidence that lesser degrees of malnutrition in infancy could harm the brain. Nevertheless, a proper balanced diet is important for normal bodily growth in all children.

THE EFFECTS OF BRAIN DAMAGE

Brain damage produces widely differing effects depending upon the degree of damage, the parts of the brain involved and the age at which damage occurs.

Mental Handicap

Severe mental handicap usually means that there is widespread brain damage. More circumscribed brain damage does not cause mental handicap as the processes of thinking and learning are not localised to one particular part of the brain.

Mentally handicapped children often have varied levels of skill. Some may have abilities with drawing or memory or speaking which are clearly much more advanced than their other abilities. This would imply that certain areas of the brain have been relatively undamaged. Educational programmes can be contrived to exploit and build on such strengths once they have been identified.

Associated handicaps, such as problems with vision, movement, behaviour, language, epilepsy or hearing, are not uncommon in mentally handicapped children. Careful assessment is important if associated handicaps are to be detected and appropriate treatment commenced early on.

Cerebral Palsy

Damage to the parts of the brain responsible for movement, co-ordination or posture results in cerebral palsy. The type of cerebral palsy depends on the site of the damage.

Spastic cerebral palsy occurs when there is damage to the frontal cortex or to the axons passing down from the frontal cortex to the spinal cord. The muscles of the affected limbs are weak and stiff (spastic). When only one cerebral hemisphere is damaged there is spasticity of the arm and leg on the opposite side of the body (a spastic hemiplegia). When the movement areas of both cerebral hemispheres are severely affected, all four limbs are weak (a spastic quadriplegia). Spastic weakness may be limited to the legs (a spastic diplegia) if the damage to both cerebral hemispheres is less severe.

Ataxic cerebral palsy is due to damage to the cerebellum or its connections with the rest of the brain. All movements are unco-ordinate and tremulous (ataxia) and balance is impaired.

Damage to the basal nuclei affects posture and may be associated with writhing movements (athetoid cerebral palsy) or fluctuating rigidity (dystonic cerebral palsy).

Epilepsy

An epileptic attack usually takes the form of a convulsion (*grand mal* attack) or a loss of awareness (*petit mal* or absence attack). Both are due to uninhibited over-activity of neurones in the brain which interrupts its normal functioning. Many children without brain damage suffer from epilepsy, but epilepsy is relatively more common in brain damaged children. Epilepsy is thought to be due to a defect in the mechanisms which normally inhibit excessive neuronal activity and prevent its spread to other parts of the brain.

Hearing Impairment

Deafness is more common in brain damaged children than in other children. This is because the cause of brain damage may also involve the inner ear or auditory nerve, or because the parts of the brainstem or temporal lobes which subserve hearing are included in the brain damage. Athetoid cerebral palsy used to occur more frequently before effective treatment became available for severe jaundice in new-born babies. As well as damaging the basal nuclei, severe jaundice frequently damaged the hearing centres in the brainstem so that deafness was often associated with athetoid cerebral palsy.

Deafness can often go unsuspected in brain damaged children as it is all too easy to explain unresponsiveness and delayed speaking on the basis of mental handicap. Careful routine hearing tests are essential for all brain damaged children if deafness is to be detected and treated early on.

Visual Impairment

Defective vision is also more common in brain damaged children. The developing eyes may be affected by the cause of the brain damage or the damage may involve those parts of the brain (optic nerves and tracts and occipital lobes) which transmit, process and interpret visual information. Some brain damaged children, despite good vision, may have difficulty interpreting shapes and spatial relationships (visuo-spatial perceptual disorders) because of damage to the parts of the brain which carry out these functions.

Behaviour Disorders

Many brain damaged children are well behaved, but behaviour disorder is said to occur five times more commonly than in ordinary children. Brain damage may be directly responsible for disturbed behaviour, or it may interfere with the learning of socially acceptable behaviour, or the presence of a handicapped child may so alter family relationships as to produce behaviour disorder.

No single type of disturbance is seen in those brain damaged children with behaviour disorder. Some are shy, clinging, easily upset and fearful of change or of making new relationships. Some are destructive, violent and anti-social. Some are hyperactive, impulsive and restless and have poor concentration and a short span of attention. Some have poor tolerance of frustration with frequent outbursts of temper. Some brain damaged children show autistic behaviour which includes obsessional play, dislike of changes in routine, gaze avoidance, inability to give or receive affection and limited communication whether by speech or gesture. Some children show repetitive behaviours such as head banging, body rocking or hand flapping. Some may constantly mouth or swallow inedible objects (pica) or bite themselves or others. Difficulties with feeding, sleeping and toileting may also be symptoms of disturbed behaviour.

Language Disorders

Some brain damaged children have particular difficulty understanding what is said to them (comprehension of language) or in learning to speak (expressive language). The left temporal cortex (Wernicke's area) is normally responsible for interpreting language and the left frontal cortex (Broca's area) for generating language from thought prior to speaking. However, damage restricted to either of these two left sided areas before five years of age is not usually associated with permanent language disorder, as the immature brain is able to learn to use the corresponding areas in the right cerebral hemisphere. Permanent specific language disorder before the age of five years usually implies damage to these areas in both cerebral hemispheres. After the age of five years, brain damage involving the language areas in the left hemisphere alone can produce permanent language disorder.

Learning Disorders

Many brain damaged children have more difficulty with school work than might be expected from their abilities in other areas. Learning to read, write and calculate requires the co-ordinated working of many different parts of the brain. If one of the parts involved in this process is not functioning as well as the others, or if the connections between the parts are inefficient, the whole learning process tends to suffer. In children with specific learning disorders the main problems may be with concentration, or memory, or language comprehension, or with visuo-spatial perception. Inefficient connections between the visual cortex and the language comprehension area may severely interfere with the normal process of learning to read and is one possible cause of dyslexia.

Clumsiness

Normal children vary considerably in their agility and dexterity, but some brain damaged children are so clumsy that it amounts to an extra handicap in its own right. Clumsiness may be caused by damage to any part of the brain which is normally involved in the control of movement, co-ordination or posture but which is not sufficiently severe to cause cerebral palsy.

Agility in whole body movements may be affected, the child having difficulties with such activities as hopping, balancing, running, jumping, cycling, P.E. and games. Dexterity in hand movements may be affected, the difficulties being with activities such as drawing, jig-saws, model making, using scissors, fastening buttons, tying shoe laces and writing. Usually agility and dexterity are both involved, but occasionally one or other is relatively spared.

When clumsiness is due to brain damage it is usually associated with some other disorder such as mental handicap or language disorder. The term minimal cerebral dysfunction (MCD) has been used to describe some children with varying combinations of learning disorder, clumsiness and hyper-activity or other behaviour disorder. The term has largely fallen into disuse as it has tended to be used by different people to mean different things.

TESTING FOR BRAIN DAMAGE

Brain damage generally presents as failure of normal develop-ment in some way. In order to evaluate the problems of an individual child it is usually necessary to refer to a multi-disciplinary team in a child development centre (or paediatric assessment unit) as described in Chapter 2. The paediatrician member of the team is trained to assess the effects of brain damage on the child's development, to diagnose the type of handicap produced by the brain damage and to find the cause of the brain damage if this is possible. By history and examination he is able to diagnose such conditions as Down's Syndrome, oxygen lack at birth, cerebral palsy, hydrocephalus and epilepsy. He may also wish to request various tests to aid his assessment.

Blood Tests

Some tests are carried out on all babies soon after birth (screening tests), so that rare inherited conditions, which may not show when the child is born, can be treated promptly to prevent brain damage from occurring. This is possible in cases of thyroid hormone deficiency (which causes cretinism and is treated with thyroid hormone medicine) and phenylketonuria (which causes severe mental handicap and is treated with a special diet). Children on treatment for thyroid hormone deficiency or phenylketonuria require regular blood tests to monitor the efficiency of the treatment, which needs to be continued for many years.

In children with evidence of brain damage, certain features may suggest a cause which could be verified by blood testing. The cells in the blood may be examined for abnormality of the chromosomes (as in Down's Syndrome), or blood fluid may show increased antibodies (as in damage due to German measles) or chemical substances (such as lead). Some of these conditions can be treated, but usually those caused before birth are irreversible.

Some forms of medical treatment can be monitored by occasional blood tests. This is particularly true with anti-convulsant medicines given to treat a child with epilepsy. A measure of the amount of medicine in the blood is very helpful when the dose needs to be adjusted.

X-ray Tests

Ordinary head X-rays give limited information about the brain as only the skull bones show on the films. However, the skull bones are sometimes affected by the underlying brain (eg. in hydrocephalus) and changes in the brain can be inferred.

A new X-ray technique known as CAT or EMI scanning represents a major advance as it actually produces a picture of the brain in cross section at different levels. CAT scanning is not required to evaluate most children with suspected brain damage but is invaluable when certain conditions such as hydrocephalus or tuberous sclerosis are suspected. The advent of CAT scanning has meant that the more dangerous X-ray investigations to show details of the brain, known as air encephalography and arteriography, can now be avoided in most cases.

Electroencephalography (EEG)

The brain produces minute electrical currents as it carries on its normal work. These can be recorded by sticking a number of small disc electrodes to the scalp and amplifying the currents they detect. The amplified signals are then fed to a pen recorder which writes them as a series of traces on paper – the brain waves (Fig 5).

Changes in the brain waves localised to one area of the scalp may indicate damage to that part of the underlying brain. However, the EEG is most valuable when epilepsy is suspected.

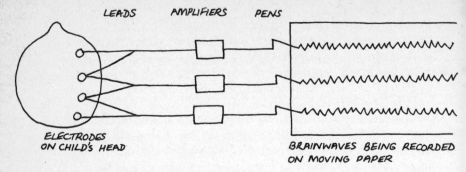

Fig 5. Diagram to show how an EEG is recorded from a child.

Even in between attacks, the EEG usually shows episodes of spiky waves corresponding to the uninhibited over-activity of the neurones responsible for the epileptic attacks.

Cortical Evoked Responses
The brain's response to noise and light can be measured if the more usual tests of hearing and vision are difficult to interpret. Two electrodes are attached to the scalp and the currents recorded are amplified and fed into a small computer. To test hearing, click noises of known pitch and loudness are made at regular intervals. For vision, a bright flashing strobe light is used. The computer picks out the brain's response to the clicks or flashes and prints it out as a trace on paper.

Psychological Tests
A wide variety of psychological tests is available for testing the abilities of children of different ages. Some assess specific areas such as language, while others measure overall abilities. Psychological testing allows a child's strengths to be recorded as well as his weaknesses, which is very important when educational or therapy help is being planned.

Vision Tests
Some estimate of vision is possible even in young babies or very handicapped children and these tests are described in Chapter 6. All brain damaged children should be seen by an eye doctor (ophthalmologist) as squints, cataracts and focusing errors are common and need early treatment.

Hearing Tests
Hearing should always be tested carefully in children with suspected brain damage and this requires the skilled services of a specially trained paediatric audiologist as described in Chapter 7.

TREATING BRAIN DAMAGE
This section considers briefly some treatment approaches but purposely omits educational programmes, social supports, genetic counselling, parental self-help groups and many other important areas which are covered elsewhere in this book.

Medicines and Diets
Brain damaged children who have epilepsy usually need to take regular medicines (liquid or tablets) called anti-convulsants which reduce the frequency of the attacks. Anti-convulsant medicines act to increase the normal inhibition which prevents the excessive activity of neurones responsible for the attacks. There are many different anti-convulsant medicines but the commonest prescribed include phenytoin (trade name 'epanutin'), carbamezepine ('tegretol'), valproate ('epilim'), primidone ('mysolin'), ethosuximide ('zarontin') and clonazepam ('rivotril').

Most anti-convulsant medicines are free from serious side-effects, even when taken for many years. Usually they are discontinued when a child has managed to go two or three years on treatment without having had an attack.

Some medicines are able to reduce spasticity when given to children with cerebral palsy and may produce a corresponding increase in normal movement and function. They do not seem able to help all children with cerebral palsy but a few show worthwhile improvement. Anti-spastic medicines include baclofen ('lioresal'), dantrolene ('dantrium'), and diazepam ('valium').

There is no evidence that vitamins in normal or high dosage help brain damaged children although there have been vogues for such treatment.

Behaviour disorder in children with associated brain damage can sometimes be improved with medication. Medicines such as methylphenidate ('ritalin') or pemoline ('kathomed') can help concentration span and reduce hyperactivity in some children where these are troublesome and are causing poor school progress. Tranquillisers such as haloperidol ('serenace') or thioridazine ('melleril') may be necessary if a brain damaged child with aggressive anti-social behaviour is going through a particularly difficult phase, but tranquillisers are rarely indicated for long term use.

Diets are not often prescribed. Rarely, when epilepsy is severe and not controlled by medication, a ketogenic diet is recommended. This diet gives a child a normal protein intake but carbohydrates are largely replaced by oils and fats; the body is made to burn fat instead of carbohydrate and this change in metabolism has a beneficial effect on epilepsy in some children. Recently a diet avoiding artificial food colouring and preservatives (the Feingold diet) has been tried for children with hyperactive behaviour disorder; the diet is not difficult and there is some evidence that it helps certain children. The theory that brain damage may be due to food allergy has been responsible for various exclusion diets, but there is little to support the theory and these diets can be unpleasant and dangerous if taken to extreme. Relatively immobile handicapped children are at risk of becoming overweight, which may add to the child's disability, and suitable weight reducing diets would then be required. It is also important to note that glucose is a sugar and substituting it for cane sugar does not prevent a child from getting fat.

Surgery
Brain surgery is usually required in hydrocephalus to prevent progressive brain compression. One end of a tube made of biologically inert silastic rubber is inserted into a lateral ventricle, and the other end passes into a heart chamber (ventriculo-atrial shunt) or into the abdominal cavity (ventriculo-peritoneal shunt). The excess CSF drains continuously from the ventricle, either directly into the blood stream or following absorption in the abdominal cavity. Thus the obstruction is by-passed, but the shunt must remain indefinitely. Complications may arise from infection in the valve.

Brain surgery is rarely indicated for other reasons. When severe epilepsy is known to be due to neuronal over-excitability in one temporal lobe surgery may be successful in reducing the attacks. Recently, implantation of pace-maker electrodes near the cerebellum, with subsequent long-term stimulation of that part of the brain, has been claimed to improve some patients with intractable epilepsy or cerebral palsy. It will probably be some time before this new treatment is properly evaluated.

Orthopaedic surgery is frequently required for children with spastic cerebral palsy. Because of the spasticity, certain muscles and tendons tend to shorten over the years, producing deformities. Physiotherapy can reduce the risk of this happening but cannot always prevent it completely. Various orthopaedic operations have been devised to lengthen muscles and tendons, transfer muscle attachments, and free stiff joints. All the operations aim to reduce deformity and improve mobility.

Eye surgery may be required to straighten a squint by shortening or lengthening one of the eye muscles. A severe cataract (lens opacity) would need removal to improve vision, but glasses or contact lenses are required after surgery.

Appliances

All manner of appliances are available to help children with various handicaps. It is easy to recommend them and feel that something has been done to help. However, they should not be used unless there is clear benefit to the individual child, as appliances label the child as handicapped both in his eyes and others. Any appliance must be prescribed on an individual basis to comply with the child's needs. The need for it and the way it should be used must be carefully explained to the parents and other care attendants including teachers, and to the child himself if he is able to understand.

Appliances may be used to aid posture, mobility, feeding, toileting, bathing and all activities of daily living. Postural aids include foam wedges for lying, special seats and tables, standing frames, calipers and braces. Rollators, special shoes or boots, walking frames or trolleys, buggys, stair lifts, ramps and various wheelchairs can be classed as mobility aids. Aids for feeding, toileting and bathing include non-slip table mats, easy to grip cutlery, feeder beakers, potty chairs, enuretic arms, musical potties and toilet rails allowing easy wheelchair transfer, bath hoists and shower units. Advice on the use of these aids is usually given by a physiotherapist or an occupational therapist.

Sensory aids to improve vision, hearing and communication are of great importance, and hearing aids, auditory training units, spectacles and low vision aids come into this category. Communication aids are undergoing a rapid revolution due to progress in electronic engineering; they include communication boards, Bliss symbolic materials, Possum equipment, language processors, special typewriters with key guards and speech synthesisers. Continuous supervision of the use of these aids is carried out by orthoptists and opticians, teachers of the deaf, speech therapists and language teachers as appropriate.

Therapy

Various therapies are available for the brain damaged child. They are mentioned here briefly for the sake of completion but are discussed more fully elsewhere in this book.

Physiotherapy and occupational therapy are particularly valuable for children with cerebral palsy and for clumsy children. Therapy aims to inhibit abnormal and encourage normal motor development and to prevent deformities developing. Its use is described more fully in Chapter 5.

Speech therapy is helpful for brain damaged children with language disorders. The aim is to encourage normal speech and language development. Nowadays emphasis is placed on the acquisition of language concepts to aid learning rather than the correct enunciation of sounds. Sometimes this can be helped by using a special series of visual symbols (Bliss-symbolics) for initial communication or even a sign language such as the Paget-Gorman system. Communication aids may be required for some brain damaged children who can understand language but who are unable to produce intelligible speech. The use of speech therapy is described in more detail in Chapter 7.

Behaviour therapy can modify undesirable behaviour in brain damaged children. It is usually planned and supervised by a psychologist, although the parents do most of the work with the child. Firstly, a careful analysis is made of the undesirable behaviour and the factors which maintain its continuation. Then goals are set to abolish or reduce the behaviour in a certain time scale. The way in which the parents are to do this is broken down into smaller goals or steps.

Desirable behaviour is rewarded consistently by praise, attention, tokens or other reward. Undesirable behaviour is consistently ignored or may result in loss of privileges. Gradually a 'shaping' of the child's behaviour is brought about in the direction of the originally planned goals. The indications for and the use of behaviour therapy are described in greater detail in Chapter 10.

References

GRAHAM, P. and RUTTER, M. (1968). 'Organic brain dysfunction and child psychiatric disorder', *British Medical Journal*, 3, 695.

GUBBAY, S. S. (1975). *The Clumsy Child: A Study of developmental apraxic and agnosic ataxia.* London: W. B. Saunders.

LANSDOWN, R. (1980). *More than Sympathy: The everyday needs of sick and handicapped children and their families.* London: Tavistock Publications.

NATHAN, P. (1982). *The Nervous System.* Oxford: Oxford University Press.

RITCHIE RUSSELL, W. with DEWAR, A. J. (1975). *Explaining the Brain.* London: Oxford University Press.

A SCIENTIFIC AMERICAN BOOK SERIES (*c.* 1979). *The Brain.* San Francisco: W. H. Freeman.

5 Motor Development and its Disorders

By Mary Clegg and Margaret Griffiths

Introduction

At birth the human new-born infant is highly dependent upon the mother for survival. In contrast to many species of mammal which can move freely on all four limbs soon after birth, the human infant is totally helpless in his ability to move from place to place and has to be carried in some fashion for several months. It is a year or so before the motor pathways from the brain have matured sufficiently for the child to have established enough control of his body to be able to walk. Other parts of the brain, responsible, for instance, for vital functions such as breathing, swallowing and coughing, have come into action with great rapidity as they are necessary for survival. Some higher functions such as smiling, reaching, vocalising, which involve the cerebral cortex, are present long before the child is fully mobile.

Development of the brain thus does not follow an 'ascending' function but centres mature selectively as they are needed. (Prechtl, 1981). Ability to walk on two legs is clearly an important characteristic of the human as it frees the hands for manipulative skills. It also enables confrontation for communication, even more the mark of mankind, which is manifested early in the infant before full mobility has been achieved.

However, control of both gross and fine movement is essential for us to perform ordinary everyday tasks, as well as skilled athletic activities or manual crafts. This chapter will be devoted to consideration of how these skills are developed, how they may be affected by disablement, and how intervention may to some extent restore them.

NORMAL MOTOR DEVELOPMENT

In observing normal development we are seeing the effect of

the joining of nerve processes from brain cells to nerve cells in the spinal cord, which are the final link to individual muscle cells which they excite to contract or relax. At birth, very little of this process has taken place, and the baby, although moving arms and legs, is doing this in a seemingly random way. Gradually, with maturation, voluntary control is acquired, starting with the head and neck, through trunk and arms to the legs. Also over this period the movements of the baby, crude at first, become smoother, finer and more graceful. It is possible to see an element of practice coming in. Moreover, these movements are active and voluntary, the baby moves himself in response to an external stimulus of his senses, such as seeing an object he wants, or in response to his mother's voiced encouragement.

The Unfolding of Motor Development
The control of movement is a very complex process; our muscles are continuously in action all the time we are awake, regulated by several centres in the brain. These centres are set up before birth by the positioning of nerve cells allotted specific functions. At full term birth the infant's brain has the same structure as that of an adult but is much smaller. The size is dictated by the diameter of the pelvic orifice through which the baby's skull must pass. The very rapid growth of the brain in the first two years is shown by the growth in size of the skull and is due to a vast increase in the number, complexity and efficiency of the connections between the nerve cells already present.

The centres concerned with movement (see Chapter 4) are situated in the cerebellum (mainly concerned with balancing mechanisms), the basal ganglia (co-ordinating muscle groups to give free-flowing movements) and the motor cortex in the cerebral hemisphere (controlling voluntary movements). All these centres mature synchronously, gradually bringing the eyes, face, tongue, neck, trunk, arms and legs under control of the three systems which send messages down the spinal cord to the cells activating individual muscle fibres.

There are however, other phases affecting motor development during the first year of life. From birth until the third or fourth month, in addition to his kicking, arm waving and his social responses to his mother, the baby shows reflexive patterns of movement. These primitive reflexes (also seen in other primates) are closely associated with nourishment and protection of the infant (Gallahue, 1982). These reflexes, which disappear around the fourth month, will not be described in detail but can be explored in accounts by Nash (1977), Bobath (1981) and Gallahue (1982).

The postural reactions which develop from four months onwards automatically provide for maintenance of an upright position of the individual in relation to the environment and gravity (Gallahue, 1982); these persist throughout our lives and appear to be unconnected with the primitive reflexes, indeed for a time both may be seen in the one baby (Prechtl, 1981).

As these reactions become established the baby is able to use them for increasing mobility (Figs 6 and 7) and increasing skills in manipulation (Figs 8 and 9). And with the attainment of control of his body the way is opened for further development in social activity, exploration of objects in his environment and wider relationship (Fig 1, p. 20).

THE EFFECT OF BRAIN DAMAGE ON MOVEMENT

It has already been explained that the function of the brain in controlling movement depends partly on the intact condition of the motor pathways which have been described and partly on the stimulus the baby or child receives to make him want to move. It must rely upon the integrity of the final path from the spinal cord by which individual muscle fibres receive messages which make them either contract or relax. The major part of this chapter will be concerned in considering the difficulties that a child will have when the specific motor pathways from cerebral cortex, basal ganglia, or cerebellum are damaged.

However, it is probably wise, in addition, to consider the other factors which may affect a child's skill in moving.

1   Lack of stimulation or motivation

A blind child is unable to see the world around him, to see his mother's face, and learn about objects except by hearing, tasting and touching. It is not surprising, therefore, that many blind children are delayed in their motor progress and this will be considered more fully in a subsequent chapter. The

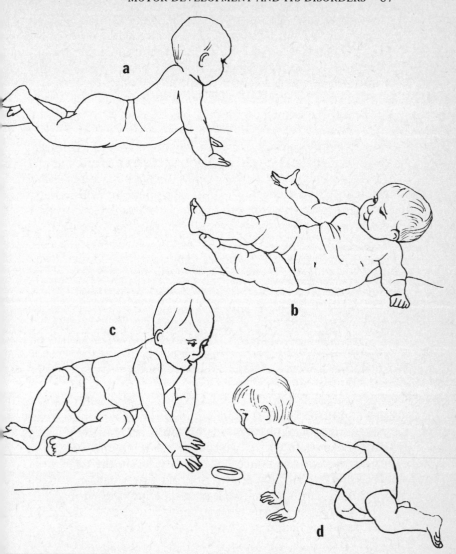

Fig 6. Paths to Mobility I
a) Child of six months able to hold up the head to support the body on outstretched arms.   b) Child of eight months rolling over (note the way the right leg is coming over the left and the right arm is swinging over. The head is flexed and the spine is curved).   c) Child of eight months turning to pick up object from the floor and from this position will easily get into a crawling position.   d) Child of nine months with good crawling pattern.

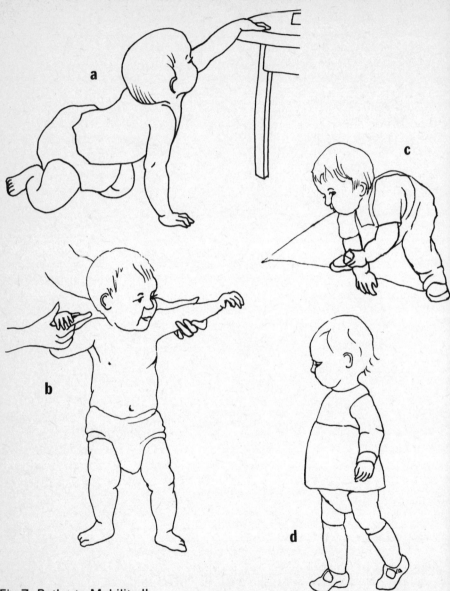

Fig 7. Paths to Mobility II
a) Child of nine months reaching to pull up to standing.   b) Child of nine months standing when held up but taking all the weight on straight legs and firmly planted feet.   c) Child of 15 months able to pick up object from ground when standing (note wide base of feet).   d) Child of 13 months walking alone.

Fig 8. Manipulative Skills
Once a child has firm sitting balance, hands and eyes can be used
together: a) Child of eight months passing toy from hand to hand,
and   b) able to hold two objects at once.   c) and   d) Child of ten
months not only holds an object but takes an interest in the bell and
plays with a cup and spoon.   e) Child of ten months looks at pictures.
(*Note*: in all these, the child holds an object at the optimum distance for
vision at that age.)

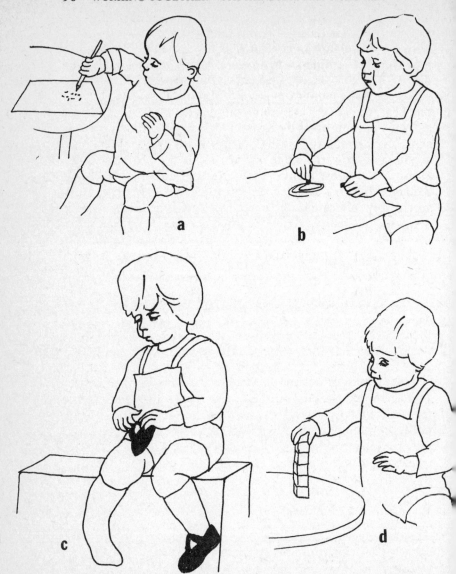

Fig 9. Increasing Manipulative Skills
a) One year-old child holding pencil in primitive all-finger grip and making
marks on paper. b) 22 month-old child copying a circle, c) taking off a
shoe, d) making a tower of five bricks.

motor patterns shown by a blind child, unless there is associated brain damage to the motor pathways, are quite normal, although he may not have either the stimulation to move nor the confidence to do it and will therefore need a good deal of help and encouragement during his early life.

The mentally handicapped child, although he can usually see and hear, shows very poor motivation in the things that he does and may in some cases therefore be delayed in acquiring motor skills. In the majority of these children the motor skills, once acquired, follow the same pattern as in the ordinary child. However, in some mentally handicapped children, the brain damage which has affected their mental development may also specifically affect motor pathways; such children will be discussed in Chapter 11. The routines described in this chapter, for helping any child with disordered or deviant motor development, are applicable with modifications to children with other handicaps.

2   Disorders of spinal and peripheral motor pathways

This group of children may be severely physically handicapped; those with spinal lesions have spastic limbs and loss of sensation below the lesion; those in whom the peripheral nerves are involved have loss of use of groups of muscles.

These children do not experience the associated problems that accompany motor difficulties due to impairment of brain function and their disability is more circumscribed. Their needs are predominantly medical, and their educational needs are very much related to their physical difficulties. Vision, hearing, speech and their capacity to learn are relatively unimpaired.

3   Children with motor disability due to damage to motor pathways in the brain

a)   *Cerebral Palsy.* The vast majority of children who suffer from disordered motor development due to brain damage are found in the group of children described as suffering from cerebral palsy. This is an umbrella word which has been coined to describe children with a wide variety of disability but in whom there is clear evidence of malfunction of one or more of the motor pathways which have been described. (Another less accurate term to describe these children, which is commonly used in everyday parlance, is 'spastics'.) It is true that children with spastic disability form the largest group within the condition of cerebral palsy. Spasticity is associated with damage to the nerve cells in the cerebral cortex or their processes. These children are stiff, their muscles are tense, and they find it difficult to change the position of the affected parts of their body. They frequently retain some of the primitive reflexes which should have disappeared before the age of four months (Nash, 1977; Bobath, 1980 and Gallahue, 1982); these are movements over which the child has no control. Therefore, these children not only have difficulty in moving, but if they are allowed to remain in abnormal positions they may gradually become deformed. Their difficulties will be discussed in much more detail when we consider how they can be helped.

The second group of children with cerebral palsy are known as 'athetoid'. These children have damage to their basal ganglia and their voluntary movements are very uncontrolled because the co-ordinating function which has been described is lacking. They may also show persistence of primitive reflexes.

The third group are those who have disorders of their cerebellum. Their type of movement is usually described as 'ataxic'. Because of their lack of balance they tend to stagger rather like a drunken man and may also have a similar jerky speech. One other characteristic is that, rather than their muscles being tense, they may be very weak and flabby, and this again may delay the child's ability to move about and use his hands.

In children suffering from any form of cerebral palsy, the brain damage which has caused the motor disorder may also have affected other parts of the brain leading to difficulties of other kinds which may include visual handicap, auditory handicap, speech disorder, behaviour disorder, mental handicap, epilepsy or specific learning difficulties.

b) *The 'Floppy' Infant.* During the first year of life a child may show a delay in motor development associated with weak and floppy muscles. This condition may be due to a variety of causes, some of which are associated with brain impairment, others not. Many forms of cerebral palsy already described, may present in the early days of the child's life as a general weakness and floppiness of the baby. And quite often it is only as the child grows older that it is possible to decide whether he may have an athetoid or ataxic form of cerebral palsy. As the child grows older the typical motor disability begins to appear: a spastic child will become very stiff, an athetoid child will show the typical excessive movements and it is only the child with ataxia due to a cerebellar disorder who may remain floppy.

Other brain conditions associated with floppiness are encountered in certain forms of mental handicap in which the most common is that of Down's Syndrome. These children are always very floppy in the early months and may continue to show this kind of weakness. It is known that their cerebellum is not well developed and it is thought that their lack of tone is associated with this. Such children show normal but delayed patterns of development in contrast with children with cerebral palsy who, in addition to their floppiness and their later development of typical motor abnormalities, very often have persistent primitive reflexes and very abnormal posture. Other conditions due to nerve or muscle disorders are beyond the scope of this book.

c) *Hydrocephalus.* Hydrocephalus is derived from Greek words meaning water/head. These children have very large heads due to the fact that the circulation of the fluid within the brain has been obstructed and tends to accumulate. Because the baby's skull has not joined up, the increasing fluid distends the brain, which is able to grow, separating the individual bones of the skull and distorting the motor pathways and other pathways in the brain. Increasing pressure may lead to blindness from pressure on the optic nerve and may also produce motor disabilities of either spasticity, if it affects the pathways from the cerebral cortex, or flabbiness and ataxia, if the pathways from the cerebellum are involved. Also, perception of shape and form and language development in these children may frequently be affected by these distortions. In some children, hydrocephalus is associated with spina bifida and the movement disorder in the legs is due to the damage to the spinal cord, causing flabbiness and weakness.

d) *'Clumsy Children'*. There is a small group of children in whom early motor development may be slightly delayed; their gait may be rather clumsy and their ability in manual dexterity may not be as good as that of their fellows. This degree of difficulty does not produce a handicap unless, as so frequently happens, there are associated learning difficulties. These will be dealt with in Chapter 8, but there is also very often a clear difficulty in movement, and some writers (eg. Grimley, 1980) have found that physical treatment to help co-ordination both in manipulation and mobility, very often increases their ability to learn.

CAUSES OF MOTOR DISABILITY

The ways in which impaired development of brain function may be caused have been considered in general terms in Chapters 1 and 4.

The same principles apply to causation of motor disability, although certain factors may be identified as being more important than others.

1 Genetic Causes

Some rare conditions, particularly those involving the peripheral motor pathways, have a clear familial incidence and mode of inheritance, (one example is muscular dystrophy). These children very often appear to develop normally for the first months or years. After the difficulties of movement appear, unfortunately, these tend gradually to become more severe. Neurological examination, biochemical tests and other investigations may then reveal the nature of the condition.

2 Acquired Conditions

When a child who is handicapped has been exposed to adverse factors during development, it is sometimes difficult to be certain of the link between them. However, when a number of children reveal the same medical history and have similar disabilities, it is reasonable to conclude that the two are related.

a) *Prenatal.* Certain adverse factors during pregnancy are known to be associated with motor disability. Exposure to irradiation, some chemical substances, and some virus infections, such as German measles, are known to affect the embryo during the first thirteen weeks of pregnancy. After this time the foetus may be affected by conditions in the mother which may lead to damage during pregnancy or make the baby more liable to hazards at birth.

b) *Perinatal.* Premature infants develop cerebral palsy more often than mature infants; the smaller and more premature they are, the more likely it is that they will be affected. It is difficult sometimes to decide whether the baby was born early because there was something wrong, or whether factors after the baby's birth have caused the condition.

One type of cerebral palsy appears to be specifically related to prematurity and that is 'spastic diplegia' in which the spasticity is largely confined to the legs and the ability to learn is unimpaired.

Athetosis can be caused by some forms of jaundice in the new-born. That due to haemolytic disease caused by rhesus incompatibility is now fortunately rare, as the blood condition can usually be prevented and, if it occurs, may be successfully treated. However, premature babies may develop jaundice in the absence of blood incompatibility and this will be treated.

States of emergency leading to poor supply of oxygen may affect both mature or premature babies; prompt measures for resuscitation are needed, and in some instances the facilities of a 'special care baby unit' may be required.

c) *Postnatal* (ie. once the child is one month old). It is always easier to define an adverse factor occurring in the postnatal period. These are usually serious conditions that certainly require medical, and may require hospital, treatment. Infections and accidents involving the head or the spine are the most common factors.

ASSESSMENT
Assessment of a child with motor disability will require the help, at some time or another, of several members of the team whose skills are outlined in other chapters, but at the outset the paediatrician and physiotherapist will be predominant.

1 Medical Assessment
Children whose developmental milestones are delayed, may be seen first by their health visitor and family doctor, who will

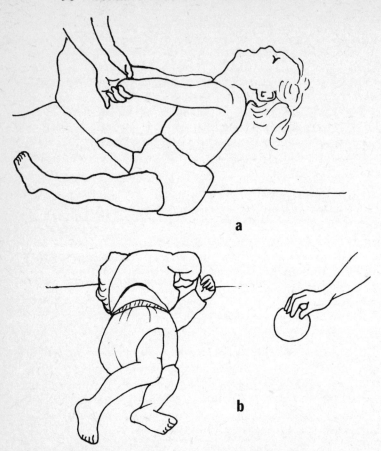

Fig 10. Limitations of Movement (in children with spastic cerebral palsy)
a) Shows the difficulty a spastic child may have in raising the head when being pulled up to a sitting position. Note also the stiffness of the shoulder and the straight arms. A normal child would lift up his head first and bend his arms to help with the pull.   b) Shows the difficulty a spastic child has in rolling over. In contrast with the normal child in Fig 6b, the spine is stiff, the head is held back and movement at the hips is limited.   c) and   d) Contrast the ability of a child who is able to sit alone and reach for a toy and grasp it with the limited sitting balance of a spastic child (Fig e)) whose reach is diminished and who would fall over if he were able to grasp the toy.   f) (Compare with Fig 7a.) Illustrates the difficulty that a spastic child has in pulling up to stand (note the stiff back, the hunched shoulders, and the stiff legs held on tip-toe).

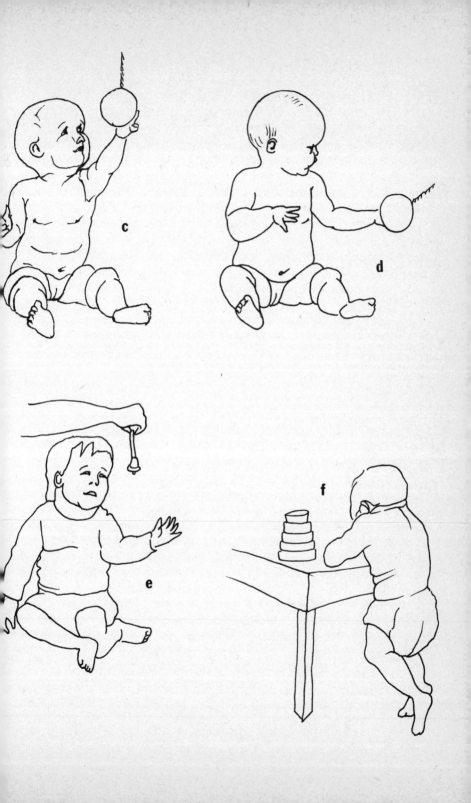

c

d

e

f

detect the underlying disorder of movement; alternatively, the baby may be attending a hospital clinic regularly, where the doctor is on the lookout for signs of brain damage based on a knowledge of risk factors identified during the pregnancy or around the time of birth; sometimes a previously unsuspected movement problem may be noticed by a stranger meeting the child for the first time, for example at playgroup or nursery school. At some stage during early identification, it is likely that the child will be referred for further examination and investigation to the paediatrician. This doctor will want to define the extent and severity of the brain damage by comparing the child's performance with that expected for his age, taking into account such factors as prematurity, other illnesses and life experience. A careful history of the pregnancy, birth and medical events in the child's life up to the present, may help pinpoint the cause and this, along with family history, may give the doctor sufficient information to be able to predict the risk and possible preventive measures to be taken during a subsequent pregnancy.

2   Physiotherapy Assessment

The physiotherapist looks for the stages of motor development and the patterns of movement which the child uses to achieve them, and she does this, with the mother, first by observation and then by handling the child. She will note how he watches his mother, follows her or other objects with his eyes, whether he smiles, how he kicks, whether he is passive or active and, at appropriate ages, whether he is able to control his head (Fig 10a), whether he rolls over (Fig 10b), attempts to crawl, is able to sit alone (Figs 10c, d, e), can pull to stand (Fig 10f), and so on through his motor milestones. She is not only looking to see if he *can* do it, but *how* he does it: whether the primitive reflexes are present or not, what postural movements he uses to attain his objectives, whether he has motivation to move. These original observations may lead her to wonder whether the child sees or hears properly, whether he understands appropriately for his age and whether there may be mental factors leading to a lack of response. If she has these doubts she will be able to approach her professional colleagues in other fields for help and advice.

She will then need to undertake a more detailed examination by handling the child; to note his muscle tone, whether he is stiff (hypertonic) or flabby (hypotonic) and whether this alters with posture; she will deliberately try to elicit primitive reflexes and the unfolding of the essential normal postural responses in due order. She will record any unco-ordinated movements and any asymmetry between the sides of the body, and she will evaluate the possible range of movement at large and small joints.

3 Overall Assessment
As a result of this careful analysis, the movement disorder will be defined and appropriate help can be planned in consultation with other members of the team.

The child's abilities and disabilities in other fields – vision, hearing, communication, 'drive' and intellect – need to be evaluated, within the family situation and with the parents as important members of the team, so that a carefully structured programme tailored to the one individual may be carried out. The presence of handicap in one area of development should always invite a thorough examination of all other skills in case the agent causing the handicap has been more widespread in its effect both within and beyond the brain. Failure to detect other problems could adversely affect progress in overcoming the physical handicap, leading to disappointment with the lack of progress. A physical handicap always makes it more difficult for the child to co-operate in tasks which are designed to show ability in other fields in children who have full control of their movements. These problems will be discussed in Chapter 11.

WHAT CAN BE DONE TO HELP?

1 Encouragement of Motor Abilities
Children with normal but delayed motor development profit from physiotherapy help, and this is particularly beneficial in children with visual impairment (Sykanda and Levitt, 1982) and in some mentally handicapped children. More general developmental measures (Cunningham and Sloper, 1978; Simon, 1980; Cameron, 1982) are appropriate for disadvantaged and many mentally handicapped children. In such cases it is

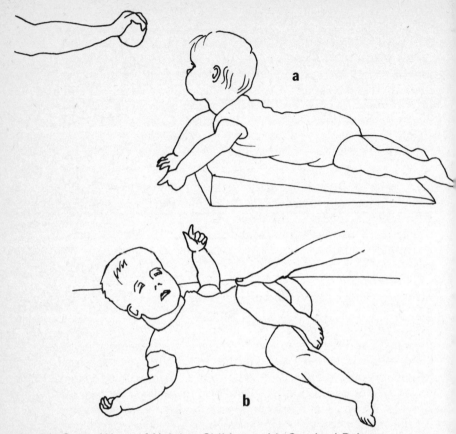

Fig 11. Some Ways of Helping Children with Cerebral Palsy
a) (Compare with Fig 6.) Shows how a spastic child with poor head contro
and inability to take his weight on outstretched arms can, by being placed
over a wedge, lift up his head and play with toys.   b) Rolling over (compare
with Figs 6b and 10b). This spastic child is being helped to roll over by gently
bending his left knee and drawing it over towards the right. The rest of his
body will follow until he is lying on his front.   c) This mother is undressing
her spastic child who is lying on his tummy. In contrast to children with
normal movement patterns, spastic children are much stiffer when lying on
their backs, so that rolling them over onto their fronts makes it easier to get
clothes off and on.   d) Shows how a severely athetoid child may be helped
with feeding. Note that he is sitting up to a table, the therapist is controlling
his back and his left hand, and is holding his right with the spoon in it. This
help with feeding from behind encourages the child to learn to feed himself

very often helpful at the outset for the physiotherapist to demonstrate to the mother or the home visitor the underlying pattern of the postural reflexes as they need to develop. This is particularly the case in some children with Down's Syndrome as their extreme floppiness is thought to be due to poor development of the cerebellum.

Treatment and management of a child with abnormal patterns of movement should not be thought of in separate terms. In other words, the everyday management of the child should be his treatment. His life style should be such that he is receiving continuous treatment in the way he is picked up, carried about, seated, talked to and further encouraged to meet the needs of his condition and to improve his potential.

Initial advice from the physiotherapist is nearly always given in the home: in this way she gets a better idea of the needs of the child and the problems the parents are having to cope with. More constructive, helpful advice can be given when the therapist knows about the home environment and can show the parents how to handle their child (Figs 11a & b), how to play with him and how to use the facilities they have to the best advantage.

During these first visits, the therapist builds up a relationship with the family, which lays the foundation for the future. The therapist needs to be integrated into the family, as the relationship is almost always long-term; although she becomes a friend she must retain her professionalism to give the family a foundation for confidence in her advice. This is not always easy to achieve, but must be recognised by the therapist and the parent or it will lead to a breakdown in communication.

What do we look for? To start with, it will be the everyday things which will worry the mother: the child is probably not sleeping at night, he is difficult to feed, she may already be finding that he is difficult to pick up, to hold, to dress, although at this stage she may not realise why this is so. These are the areas where help can be given and where the quality of life that she and her baby are experiencing at the moment can be improved. So at this stage we need to look at what she is doing with him from the time she gets up in the morning. Suggest to her where she can put the cot to give the most stimulation. Where is the door in the room? Where is the window? Where will she come from every time she goes in to pick him up? Can she change this round to give better stimulation, ie. stimulation from both sides?

We may not know as early as this whether he has any disabilities with regard to sight and hearing, so we suggest ways in which these can be stimulated until such a time as we know what the problems are. We teach her how to pick her child up in ways to encourage a natural balance reaction. If he has poor head control, she is shown how to roll him onto his side *before* she picks him up (Plate 1), so that his head will not flop, even if she does not hold it; in this way the head is supported through the shoulder girdle. We teach her how to hold him, so that he is easier to dress (Fig 11c), in a position promoting motor development, but inhibiting abnormal reflex activity. We teach her how to position him for feeding (Fig 11d), in a position

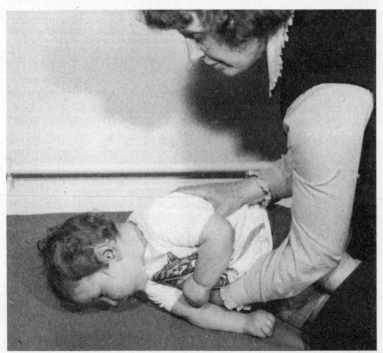

Plate 1.   Rolling a spastic child onto his side before picking him up to prevent his head from dropping back, as in Fig 10a. *Photo: A.J. Coote, Dudley Health Authority.*

comfortable to mother and child, promoting contact and interaction between the two of them; feeding must be enjoyed by both, thus leading to a contented, happy child. We teach her that 'treatment' is done through management and handling; it is a cautious process to be enjoyed, so that she feels from the outset that she is contributing something to her child's development. We can help with the position for sleeping, ways of seating, types of prams, ways to bath him; this is immediate aid, it is finding ways to help both mother and baby towards a more comfortable life. The mother will begin to feel easier with her child, to be able to behave more naturally and feel less pressure and stress. Once she starts to do this she is already on the way to helping her child develop as any other child would, in his interaction with her and the way she is handling him. She needs to be taught how to handle him slowly, to encourage him, to talk to him all the time (Plate 2), explain to him and give him the encouragement through her voice, through her handling, through her touch (Plate 3), so that he gains confidence in her and she in him. The more she handles him correctly the more confident she will become, because his responses will be more normal.

If she handles him incorrectly, she will begin more and more just to leave him lying on the sofa because she will be afraid to pick him up. This is where we, as professionals, must help her. This is the way we can help, in the very early months, to give the mother confidence to build up her feeling that she and she alone can help her child. She must be made to understand that it is what she does, not what we do in the few minutes that we are with her, or the hour that we spend once or twice a week. She is with him all the time; the more that she can be encouraged to be with her child and the more natural she feels with him, the better he will develop (Plate 4).

So, from the outset, without long periods of prescribed exercises, or interference with their family life, the mother finds herself in a natural and unstressful way the child's main therapist, and the child begins to become a part, but not necessarily the focus, of family existence. The importance of directing the physiotherapy 'treatment' to practical aspects of daily living and the development of social skills is particularly relevant in the preparation of the child for formal schooling.

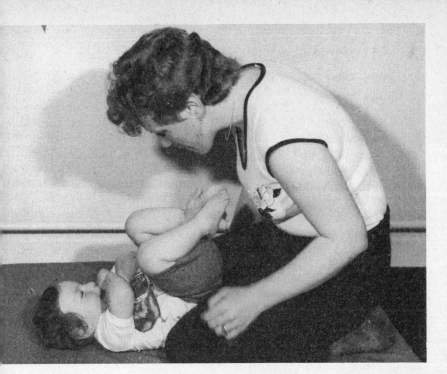

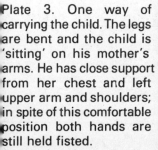

Plate 2. Mother talking to her child and getting his attention before picking him up.
Photo: A.J. Coote, Dudley Health Authority.

Plate 3. One way of carrying the child. The legs are bent and the child is 'sitting' on his mother's arms. He has close support from her chest and left upper arm and shoulders; in spite of this comfortable position both hands are still held fisted.
Photo: A.J. Coote, Dudley Health Authority.

Plate 4. Another way of carrying, with legs each side of the adult's hips, sitting on the right arm and supported by the left. In a good position for being talked to. *Photo: A.J. Coote, Dudley Health Authority.*

However, this transfer of handling skills from therapist to parents, teachers and other care givers, makes the task of the physiotherapist more, rather than less, demanding. It means that the skill of the therapist in selecting the best way of handling each individual child must rest upon extensive experience and deep knowledge of the basis of disorders of movement and of the various ways in which these can be tackled. Levitt (1975) advocates an eclectic approach which is favoured by many of her colleagues who are able to select from well established approaches (such as Bobath, 1980; Knott and Voss, 1968), and from new techniques as they are described, the most appropriate patterns of treatment for each individual. These tailored programmes can be grafted on to simple instructions (Finnie, 1974) and reinforced by a set of universal 'do's' and 'don'ts' set out by Yorke-Moore and Stewart (1984). Developmental physiotherapy is the hub of support for children with disorders of movement, particularly during the first few years, but other sources of help should not be neglected.

The child's motor ability is involved in other activities besides locomotion and manipulation, and the physiotherapist has to be concerned with other professionals and the parents in important social day-to-day activities:

Speech. The motor disorder may affect all the aspects of production of speech. The physiotherapist can advise about the posture of the child and, with the occupational therapist, suitable seating, so that the child can control his breathing and head posture, thus enabling him to co-operate better with the speech therapist in using the more specialised muscles for speech.

Feeding and toilet training. A stable and comfortable sitting posture is essential and needs to be individually organised by the physiotherapist and occupational therapist and parents for each child.

2 Drug Treatment
Relief of spasticity with drugs has resulted in improved function for some children with restricted voluntary movement due to muscle spasm. This improvement can be capitalised by

the physiotherapist to extend the range of the child's experience of movement, and may also allow the child to be seated more comfortably for feeding and playing. Unfortunately, joint contractures due to muscle and tendon shortening cannot be helped, as the relaxing effect of the drug is incapable of mobilising a fixed deformity. Most drugs in common use act on the brain, so are liable to cause unwanted side-effects of drowsiness, or lack of interest. Occasionally, the reduction in muscle spasm may lead to a deterioration in function, so drug treatment must be closely monitored by the doctor and physiotherapist lest it does more harm than good.

3 Orthopaedic Treatment

The help of the orthopaedic surgeon will be requested on occasions where examination reveals that the abnormal muscle action consequent to the brain damage has led to deformity, threatened dislocation, shortening of muscle tendons or a diminished range of movement of joints. The hips are particularly prone to dislocation which, if left untreated, will reduce the potential for stable sitting and interfere with normal walking. Low muscle tone or muscle spasm around other joints may lead to difficulty in maintaining an upright position, cause deformity of the ankle and foot, prevent arm straightening, and restrict neat movements of the hand and fingers. Careful assessment by the surgeon and physiotherapist will determine the need for supports, splints and surgical treatment to prevent, delay, or alleviate deformity and encourage complete mobility of joints (for more detail see Samilson, 1975).

4 Group Therapy

As soon as the parents feel up to it, it is important to start some involvement outside the home. This is always a big milestone to be overcome, as it means that they must have some acceptance that their child has a problem.

One of the most successful ways of achieving this adventure into the world is by attending a parent and baby group. These may be run by therapists or nursery teachers who should invite other members of the team to come along whenever they wish. By doing this the parents will realise that everyone is working together for the good of their child. It will also go a long way towards avoiding any misunderstanding. The paediatrician may also be present at the group from time to time, thus creating a more informal atmosphere in which the parents may chat to him. These groups may be run almost anywhere in the community that has a facility – perhaps in a children's unit or a physiotherapy department in a hospital, attached to a nursery school or run by a voluntary society. The groups should be of such a number that an informal atmosphere is obtained. The parent works with her child under the guidance of the therapist, but must not feel threatened or that she has to prove herself or her child. There must be room for the parents to chat and exchange ideas, thereby offering one another mutual support. The group need not be of one handicap: the parent of a baby with Down's Syndrome may get invaluable help from a parent of a child with spasticity. By mixing the handicaps the parents are less likely to compare and feel their child is failing. The grouping will be by age and ability and this allows the therapist to structure the session. These groups must not be confused with the more formal assessment situation which occurs at a later stage. They will, however, be an excellent introduction to the medical and educational assessment which must take place before the child is placed in school.

5   Other Ways of Helping

a) Swimming and Riding groups provide not only a therapeutic session but also social contacts. *Hydrotherapy* may be introduced at a very early age, providing the water temperature is high enough. It can be beneficial for almost all handicaps, with perhaps the exception of the child with a heart or chest condition or severe epilepsy. There may be intermittent reasons why a child may not go into the water. It can be helpful in severe spasticity to gain relaxation and joint mobility; in other conditions such as athetosis and ataxia the water buoyancy eliminates the difficulties caused by gravity, improves co-ordination and increases confidence (Plates 5 & 6). Children with visual (Plate 9, p. 134) or mental handicap and associated delay in motor development also gain in confidence by pool sessions. Some spina bifida children may gain complete independence in the pool and will improve muscle strength, especially in the arms.

Plates 5 and 6. In the pool. The child is still somewhat stiff. Plate 5 shows relaxation of the shoulders and hands when the head only is supported by the therapist and the buoyancy of the water floats the body. *Photos: A.J. Coote, Dudley Health Authority.*

Riding is usually introduced from the age of three-and-a-half to four years. In some cases it may be earlier. Children with many forms of brain damage improve with riding. The child with total paraplegia will be completely mobile on a horse; spastics and low tone diplegias usually learn to ride well, the abduction of legs in the riding position, together with the movement of the horse, improving balance, promoting relaxation and reducing spasticity; the ataxic child learns balance and the athetoid child learns to co-ordinate his movements better, as does the child who comes under the heading of 'clumsy' (Grimley, 1980). Children with visual, communication and mental handicap also gain in confidence.

b) Soft Play Areas. A total soft play environment is invaluable when working with the hyperactive, clumsy children and active children with mental handicap. It provides an area in which they can learn many gross motor, spatial and perceptual skills (Knight, 1984).

c) Aids and Equipment. Aids should be looked upon as something which helps a child to perform better. Equipment such as chairs and seating is highly specialised. Seating must hold the child correctly and, since it will be used during the greater part of his waking hours, must be comfortable and prevent deformity as much as possible. The use of equipment should be kept to a minimum and normal everyday things used (Caston, 1981); it will often be better to make a small adaptation to a piece of household furniture than to purchase an expensive piece of equipment which will not be used after the first week. Barton *et al* (1980), Finnie (1974) and others describe in detail many excellent devices for making children more mobile, easier to bath and feed, improving their sitting posture and their ability to communicate.

Wheelchairs are normally available in the United Kingdom from the DHSS on prescription from a doctor who, hopefully but not invariably, will seek advice from a therapist as to the best type, measurement and modifications. Where necessary, other more suitable models will be suggested by the therapist. The decision as to whether or not a child needs to use a wheelchair is often a very difficult one. For some children, it aids mobility to such an extent that ways are opened to leisure activities and their lifestyle is widened and normalised (as any who have watched wheelchair athletics will agree). In other cases, the child may abandon the struggle for independence through walking, when this is an achievable goal, and subside into wheelchair existence as an easier option. A recommendation should never be made in haste, and there should always be thorough consultations between parents, therapists, teachers and doctors before a decision in principle is made. The type of wheelchair (Russell, 1984) can then be selected by parent and therapist, preferably on a trial basis. Once a child is given a wheelchair it should be looked upon as an additional means to freedom; training in transfer from wheelchair to ordinary chair, to bed, to toilet seat should be started in every child who is able to co-operate, and lifting by parents and colleagues should be eliminated as much as possible; when it is necessary, however, thcy should receive careful instruction in how it can best be done to avoid back problems.

Formal Education
Early training towards normal posture, mobility, communication, social and manipulative skills, is the foundation upon which continuing education must be based. Failure to obtain the right kind of help in the early years compounds the handicap by allowing permanent deformities and lack of sensory stimulation. On-going assessment, coupled with individual programmes of management, enable the team, and in particular psychologists and teachers, to build up a picture of the child's strengths and weaknesses to enable them to advise and, with the parents, to recommend the most suitable educational placement for each child. Some children flourish in response to the challenge of life in an ordinary school; others do better in the more sheltered environment of a special school, where smaller classes and skilled teaching enable them to learn in the best way and at their own pace; for others a compromise may be found in a special unit within the campus of an ordinary school. Parents and professionals need to shed their personal prejudices in these decisions, and seek the available placement most suited to the child.

Education and the Physiotherapist

The handicapped child is now being offered nursery placement by the Education Authorities at a much earlier age. The therapist will be asked to give a report on the child's abilities before he is admitted to school. This report should include gross and fine motor skills, self-help skills and details about environmental needs, together with equipment needs. She should visit the school or nursery to advise the staff on the child's ability, how to handle him if necessary and the best positions for him to work in throughout the day. She will also need to give advice on the 'do's and don'ts' for physical education (George and Hart, 1983).

The child who is admitted to a normal school should integrate as much as possible and must not be made to feel different. If physiotherapy treatment is to be continued, this must be done at a time suitable to both the school and the child.

In most schools for children with handicaps, there will be a physiotherapist on the staff or visiting the school on a regular basis. Many special schools for physically handicapped children have excellent facilities for physical treatment, but the therapist should never be confined to these quarters. Classrooms, gymnasia, swimming pools, playgrounds and playing fields are the places where movement happens and where staff and children can learn ways to make this easier and more effective under the therapist's guidance.

Growing up

The test of the adequacy or otherwise of measures taken to help a physically handicapped child during the school years is his ability to integrate into an adult world. Hopefully, most children will be able to continue education and training beyond school leaving age and find employment or occupation in some aspect that interests them and is within their competence. Attendance at any ordinary school does not always give a handicapped child an advantage over his fellows who have been educated in a special school; the nub of the problem is whether the school has been able to meet the child's need for social independence and for striving to reach realistic goals of which he may be capable.

The academic children should be trained for exams,

instructed in the use of aids to expressing themselves and encouraged to seek a career which is suitable for their intellectual level and compatible with their physical difficulties. Those who do not favour an academic approach but who are capable of employment on the open market should be offered work experience while they are still at school so that both they and prospective employers may be made aware of the difficulties that they will have to face. More severely handicapped young people may need to be accommodated in sheltered workshop provision.

References

BARTON, E. M., HOLLOBON, B. and WOODS, G. E. (1980). 'Appliances used to help the handicapped child under three to follow the normal developmental sequence', *Child: care, health and development*, **6**, 209–232.

BOBATH, K. (1980). *A Neurophysiological Basis for the Treatment of Cerebral Palsy*. London: Heinemann Medical Books. Philadelphia: Lippincott.

CAMERON, R. J. (ed) (1982). *Working Together: Portage in the U.K.* Windsor: NFER/Nelson.

CASTON, D. (1981). *Easy to Make Aids for Your Handicapped Child*. London: Souvenir Press.

CUNNINGHAM, C. and SLOPER, P. (1978). *Helping Your Handicapped Baby*. London: Souvenir Press.

FINNIE, N. R. (1974). *Handling the Young Cerebral Palsied Child at Home*. London: Heinemann Medical Books.

GALLAHUE, D. L. (1982). *Understanding Motor Development in Children*. New York, Chichester: Wiley.

GEORGE, S. J. and HART, B. (1983). *Physical Education for Handicapped Children*. London: Souvenir Press.

GRIMLEY, A. (1980). 'Physiotherapy' in *Helping Clumsy Children* (pp 56–72), GORDON, N. and McINLAY, I. (eds). London, Edinburgh and New York: Churchill Livingstone.

KNIGHT, L. (1984). 'Soft play – movement, motivation and fun', *Newsletter*, February 1984, 7–8. Association of Chartered Physiotherapists.

KNOTT, M. and VOSS, D. E. (1968). *Proprioceptive Neuromuscular Facilitation*, second edition. New York: Hoeher.

LEVITT, S. (1975). 'Stimulation of movement; a review of modern therapeutic techniques' in *Movement and Child Development*, HOLT, K. (ed). London: Heinemann Medical Books.

NASH, M. I. (1977). 'Assessment of gross and fine movement in cerebral palsy' in *Neurodevelopmental Problems in Early Childhood*, DRILLIEN, C. and DRUMMOND, M. (eds). Oxford: Blackwell.

PRECHTL, H. F. R. (1981). 'The study of neural development as a perspective of clinical problems' in *Maturation and Development* (pp. 198–215), CONNOLLY, K. J. and PRECHTL, H. F. R. (eds). London: Heinemann Medical Books. Philadelphia: Lippincott.

RUSSELL, P. (1984). *The Wheelchair Child*, second edition. London: Souvenir Press.

SAMILSON, R. L. (ed) (1975). *Orthopaedic Aspects of Cerebral Palsy*. London: Heinemann Medical Books. Philadelphia: Lippincott.

SIMON, G. B. (1981). *The Next Step on the Ladder*. Kidderminster: British Institute of Mental Handicap.

SYKANDA, A. M. and LEVITT, S. (1982). 'The physiotherapist in the developmental management of the visually impaired child', *Child: care, health and development*, **8**, 261–270.

YORKE-MOORE, R. and STEWART, P. (1984). *Management of the Physically Handicapped Child. Pamphlet 1* Guidelines to Handling. *Pamphlet 2* Guidelines to Lifting, Carrying and Seating. Kidderminster: British Institute of Mental Handicap.

Background Reading

BLECK, E. E. and NAGEL, D. A. (1975). *Physically Handicapped Children: A Medical Atlas for Teachers*. New York and London: Grune and Stratton.

GORDON, N. and McINLAY, I. (1980). *Helping Clumsy Children*. London and Edinburgh: Churchill Livingstone.

HOLT, K. S. (1975). *Movement and Child Development*. London: Heinemann Medical Books. Philadelphia: Lippincott.

LEVITT, S. (1977). *Treatment of Cerebral Palsy and Motor Delay*. Oxford: Blackwell.

SCRUTTON, D. and GILBERTSON, M. (1975). *Physiotherapy in Paediatric Practice.* London: Butterworth.

SHEPHERD, R. B. (1974). *Physiotherapy in Paediatrics.* London: Heinemann Medical Books.

6 Vision and Visual Handicap

By Margaret Griffiths and Sister John

WHAT IS VISION?

Sight is an important sensory pathway by which we learn about our environment. Vision implies a complex activity in which sight is used to collect visual impressions which, on transmission to the brain, must be analysed, sorted, recalled and synthesised before meaning is given to the objects and activities that are 'seen'. Clearly it is essential that the collecting mechanism (the eye) should function perfectly to provide accurate and well-defined images on the retina prior to transmission to the brain. Equally, perfect 'photography' by the eye is useless unless the mechanisms within the brain are able to utilise the messages which the eye produces. Well might Jan and his colleagues (1977) state that 'it is the brain that sees'.

When we say that a child can see, therefore, we mean that the eye is able to catch and record a visual image and that the child, through his brain, can use such stimuli to make sense of the world around him. He builds up a series of responses and actions which eventually make him an independent person.

The importance of these processes for learning and development cannot be overestimated and, particularly in early life, an impairment in any part of the chain is bound to lead to impoverishment of experience and skills in more than one field of ability.

THE DEVELOPMENT OF VISION

Up to the time of birth the developing baby is not exposed to sources of light, but during this period the eyes develop fully and the parts of the brain designated to respond to stimuli from the retina, and to analyse or store them, are prepared at the time of full-term birth to take up their function immediately visual stimuli are presented.

At birth normal eyes are potentially perfect cameras in which the focusing mechanisms and the means by which both eyes together can fix on an object are not fully mature. However, at the end of the first year of life the definition of an image is as good as that in an adult (Catford and Oliver, 1973).

Even during the first few months of life, when the optical images may not be perfect, the infant is able to make use of his vision in a way that shows the higher brain mechanisms have come into play. He responds with a smile to his mother and other members of his close circle, he reaches for objects which please him before he is able to handle them. He shows a preference, very early, for the human face, and for pictures resembling it (Brazelton, *et al*, 1966). With increasing steadiness in sitting, he begins to manipulate objects and to combine the senses of sight, touch, hearing and taste in appreciating the various shapes, textures and functions of the structures he handles. With increasing mobility, he learns to find more distant objects and to be aware of their constancy.

By the time the child is two years of age, he is able to use two-dimensional reproductions (pictures) and small three-dimensional objects (toys) to represent real articles in the world around him.

In observing the normal child we come to realise how, in his development, he combines vision, hearing, mobility and communication skills, social needs and emotional responses in a global fashion – in his emergence as a person. The close interaction between different skills as they develop also implies interdependence. Delay in the acquisition of one is bound to affect the acquisition of others. This is particularly true in the case of children with visual impairment, when delayed development is likely to occur in all fields unless very early intervention is possible (Fraiberg, 1977; Scott, *et al*, 1977).

WHAT IS VISUAL HANDICAP?

As adults we may try to imagine what blindness is like by providing ourselves with blindfolds and trying to eat, to dress, to get about the house or to communicate with one another. Difficult as these tasks may be under such circumstances, we have the advantage of an immense store of images, moving or still, which have been built up over the years and which, with auditory and tactile clues, are available to help us solve our problems. Children who are visually handicapped from birth have none of these memories, and the auditory and tactile clues they receive are meaningless until they are helped to understand them.

Not all visually handicapped children are totally blind; some are able to perceive differences in light and shade and others receive images which are so distorted, blurred or fragmentary that it is difficult or impossible to extract meaning from a visual world.

Other children may start life with normal vision, and will have a store of visual memories, their associated meanings and emotional links, until an accident, infection, tumour or degenerative condition leads to loss of sight. In these children, in addition to blindness, the sudden, inexplicable loss of such an important sensory channel may give rise to psychological upset.

The correlation of function between eye and brain has already been emphasised; it follows therefore that visual handicap may be produced:

a) when the eyes only are affected;
b) when the eyes function normally but the brain is unable to use the messages they send;
c) when eyes and brain are both affected.

In figures quoted for the United Kingdom in the Vernon Report to the Department of Education and Science (1972), and for British Columbia by Jan, *et al* (1977), the proportion of children in whom the complex handicap suggested by alternative c) is present is found to be just over 50 per cent. This very high proportion of children with multiple handicap offers a challenge to all who work with the visually handicapped. In particular, it underlines the importance of careful, comprehensive assessment to evaluate the interplay of several handicaps in one child, the often global effect of visual handicap and the necessity to distinguish this from mental handicap. This assessment procedure should always be associated with continuing programmes of support for the child and family, with careful evaluation of progress.

ASSESSMENT OF VISUAL HANDICAP
In some children there may be an obvious defect of the eyes at

birth, in others the mother may very soon notice that her child does not appear to see; but, however it is discovered, severe visual impairment from birth usually becomes obvious during the first year of life. Less severe disability may be detected later.

Screening tests for the detection of a squint and a rough estimate of visual acuity using white balls of graduated size (Sheridan, 1969; Gardiner, 1982), are carried out on all children. This is not an assessment but a pass/fail test which will indicate whether a fuller examination is necessary.

The fuller assessment procedures for a child who is suspected to have visual impairment can be considered in two parts:

a) *The ophthalmological assessment* (evaluation of visual function). This will be undertaken by a paediatric ophthalmologist assisted by an orthoptist who is usually a member of the multidisciplinary assessment team and who may have carried out the preliminary screening tests for squint and visual acuity. These will probably be repeated in the eye clinic; further examination will require the administration of drops or ointment so that direct and indirect ophthalmoscopy can be carried out (Gardiner, 1982); the eyes will be inspected for the clarity of the media, the condition of the lens and the retina; and any errors of refraction will be evaluated. This is an objective examination which needs to be carried out in optimal conditions for the child and does not usually need a general anaesthetic. Tests of electrical function (Hosking, 1984) of the retina (electroretinogram, or ERG) and of the occipital cortex of the brain (visually evoked response, or VER) can be useful in investigating some of the rarer conditions associated with disorders of the brain and retina.

This assessment will identify those disabilities in which improvement can be effected by operation or the provision of visual aids. These should be prescribed and used as soon as possible if they are needed. Parents will need help from professionals at this time, to ensure that the use of the aids is understood and effective. It is essential that children with other handicaps should have even minor impairments corrected as far as possible.

b) *General paediatric assessment.* It is essential that the assessment of a child with visual impairment should include evaluation of hearing, motor skills, language and communication, social, mental and emotional development. Delay in any of these fields may be due to visual handicap alone, but it is particularly in the last three modalities that confusion is likely to arise.

It is difficult, but not impossible, to interpret results of hearing tests in children with visual impairment. It is usually easy to decide whether the child's delay in mobility is associated with normal or abnormal postural reactions. Delay in understanding and expression of language may come from lack of experience; social skills may have had similar cause for delay; behaviour problems may result from frustration and the delay in global attainment may lead to suspicion that the child is mentally retarded. Assessment will now depend upon monitoring the child's response to optimal help for his visual and any other disabilities. It is essential that overall delayed development in a visually handicapped child should never lead to a label of 'mental retardation' until the child has had a lengthy period of skilled support for the problems arising from his visual disability.

At some time it will become necessary to decide whether a child with visual impairment will be able to use the sight he has in a formal education setting or whether it will be necessary to concentrate on auditory, verbal and tactile means of communication. Younger visually handicapped children should be encouraged to develop their skills in all three modalities and to use their residual vision to the utmost before the point of decision is reached.

Formal psychological testing in visually handicapped children has limited value. The Reynell-Zinkin scales (1979) help to define the younger child's developmental level; objective recording of the child's social development on the Maxfield-Bucholz scale (1957) can be a useful method of monitoring a child's progress over the years; for children with no other disabilities the Williams test gives an indication of a child's cognitive abilities (Chapman, 1978).

EFFECT OF VISUAL HANDICAP ON DEVELOPMENT AND HOW IT MAY BE HELPED

When a child has a handicap, the age at which specific skills are accomplished may vary, although development usually follows the normal sequence unless the form of handicap precludes certain activities. Children who have a severe visual loss from birth begin life at a great disadvantage, but first and foremost it must be realised that they have the same basic needs as any other baby. They need affection, security, new experiences, independence and recognition, but their visual handicap makes it just that more difficult for these situations to be adequately provided.

1   General Effects

a)   *Parent's problems*
One important aspect of growing up is that a mother should enjoy her baby. This is not always easy when a child is handicapped.

Blindness, by interfering in the visual facial interplay between mother and child, blocks one of the first ways of establishing rapport. This may cause the mother to feel defeated because her baby is unresponsive, but with a little more than the usual amount of cuddling, more mutual laughter, more audible murmuring, the baby will soon respond to the sound of her approaching footsteps with gurgles of satisfaction, demonstrating the close, affectionate bond between them.

In addition to the particular problems associated with day-to-day living with disability, awareness of the difficulties which may have to be faced in the future may inhibit parents from enjoying present opportunities. An experienced adviser, who can give the family emotional support as well as educational advice, can be invaluable. Opportunities for sharing with other parents who have children with similar handicaps, also helps to ease tensions.

b)   *Need for stimulation*
A young blind child is more dependent on others for stimulation than is the sighted child, for he cannot see the attractive objects around him. Left in a cot or pram for long periods, the blind infant will find an outlet in self-stimulating activities such as hand flapping, head banging, rocking, etc. Once these habits are established they are very difficult to eradicate. Prevention is far more effective than any kind of

'cure' and, for this, baby needs to find the outside world interesting and stimulating. There is on the market a great variety of rattles and musical toys which can be attached to the cot or pram; the bright colours of these can stimulate vision when the eye still has some residual function. These aids to development cannot replace the most important one of interaction with people and the baby gains far more from being near his mother than from a cot full of educational toys. 'Blindisms', such as hand flapping and rocking, are far less common in cultures where the baby spends most of the day fastened to the mother as she goes about her work.

c) *Need for exploration and experimentation*
Once a seeing child is able to propel himself about, the quest for adventure comes naturally and the child usually finds the world a friendly and enticing place to explore, thus learning a great deal about it. In contrast with this, a blind infant's world is limited; venturing into the unknown does not provide the kind of information which the sighted child discovers. The consequences of being too keen on exploring can end in disaster and the child being labelled 'destructive', so that it is good to enquire into a child's actions before interpreting them. Also, the visual features of the discoveries will need to be described in words. Independence in acquiring skills takes extra time and effort because sight plays an important role in learning how to guide and control hand movements.

2 Learning Specific Skills
Parents need endless patience in teaching ordinary living skills that are normally assimilated by imitation. It may help to take a closer look at some of these.

a) *Sleep*
It may be objected that sleep is hardly a skill, but it is certainly a major issue in the lives of many parents of young infants. Children's activity levels vary widely and so do their sleep rhythms, but irregular sleep patterns tend to be more common in blind children. Several factors may account for this. It is important that an active programme should be encouraged during the day. This does not mean over-stimulation which will

only have an adverse effect. Even a very active blind child does not use as much energy as a sighted child of the same age – lack of sight does slow people down. If an infant does not appear to need as much sleep as one would normally expect, this is not in itself a problem and the management task is to organise the schedule so that other members of the family can enjoy their own sleep. This may entail allowing the child to settle down later than would be normal practice. Some young blind children go through a phase when they wake in the very early hours of the morning and sit rocking and singing for an hour or more before dropping off to sleep again. This can be distressing for others if they share the same room. If accommodation can be re-organised so that other family members are not disturbed, the problem often resolves itself. Before going to bed, the establishment of a quiet, soothing few minutes is helpful – time for the goodnight story or the lullaby. A blind person may not experience the difference between light and darkness and so may not experience 'night' in that sense, but that is not all that tells us night has come. There is a stillness and a quiet that is just as telling. This possibly causes the fear of darkness as much as the darkness itself, and the blind child may also experience this fear. Many children like to have a small light for reassurance; the tick of a familiar clock may serve the same function for a blind child.

b) *Feeding*
From the beginning, eating should be an enjoyable experience for both mother and child, but it is naturally a time of strong emotions which can all too easily get out of hand. It is an area of life in which a baby quickly learns how to dominate mother. What is more anxiety-provoking than a child refusing to eat? In the early stages the pleasure associated with feeding has nothing to do with sight. All babies find comfort in contact with the breast or bottle and the sucking is itself pleasurable. The seeing child soon associates this with visual cues but there is no reason why the blind child should not make equally strong associations with sound, touch and scent. The comforting voice of the mother, the smell of a particular soap or perfume, the special way of cuddling which precedes feeding, can all become important sources of security. If life goes smoothly

at this stage it is less likely to be accompanied by problems at the next. When weaning begins, it may be necessary to anticipate a little more than one would with a sighted child, talking about what is happening and allowing time for exploration of the plate or cup. Attention to small details such as using a cup with a wide handle which the child's hand can slip through can help to simplify life. Whether drinking or feeding from a spoon it is good to hesitate for a moment as the spoon or cup touches the lips so that the child has time to smell or feel it (Plate 7). Finger feeding is an important stage in growing towards independence in eating habits. Difficulties in eating tend to rise from two principal sources: 1) the child is too immature to take the step, or 2) the parent is over anxious. Try

Plate 7. Visually handicapped child learning to feed with a spoon. *Photo: Timothy Woodcock, by permission of the Royal National Institute for the Blind.*

eating a meal blindfolded. This can help towards understanding the task the child is trying to master and so help one to
be more imaginative in providing the best conditions for
learning, by giving thought to the shape of the plate or dish and
the size and weight of the spoon. Once these early skills are
mastered, graduation to using a knife and fork and eating in a
socially acceptable way is relatively simple (Kitzinger, 1980).

c) *Toilet training*
This is another developmental task which should be no
different for the blind child in its basic requirements. Parents
may associate delay with mental retardation, although the age at
which children become independent in toileting varies greatly.
Once again it is important to use imagination in order to
understand the difference that lack of sight makes. The sighted
child will have grown familiar with the bathroom and toilet
long before he or she will be expected to use them. Even so,
some children find it quite frightening to be placed in a large
bath or perched on the seat of a toilet with legs dangling in mid-
air. It can be doubly traumatic for a blind child to be picked up
suddenly and be expected to perch on the toilet seat while his
feet are suspended in space. A simple solution can be to use a
small stool so that the child can climb up and find the seat and
then use the stool as a foot rest.

As with any child, bedwetting and soiling may occur as a
symptom of emotional stress, but before allowing anxiety to
escalate while one searches for psychological causes, it is worth
first considering other possibilities. Changes in sleep pattern,
the ability to cope with getting to the toilet during the night, the
effects of a cold or other infection, can all cause temporary
lapses which, if handled appropriately, will pass. It sometimes
happens that a child who had no problems in bowel training
may, as a four or five year-old, have an episode of soiling,
possibly precipitated by a slight bowel infection, and faeces
may be smeared on the hands. It will also be on whatever the
hands touch and the result can cause great distress to parents.
An over-reaction can foster a major problem. If it is a first
occasion it is wise to accept it as a 'one off', but when there is
cause for anxiety it is advisable to seek professional help before
the habit becomes intractable.

d) *Mobility*

The quest for adventure seems to come naturally to most children. A blind infant needs extra guidance in order to make first discoveries (Sykanda and Levitt, 1982), but can then become as full of curiosity as any infant. The first need will be for encouragement to reach out and find the interesting objects in the cot or playpen. Then, as the ability to move around develops, the child will learn to track voices and find objects in an ever widening space. In the first place it is good to use a string or cord for the child to follow. Sometimes children with a very mild degree of brain damage have great difficulty with any task involving understanding of spatial concepts; this has nothing to do with intelligence but is important for good orientation. The use of sound cues is also important. For man as well as for the bat, high frequency sound waves can be useful in getting around and identifying obstacles. Visually handicapped children find their own ways of 'space testing'; snapping fingers, clicking or plopping the tongue. Don't discourage these too soon!

Most people believe that the blind person – child or adult – leads a far more hazardous life than that of his sighted neighbour. Parents may fear that the child will hurt himself in getting about, when playing or working or in other activities; just as employers are often unwilling to employ blind adults because they believe that blindness will cause greater proneness to accidents. However, there is no evidence to substantiate these fears and it is very probable that, if statistics were available, the blind person would be shown to have fewer accidents. We tend to imagine what we would be like if we lost our sight, but the child growing up without it knows no other world. Of course, the normal hazards of childhood will be there, but these are hazards of childhood, not of blindness. Unless the child is protected to such an extent that he is deprived of vital experiences, he will learn how to cope with accidents and how to avoid future ones.

e) *Speech and language*

The importance of the sound of mother's voice in establishing the initial bonds with her baby has already been mentioned. The value of talking to the child cannot be over-emphasised, for the blind child depends on adults to impart to him knowledge of many aspects of the world around him which are more directly accessible to the sighted child. Conversation is a bridge which brings meaning into a world that is perceived by touch, smell or hearing. To be an adequate bridge it must link the perceiver and the thing perceived. It should be related to actual objects and not just a matter of 'talking about' things or abstract events. In everyday conversation we depend on facial cues for certain aspects of information, and we may need to remind ourselves that these are not available to a blind person who is much more sensitive to auditory cues. While discussing the role of conversation in the development of the blind child, warning should also be given concerning over-stimulation. Life does not have to be one continual conversation. Above all, the use of radio, television, records and tapes needs to be kept within limits. Constant exposure to any of these can obliterate other experiences. There is a place for selectivity and active recreational pursuits should be kept in balance with passive listening. In learning to be selective a child also learns to make choices.

f)   *Cognitive development*
The foundations of learning are laid in the period of sensory-motor development and are closely related to the acquisition of both non-verbal and verbal communication skills. For the infant with a severe visual loss, awareness of all aspects of the environment must be built up from information which is always received in a sequence. When investigating an object by touch there can never be an immediate perception of the whole. Relationships of objects to other objects, or parts of objects to the whole, cannot be grasped in one sensory input in any way comparable to the process achieved by vision. Similarities between an object and a model of it are not easily assimilated without sight, and the model cannot substitute for experience of the object itself. A blind child may learn what a plant pot is from feeling and using one. It is much more difficult to learn about a chimney pot!

g)   *Social growth*
Social development takes place in the context of daily living

while the child is in interaction, first with parents and then with other family members, gradually learning to adjust behaviour by gaining security in an ever widening social group. The art of behaving appropriately in group situations is one of the most difficult skills which the young person will be required to master. Perhaps the most important element in this is the art of learning to be at ease with oneself, so that embarrassing moments do not take on the dimensions of major catastrophes. For this to happen, parents need to be able to correct the child's errors as they would with any child and without being embarrassed themselves. It is an unfortunate fact that, in many situations, there will be people present who are embarrassed when they meet a handicapped person. The latter then has to carry the extra burden of adapting to the tensions such a situation can cause. Nobody can have a prescription for every occasion and we all make mistakes, but it is only when a disability, with the limitations it brings, is understood and accepted by the disabled person that social events can really become pleasurable. Acceptance begins in the early years when family members develop a matter-of-fact attitude in taking on the challenges of supporting the blind member.

h)   *Emotional development*
Emotional development is closely linked with parental attitudes which affect the development of the whole child. Once again we need to refer to the part played by language and com-munication. The importance of the parents' voices in establishing bonding with the newly born infant has been commented upon. The initial shock to parents on discovering that their child is blind can be overwhelming and have drastic effects. Some parents may be so emotionally upset that they are unable to talk while seeing to the infant's basic needs, so that the sound of a mother's voice does not take on the function of replacing the eye contact. Consequently, the baby may appear unresponsive and mother becomes more despondent.

Some parents feel sorry for the child and want to provide protection from any frustration. Every need is anticipated and no learning takes place. More often than being given an initial diagnosis of blindness, many parents experience a long period of suspense interspersed with endless visits to clinics and hospitals, and it is so easy for the infant to become the pivot around which family life rotates. This distorts family relationships and can provoke situations in which stresses due to jealousies develop. A blind baby does require more time and attention in order to grow and develop into a lively young person. Successful rearing, demanding as it does stimulation and plenty of opportunities for new experiences, is a challenging task. At the same time, the parents' needs for leisure and time together have to be safeguarded and other children in the family cannot afford to be left out. Parents can easily find themselves trapped and then may become either over-protective or rejective or deny the existence of the handicap. In providing for the emotional needs of the family, the support of other parents who have weathered the same storms can in many ways be much more valuable than that of the professionals.

This description of the impact of visual impairment on the child's whole development highlights the immensity of the parents' task, involved as they are in daily care in all its aspects. In such a total-care situation the value of regular, skilled advice and support from a member of the professional team cannot be overestimated. The parents need the help of someone with practical experience of the upbringing of a child with impaired vision; programmes must be individually tailored for each child and family with the help of an experienced regular weekly visitor and, where necessary, back-up residential support.

Emergence from the security of home is often a frightening prospect for mother and child, but contact with other young children can be very helpful for both, and these contacts will be useful as part of the assessment process and in preparing the child for more formal education.

FORMAL EDUCATION

Continuous assessment on comprehensive lines, with strong support and appropriate experiences in the earlier years, will give adequate information to professionals and parents as to the best steps to take towards formal education.

Certain clear-cut decisions will need to be made at this stage, and these will depend upon, (i) the severity of the visual impairment and (ii) the presence of other handicaps.

(i) The visual impairment

In the early years, the totally blind infant and the infant with residual vision have similar problems and needs. Firstly, the development of non-visual sensory input (hearing, touch, taste, smell), is relevant and important; secondly, the child should be encouraged to use what vision he has by selecting toys which have interesting tactile and sound features, and which are also eye-catching.

If all goes well in these years, the child whose only disability is impaired vision should have access to the same educational opportunities as any other young person and be guided by ability, aptitudes and interests. The choice of school will depend on the specific needs of the child and the availability of appropriate provision for those needs. Over the years an increasing number of children have been educated within local schools in their home areas. This has the advantage of closeness to home and participation in activities within the local community. The effectiveness of such provision will depend on the support which is available to the school and to the family.

For many children, a period in a special school or unit for the visually handicapped may be desirable. The period of school life in which this is most appropriate will depend on the individual. For the totally blind child, early introduction to an infant school programme which encourages pre-Braille skills and mathematical concepts may be the major consideration. Some children with good residual vision may cope well in a local school if classes are small enough for the children to have the amount of individual attention which all children require in these early years. The need for specialist equipment and/or teaching may come later. Many young people who spend the years up to CSE or GCE 'O' levels in special education then feel able to integrate with confidence into further and higher education.

The concept of 'special educational need' embodies an aim of education to provide an environment which helps the young person to realise a sense of personal value and satisfaction at whatever level of achievement (Plate 8). The advantages and disadvantages of 'special' versus 'normal' school, 'daily' versus 'residential' accommodation, 'visual' or 'non-visual' pro-

Plate 8. Young visually handicapped children and their band. *Photo: Timothy Woodcock, by permission of the Royal National Institute for the Blind.*

grammes, availability of educational subjects and of leisure pursuits, need to be carefully weighed up for each individual. If adequate social integration can be combined with specialist education, visually handicapped young people are able to take their place in a sighted world (Jamieson *et al*, 1977).

(ii)   The presence of other disability

Mental handicap
In their survey of visually handicapped school children aged 5–15 years in 1974, Jamieson *et al* (1977) found that 20 per cent attended schools for the blind, whereas the remainder were in other special schools (45 per cent in schools for the ESN(S)). In a similar survey of children who had attended a special nursery school (Griffiths, 1979), 45.6 per cent of children were later placed in schools especially equipped for blind children (some with other handicaps); the proportion of children attending ESN(S) schools was 35 per cent. Clearly, mental handicap is frequently found as a complication of visual handicap,

although possibly less commonly when continuous assessment and adequate early experience have been available.

Diagnosis of mental retardation in blind children is difficult and misdiagnoses are still not uncommon. This fact should serve to heighten the awareness that all educational programmes should be multi-disciplinary and incorporate a global approach to early education which encourages development of all sense modalities. At this point it may be worth summarising some of the basic principles of education which have already been referred to in relation to the visually handicapped child.

1   Education begins at birth in the first mother/child interactions.

2   The foundations of later performance are laid in infancy in the ordinary activities of daily life.

3   From this it follows that the best medium of education is good life experiences. Any child with brain damage may have difficulty in learning to make generalisations and in using conceptual reasoning. When vision is impaired it becomes even more important that learning should be centred in life experience (Plate 9).

4   The brain damaged child as well as the visually handicapped child needs to have an environment which is stimulating (Plate 10), with plenty of material to attract attention and arouse interest.

5   Conversely, in order to absorb specific information and to learn to focus on the task in hand, it is important to have some training in an environment which has minimal distractions. A 'quiet spot' has a function at home as well as at school. Education begins where the child is. Every individual, from earliest infancy to old age, needs psychological space to be themselves. I suspect that some children 'switch off' because of over-stimulation.

There are many children for whom it is not easy to decide which is their major disability. The attempt to do so can be of questionable value, but there is no doubt that any marked degree of visual impairment will profoundly influence the effectiveness of educational methods normally applicable to children with other major disabilities. Early detection of the

Plate 9. Multiply handicapped girl enjoying the pool. *Photo: Timothy Woodcock, by permission of the Royal National Institute for the Blind.*

Plate 10. 'Riding for the Disabled'. Three visually handicapped children wearing their rosettes after giving a display. *Photo: John Wright, by permission of the Royal National Institute for the Blind.*

visual impairment is important if correct guidance is to be given to parents and appropriate development programmes initiated. The needs will vary according to the pattern of disabilities. Methods used by teachers and therapists have to be adapted to non-visual forms. There are no pre-packed programmes which provide ready-made answers for all educational requirements. Each programme has to be the product of consultation between the parents and the professional therapists and teachers who know the child. Implementing the programme will also be a team effort.

Some children who appear in early infancy to be functionally blind, in spite of having no apparent defect in the eye or visual tracts, respond very positively to the early stages of intervention and visual stimulation. Development of visual awareness makes the task of the physiotherapist and speech therapist slightly easier, and some of these children who are severely intellectually retarded may become quite mobile and develop some speech. Intellectually they remain very limited, but once they have learnt to use their sight their educational needs can be met most appropriately in provision for the mentally handicapped.

If a brain damaged child has, in addition, a type of visual defect which leads to a permanent but partial visual handicap, improvement in the use of the residual vision by training will help the child to progress in other areas, but educational provision will always have to be such that the impaired vision is catered for. For the brain damaged child who is intellectually retarded and/or physically disabled and who is also totally blind, the complete absence of sight must always remain high on the list of priorities in any educational programme.

Hearing impairment
One group of children who present a rather more complex pattern of needs includes those with a visual defect who also have a severe hearing loss.

These children are often designated as 'deaf-blind' but, fortunately, usually have some useful residual vision (which tends to improve) whilst the hearing loss which becomes a more serious problem as the child grows older, may sometimes be disregarded at first with disastrous results. The needs of these children will be discussed in Chapter 11 and are very well described by Freeman (1975).

CHILDREN WITH LATER LOSS OF SIGHT

a) *Children whose vision is affected as a consequence of some form of cerebral tumour*
Improvements in the treatment of cancer conditions and the refining of methods of surgical intervention may account for the presence of a group of children in schools for the visually handicapped who were rarely seen twenty years ago. The cause of damage to their sight is related to factors within the brain, usually resulting in atrophy of the optic nerve. Many of these young people have spent their early years functioning well in mainstream education and have to adjust not only to illness but also to the long-term effects of loss of sight. The degree of visual loss varies, and some young people continue to be able to use print for reading and writing. For some, the degree of damage to the vision is such that they will need educational materials and techniques suitable for persons who are blind. A decade ago, when a child transferred to a school for the visually handicapped after having had treatment for a brain tumour, it was not uncommon to find that the biggest problem for the educator was the child's inability to retain new learning. Recall of material learnt before the illness was not affected and ability in situations requiring practical and social reasoning was adequate, but difficulty in assimilating new learning adversely affected educational progress. This picture has changed over the years, and young people may now expect to complete 'O' level courses and then move to further and higher education. Once again, programmes are needed for each individual. The appropriate educational provision for many of these children will be either in a school for the visually handicapped or in the local school within their home area, providing sufficient support is obtainable.

b) *Children with a degenerative disease of the nervous system*
There is a small group of children who, after developing through infancy and early childhood as apparently normal, healthy youngsters, begin to experience difficulties which may

be first indicated by a falling off in their performance at school. On investigation, a defect in vision is noted. As the sight continues to deteriorate this may be considered the only disability, and distortions of behaviour may be attributed to the child's problems in adjusting to the great trauma associated with loss of sight. Children with similar eye defects manage to work through the emotional crisis and acquire the skills necessary for functioning as a blind person but, because of the nature of the disease, these children do not make that kind of progress. Instead, the deterioration in vision is accompanied by intellectual deterioration which becomes more and more evident so that, eventually, the young person needs total care. Increasingly severe convulsions add further complications and behaviour can be difficult to manage.

The fundamental question has to be asked: 'What does "education" mean for a young person who is becoming more and more enfeebled and whose life expectancy is short?' A priority must be provision for a quality of life which maintains self-esteem whilst encouraging use of remaining abilities and adjusting demands to the limits within which the young person is functioning at any given time. Because of limited and inappropriate provision, frequent changes of environment are commonly added to the stresses caused by disturbing changes within themselves. They move from mainstream education to special class, to school for the visually handicapped, to school for the multi-handicapped and finally to hospital. Medical and educational advice can be confusing and contradictory. When a diagnosis has finally been made, the worries about the rest of the family begin as genetic implications are explained. Management has to be seen in the context of the whole family.

The educational programme must be designed to enable the young people to experience success and pleasure in activities which are meaningful and sensitive to the progressive diminishment in cognitive and motor functioning. Ideally, this should be within a setting which can adjust to changing needs and avoid the recurrent stresses associated with frequent changes of environment.

References

BRAZELTON, T. B., SCHOLL, M. L. and ROBEY, J. S. (1966). 'Visual responses in the newborn', *Pediatrics*, **37**, 284–290.

CATFORD, G. V. and OLIVER, A. (1973). 'Development of visual acuity', *Archives of Disease in Childhood*, **48**, 47–50.

CHAPMAN, E. K. (1978). *Visually Handicapped Children and Young People.* London and Boston, Mass.: Routledge & Kegan Paul.

DEPARTMENT OF EDUCATION AND SCIENCE (1972). *The Education of the Visually Handicapped.* Report of the Committee of Enquiry appointed by the Secretary of State for Education and Science, 1968. London: HMSO.

FRAIBERG, S. (1977). *Insights from the Blind.* London: Souvenir Press.

FREEMAN, P. (1975). *Understanding the Deaf-Blind Child.* London: Heinemann Medical Books.

GARDINER, P. A. (1982). *The Development of Vision.* Lancaster: M.T.P. Press.

GRIFFITHS, M. I. (1979). 'Associated disorders in children with severe visual handicap' in *Visual Handicap in Children* (pp 76–91), SMITH, V. and KEEN, J. (eds). London: Heinemann Medical Books. Philadelphia: Lippincott.

HOSKING, G. (1984). 'Visually evoked responses', *Archives of Disease in Childhood*, **59**, 1–3.

JAMIESON, M., PARLETT, M and POCKLINGTON, K (1977). *Towards Integration, A Study of Blind and Partially Sighted Children in Ordinary Schools.* Windsor: NFER.

JAN, J. E., FREEMAN, R. D. and SCOTT, E. P. (1977). *Visual Impairment in Children and Adolescents.* New York: Grune and Stratton.

KITZINGER, M. (1980). 'Planning the management of feeding in the visually handicapped child', *Child: care, health and development*, **6**, 291–299.

MAXFIELD, K. E. and BUCHOLZ, S. (1957). *A Social Maturity Scale for Blind Preschool Children: A Guide to its Use.* New York: American Foundation for the Blind.

REYNELL, J. and ZINKIN, P. (1979). *Reynell-Zinkin Scales: Developmental Scales for Young Visually Handicapped Children.* Windsor: NFER.

SCOTT, E. P., JAN, J. E. and FREEMAN, R. D. (1977). *Can't Your Child See?* Baltimore: University Park Press.

SHERIDAN, M. D. (1969). 'Vision screening procedures for very young or handicapped children' in *Aspects of Developmental and Paediatric Ophthalmology* (pp 39–47), GARDINER, P., MCKEITH, R. and SMITH, V. (eds). SIMP London: Heinemann Medical Books.

SYKANDA, A. M. and LEVITT, S. (1982). 'The physiotherapist in the developmental management of the visually impaired child', *Child: care, health and development*, **8**, 261–270.

Further Reading

JEFFREE, D. M., MCCONKEY, R. and HEWSON, S. (1977). *Teaching the Handicapped Child.* London: Souvenir Press.

LEAR, R. (1977). *Play Helps: Toys and Activities for Handicapped Children.* London: Heinemann Medical Books.

LOWENFELD, B. (1971). *Our Blind Children. Growing and Learning with Them*, third edition. Springfield, Illinois: Thomas.

LOWENFELD, B. (1973–74). *The Visually Handicapped Child in School.* New York: John Day. London: Constable.

MILLS, A. E. (ed) (1983). *Language Acquisition in the Blind Child – Normal and Deficient.* London: Croom Helm.

7 Communication and its Disorders

PART I SPEECH AND LANGUAGE
By Margaret Edwards

All members of the animal kingdom communicate with one another in some way. We are all familiar with bird song, with the way domestic animals express their needs; the filming and recording of creatures in the wild entrances us from our TV sets and illustrates the ways in which wild animals communicate. Mankind, however, has developed the most highly sophisticated methods of communication in language, both spoken and written. It is therefore not surprising that impaired brain function frequently prevents or delays the child's ability to acquire language skills. This chapter explores the development of verbal communication in the normal child, how this skill can be adversely affected by a number of factors (especially those affecting the brain) and ways in which a child can be helped.

DEVELOPMENT OF LANGUAGE SKILLS

1 Development in the normal child
From his earliest days the child expresses himself vocally. Following on from the early vegetative cries which serve to express feelings of hunger or pain, there develops a range of vocalisation which is essentially interactive, ie. the response of the child to his environment and in particular to those around him. This early interactive stage is of considerable importance and talking to the child during feeding, bathing, dressing, etc., is therefore a powerful influential factor in later social and linguistic development.

The baby will convey messages to its mother by the way it vocalises, and when babbling starts at about the age of six months, links are formed between sensations of all kinds and memories of previous experiences. Sounds produced by babbling begin to resemble those of the child's language environment. Then sounds begin to be associated with particular objects, people and situations, and the understanding and use of verbal symbols is built on this foundation.

As the first recognisable words appear, each one may serve many purposes. Not only is 'doggie', for example, applied to 'dog' but also, on occasion, to 'cat', 'horse', 'sheep' or 'cow'. The word may represent a whole sentence as well – 'Look at that doggie over there'; 'Go away, doggie', and so on.

Just as one word represents others, so the restricted number of sounds which the child uses meaningfully results in one sound representing a range of others, too. The sound 't' may serve for s, st, k, ch – tun/sun; top/stop; tar/car; tew/chew.

Such sounds are not used randomly but are systematised. Some are essentially more difficult because they require finer co-ordination of movement, which in the early stages the child is naturally incapable of achieving. For instance, 's, r, th' are examples of 'hard sounds', whereas 'p, m, d' are 'easy sounds' which appear early in the child's repertoire.

Language expands at first to two-word phrases which often tell the listener something about an object: 'nice mummy'; 'no sock'. Negatives in early stages are usually expressed by the addition of 'no' to a word. As sentences increase in length, the small linking words such as 'in, on, an, the' appear. Later, question words are used, although at first they may simply prefix a sentence without word reversal: 'Where it is?' Thus language grows and extends to fulfil the need within the child to interact with his environment, to assert himself as a person, and to exercise control over events. During this period, children have to learn to understand the language they hear before they can use it meaningfully and creatively. It is interesting to note that understanding of language not only precedes its production, but throughout life also exceeds it. We all understand more than we ever actually say.

Feedback is a very important factor, not only at the development stage but throughout life, in the ability to monitor one's speech, so that adjustment can be made both in the content and in the manner of production. We are still far from clear as to how this monitoring system works, but in the case of children with hearing impairment and also of many children with disorders of speech, it is deficient.

Many people think that speech is something that trips off the tip of the tongue, and therefore when a child is delayed in developing speech there is a feeling that if he can be taught the pronunciation of words all will be well. But this aspect is only one link in a chain of events which need to take place. Another commonly held view is that children's speech represents an immature, incomplete version of the adult model. This is not so and it is much more fruitful to look upon each successive stage as being a system complete in itself and appropriate to that level of the child's development.

It is apparent that the ability to speak meaningfully, to convey thoughts, wishes and instructions, is an immensely complicated process, and yet the majority of children are able to achieve this within the first few years of life. Of course, thereafter there is an ongoing process of enrichment which is dependent to some extent on interaction with others, but this relates mainly to an enlargement of vocabulary and to the opportunities for development of use of language.

The matrix of language is therefore laid down during the early years of life. For this reason it is crucial that, where there seems to be a departure from, or a slowness in, reaching successive stages, there should be help and advice available in order to reinforce this natural language learning period. The term 'stages' suggests discrete steps, but in fact, language development is an unfolding activity which is influenced by the biological development of the baby. No amount of extra stimulation will produce an appreciably earlier emergence of language, in much the same way that concentrated exercises will not result in the child being able to walk much before he is biologically ready to do so.

The terms speech and language are often used interchangeably. Language has a much wider connotation; it may be written or in the form of gesture, and indeed silence can be a highly significant form of communication. Speech, however, refers to the spoken form of language and more specifically to the manner in which sounds are actually produced. In this chapter the term 'language' refers to the spoken medium.

This brief outline of some aspects of language development

is sufficient to emphasise its complexity, and it is therefore all the more surprising that so many children learn to speak almost without being aware of it. It is essentially a flexible process, subject to variation in time of onset, and not all children go through exactly the same stages. Obviously factors such as intelligence, health and environment will exert some influence on its development.

2 *Functions which contribute to the normal development of speech and language*

a) Input is developed through a number of different pathways or channels. The *auditory pathway* is of paramount importance in learning language; children who have a severe congenital hearing impairment will not develop language spontaneously. Less obviously, the *visual pathway* is also important insofar as we extract meaning not only from the heard word but also from facial expression and gestures of the speaker. Children who are partially sighted may well be rather slow in acquiring language. *Kinaesthesis*, the sense by which we recognise our own movements, is the third important channel, and children with hearing impairment have to rely very much upon this when they are learning to speak.

b) Of itself, hearing is insufficient. The ears are good microphones, but only the brain can interpret the electrical currents generated by the ears. The *integration* essential for building up such a complex function as language is dependent on links between one part of the brain and another. In order to understand speech, it is necessary to make rapid ongoing *discriminations* between sounds within words so that they may be recognised. The words 'pat' and 'bat', for example, differ only fractionally from each other and yet have totally different connotations. Then, too, the sounds need to be heard in a recognised temporal sequence. 'Pat' differs from 'tap' mainly in the ordering of sounds. Finally, the total pattern needs to be retained so that comparisons can be made with past experience of the word and so that it may be stored for future reference.

c) Production of language. Before speaking we first of all need to have an idea about what we wish to say. To express this idea, the appropriate words have to be available within a sort of linguistic store which has been built up from past experience of language. The words then need to be arranged in an order which renders them meaningful, ie. they need to conform to the grammatical rules of language. 'Jumps man the', for example, is not a normal English sentence. Just as there is a need to conform to order of words, so also do the sounds with the words need to follow an established pattern. In English, for example, we do not normally find a word beginning with the sound 'ng'. Very young children may not have mastery of correct sequences of sounds within words and of words within sentences. Long words like 'elephant' may emerge as 'ephelant' and, indeed, as adult speakers we are all familiar with the 'slip of the tongue' phenomenon.

   d)   The actual *production of speech* involves a complicated and co-ordinated series of physical events which are programmed by the nervous system, beginning with expiration of air from the lungs, vibration of the vocal cords in the larynx, the amplification of this sound and the imposing of characteristic articulatory patterns by movement of tongue, lips and palate.

LANGUAGE DISORDER

The following section attempts to describe in outline some of the types of language disability which children may suffer. But it is important to remember that these do not necessarily occur as discrete conditions and, indeed, a confident diagnosis is rarely possible. For this reason, diagnostic labels should be used only with utmost reservation. They form a convenient shorthand, but of far more practical value is a detailed description of the specific deficits which the child may show in spoken language.

1 Delayed Language Development

Causes of delayed language development remain unknown in many cases; possibly they are associated with a corresponding lag in neural maturation, and sometimes environmental conditions provide a clue, particularly if there is a history of deprivation or, for example, if the child has been hospitalised at a critical period of language learning.

   It is usually possible for a speech therapist to pinpoint the area of greatest difficulty and to determine whether this reflects a straightforward maturational delay which may be resolved without too much difficulty, or whether the extent of handicap is such that it requires more concentrated intervention. There are, of course, grey areas where delay spills over into deviance. How, for example, may one classify a child of six who is said to have a language age of three? Certainly his speech will not be a mirror image of that of a three year-old, if only for the reason that he has three further years of experience of life. Also his efforts to respond to the delay will almost inevitably have resulted in the development of alternative strategies, so that the result may well be a mixture of delay and deviance.

Many children appear to stick at a maturationally earlier stage of language development. This may show itself in a paucity of vocabulary with which to express their ideas; it may take the form of very limited syntax (grammar), or there may be adequate expression of ideas which are rendered unintelligible because of immature phonological (pronunciation) patterns.

2 Children with Deviant Language

In the case of other children there may be some organic (physical) condition which underlies the language impairment. A very obvious example is that of cerebral palsy, when limitation of movement produces the characteristic staccato, jerky, uncontrolled utterance which is readily recognisable. Some of these forms of deviant language will be considered briefly.

a) *Hearing Impairment*

The extent of the resulting language disability is related to such factors as the severity of the hearing loss and the time of onset. At one time it was common practice to attach little significance to minor degrees of hearing loss, or to fluctuating loss such as is suffered by many young children with respiratory infection (conductive hearing loss). This attitude may well be appropriate if the onset follows establishment of language. But where the child has not yet been able to establish intelligible speech, when he is not sure of the exact nature of contrasts between sounds, even slight impairment or a variable response to sound may well have a deleterious effect upon production.

The child with congenital hearing loss of significant degree is greatly handicapped in his ability both to understand and to express himself verbally. The importance assigned to the early detection of hearing loss has done much to remedy the appalling conditions which pertained some years ago, when such children might well have been labelled 'deaf and dumb'. Even so, with all the help now available, the profoundly deaf child is still confronted with severe obstacles in the way of achieving intelligible speech.

Those with a selective sensorineural loss may find difficulty in perceiving high frequency sounds such as 's', 'th', and 'sh'. A severe hearing impairment extending through the entire range of frequencies results in a very characteristic pattern of disability. Predominantly the rhythm and melody of speech is affected. Emphasis is inappropriate and there is abnormal lengthening of words and overlong pauses. Articulation is also abnormal because the child cannot perceive differences between visually similar sounds like 'p' and 'b'; 't' and 'd'; 'k' and 'g'. Sentence length is reduced and becomes telegraphic. Correspondingly, the child is only able to receive the more obvious concrete elements of speech and thus fails to develop an appreciation of more subtle nuances conveyed by pause, emphasis and intonation changes. At a grammatical level, he will be impaired by inability to hear, for example, plural 's' endings and this will produce a corresponding error in his own speech.

b)   *Developmental dysphasia*
In this situation the child's problem may lie in the understanding of language (comprehension) or in the ability to formulate ideas in the spoken form (expression).

Comprehension. This differs from the type of disorder associated with hearing impairment in that it is a difficulty of central processing. Whereas the deaf child may have an intact potential for understanding and producing language but is prevented from doing so because of the peripheral barrier of hearing loss, the child with this type of specific language disability cannot, despite normal hearing, make sense of the linguistic world about him. Where comprehension is impaired, he will hear language but it will have little or no meaning. The degree of disorder may sometimes be masked, in that some children appear to have a facility for picking up isolated phrases which they reproduce quite intelligibly parrot fashion, without meaning. This may be more noticeable where there have been efforts to teach the child labels for objects. For example, a child shown a picture of a house immediately catalogued all the features. 'House, yes that a house. That's a window. That's a door', etc. Yet he was completely unable to apply this information to the door and window of the room in which he was sitting.

Where comprehension difficulties are profound, the child is unable to symbolise his experience. The development of spoken language is very difficult, but some success may be achieved by teaching a visual language system.

Expression. Where the problem relates more to expressive language and the child is able to comprehend the language he hears, his output will be limited to odd words which will be appropriate but may be difficult for listeners to understand. In many ways this latter type of disability, although less severe, brings with it more frustration and behavioural problems than does the receptive type. Somehow the more profound the deficit, the more the child cuts himself off, in a sort of cocooning process. This may well lead to a misdiagnosis of deafness, and often considerable time elapses before a dif-ferential diagnosis can be established.

c) *Dysarthria*
The predominant difficulty is one of articulation. Children who have cerebral palsy (especially spasticity or athetosis) may have this type of disability. Because movement of tongue, lips, etc., is slow and unco-ordinated, speech may be unintelligible. Rhythm of language is also impaired and sentence structure may be truncated because of associated difficulties in breathing. Speech may alternate between explosive bursts and weak, whispered delivery. Although the difficulty appears to be in production there may also be sensory deficits and there is a need to be alerted to other possible handicaps.

d) *Dyspraxia*
This is another type of language disability which needs to be

differentiated from dysarthria since superficially both may appear to share common attributes. This condition is often met in children who suffer from general clumsiness, although it can exist in isolation. Peripherally the child will have intact musculature capable of normal movement, but there is a failure in the programming activity which ordains the appropriate sequences of movement necessary to produce intelligible speech. On single short words there may be little evidence of difficulty, but on multisyllabic words and in long stretches, language may disintegrate into a meaningless jumble of nonsense. Careful analysis does reveal a pattern in this apparently random 'gobbledegook', but at first sign it is difficult to discern and well nigh impossible to understand. A corresponding failure of organisation may be apparent in writing and in other motor activities such as hopping, jumping, running, etc. Frequently there are reading difficulties as well.

e) *Mental handicap*
Children who are mentally handicapped may show evidence of any of these specific types of disability and it is important in any assessment that this should be born in mind. But it is also important that any expectation of improvement should be realistically related to the intellectual level of the child. Too often it is easy to be deluded into thinking that, if language skills could be extended, this would result in an all-round improvement. It is true that a child not able to exercise his full potential for language may well have further problems, but at all times one must bear in mind the limitations of that potential and not vest never-to-be achieved hopes in change that cannot be wrought. False expectations may be raised by the fact that, superficially, many mentally handicapped children appear to have a facile use of language. Closer examination, however, reveals this to be largely devoid of content. Often the questions are attention- and not information-seeking and the apparently sophisticated sentences are parrotings, evidence of no more than good gifts of mimicry. Children with severe mental handicap may be taught to communicate, sometimes using 'total communication' methods. By setting realistic goals, one's efforts are likely to meet with more success.

f) *Stammering*

In the course of normal language development, some children between the ages of three and four, or thereabouts, go through a period of non-fluency. This is at a time when there is a disparity between thought and vocabulary. Thoughts and ideas may race ahead of the child's verbal ability to express them. As vocabulary develops, however, the child becomes fluent, although occasionally he may appear to get stuck at this point and parental anxiety may take the form of drawing attention to speech by telling him to talk more slowly, to think about what he is saying, even to take a deep breath before speaking. All such advice should be avoided. In this early non-fluent stage, it is likely that the child is unaware of it. Focusing attention may bring about an awareness and a resulting attempt to repress it, and this in turn could be the beginning of a true stammer. A speech therapist should be able to offer specific guidance on the management of children with prolonged non-fluency.

ASSESSMENT

A child's difficulties in the acquisition of speech and language may be brought to attention in a number of different ways: through the parents, the health visitor, the nursery or infant teacher. At first it may not be realised that the child has a specific disability in the field of language, and concern for problems of behaviour, suspected deafness or mental handicap, may mask the true state of affairs.

Except in cases of deafness, mental handicap or cerebral palsy, it is often exceedingly difficult to define a certain cause of the impaired brain function. It is known, for instance, that some developmental conditions such as language delay or dysphasia appear to be inherited and may be passed from father to son, although the basis remains obscure. Severe language disorder is also often associated with 'autism', although it may be difficult to distinguish which is the core problem and which secondary.

1 *General development*

This will be the concern of the multidisciplinary team, and all children with significant delay in acquisition of language will need a hearing test. Vision should also be evaluated and the amount of stimulation in the child's environment carefully assessed. Delay in other aspects of development may indicate an association with mental handicap and this must be considered.

2   *Specific evaluation of speech and language*

The first task of the speech therapist is to identify as precisely as possible the nature of the language disability. Partly through the use of standardised assessment procedures (eg. Reynell, 1977), partly through observation of the child and partly through information obtained from parent or caretaker, a profile of his strengths and weaknesses in communication may be delineated.

It is generally recognised that standardised assessment procedures provide only a very limited representation of language disability and they should therefore be regarded as an adjunct to the valuable data acquired as the result of detailed observation of the child communicating in his natural environment. Most speech therapists will be proficient in the use of linguistic assessments, particularly those developed by Crystal *et al*, and which are described in detail in Crystal, 1982. Fenn (1979) has produced a measure of comprehension which is suitable for mentally handicapped children. Another frequently used test is the Boehm *Test of Basic Concepts* (1969).

INTERVENTION

There are a number of ways in which children with language disability may be helped. But because this is frequently just one aspect of a multiple disorder, it is essential that any particular method of remediation should take into account the overall rehabilitation programme to which other members of the team are contributing. It is quite obvious from this book that many different people have a role to play. However, at the heart of any remedial programme the key figures in its success are those most immediate to the child, that is, his family or caregivers. As far as language learning is concerned, this fact has been acknowledged for some time, but unfortunately the recognition has tended to be confined, in many cases, to somewhat cursory general advice and the actual involvement has been minimal. The concept of remedial work, too, has broadened considerably in recent times. From a preoccupation with how the child speaks, there has developed an increasing concern with helping him to achieve the best possible level of functional communication, with absolute correctness of articulation and grammar taking second place. To this end, in some cases, it may be necessary to consider the teaching of non-verbal types of communication if it is felt that an over-concentration on speech *per se* is unlikely to result in more than a few laboured utterances attended by much frustration.

1   The Role of the Speech Therapist

Using the information gained during the assessment procedures, the next task is to select a particular aspect of the language deficit upon which work should begin. A step-by-step programme is then drawn up to achieve the particular goal. For example, in the case of a highly distractable child, the primary task may be to improve attention. If auditory perception is found to be poorly developed, then a scheme of work designed to improve skills of discrimination, sequencing and memory will be devised. It is usual to work within a developmental sequence, and such programmes need to be systematic and well structured. Furthermore, the speech therapist needs to evaluate progress regularly to ensure that the desired changes are taking place.

Such an approach does not mean, however, that the entire treatment programme has to be carried out by the therapist. In the case of very young children this is undesirable; it is the parent who is the most suitable person to undertake the work under the regular direction of the therapist.

There is, however, a qualification about over-strict adherence to such programmes. Some children, particularly those who are mentally retarded, may succeed in learning precisely what they are taught, but will fail to generalise this to everyday speech situations. Such 'carry over' is even more difficult to achieve if all the work is done in a formalised clinical setting. For such children, flexibility of approach is essential and maximum use must be made of an environment where the child is highly motivated to use language.

2   *The Role of the Parent or Caregiver*

Over the past few years it has been increasingly common practice to involve parents actively in language learning activities and a number of programmes have been designed with this specific aim. Some of these programmes (Cook, 1979; Cooper, Moodley and Reynell, 1978: Gillham, 1979; Jeffree and McConkey, 1977) are mentioned in the References.

Important aspects of most programmes are:

(i)   The need to teach the child to attend, by developing the attention step-wise, using sight or hearing or touch. Good listening should be encouraged and overstimulation avoided. One-thing-at-a-time should be the rule.

(ii)   Specific times each day should be set aside for short periods of language work, related to everyday household duties and free from family distractions. Simple language should be used; repetition and reinforcement will be needed.

(iii)   Once a nucleus of names is understood these should be linked to actions:

baby,	baby sleeping,	baby crying
daddy,	daddy working,	daddy reading

or to attributes:

cup,	big cup,	my cup
dog,	good dog,	little dog, etc.

When the child starts to verbalise, questions should offer alternative answers, eg. 'Are you eating or drinking?' rather than, 'Are you eating?' requiring a 'yes' or 'no' (which need not be verbalised); neither should questions be open-ended, eg. 'what are you doing?'

As a general rule it is advisable to give more attention to expansion of expressive language as such, with intelligibility being of secondary importance. Articulation errors may be indicative of maturational delay and, with good models, as language expands they may spontaneously resolve.

These very general guidelines are intended solely as an adjunct to any programme which may be designed by a speech therapist and which will provide more specific instruction.

Each child really needs to be treated as an individual case; rates of progress vary so much that it is impossible, and indeed undesirable, to be too specific about ages by which children should have reached certain stages. So many factors have to be taken into account.

It is sometimes thought that contact with other children may of itself bring about improvement in language. Actually this is seldom the case. Young children do not in fact talk *to* each other a great deal. What they do is talk in the presence of other children, but there is often very little actual interchange. The most natural language learning environment is between child and adult, usually the mother. Furthermore, as has been stated, many young children with language disability are maturationally unable to cope with the demands of playgroup or nursery school.

3   The Role of the Nursery Nurse

In some cases, however, it is absolutely necessary that the child should attend a day nursery, and in such cases it falls to nursery nurses to carry out the type of programme outlined above. The important part played by nursery nurses in such cases is becoming increasingly recognised and many authorities are to this end providing work-shop type courses with ongoing supervision so that they may carry out day-to-day language work with children. To date, such schemes give every indication of considerable success. One published account is that by Bath (1981).

CHILDREN WITH OTHER HANDICAPS

For those children who are multiply handicapped, parental involvement is likely to embrace a number of different disciplines. A concerted programme in these cases is of even greater importance if confusion of purpose is to be avoided. Children with cerebral palsy (Mueller, 1974) and *clumsy children* (Gordon and McKinlay, 1980) will need the combined efforts of physical, occupational, speech therapists and teachers in the drawing up of programmes designed to improve rhythm and sequencing skills. As far as the *specific speech difficulties* are concerned, work starts at a global level and narrows down to the more specific requirements of appropriate rate, emphasis and rhythm of speech. Where there are feeding difficulties, any member of the team may well be involved in the work designed to improve chewing, sucking and swallowing.

For those children attending school, close co-operation with teachers is essential, and again this must constitute more than a token interchange of remarks about the child's progress. Where, for example, non-verbal systems such as Blissymbolic* or Makaton* are used, then a programme based on joint participation of all disciplines is essential to its success. Since the British educational system does not allow for teachers leaving their classrooms for any length of time to participate in joint discussions, in the case of children with significant handicap who attend special schools or units for cerebral palsied or visually handicapped children, it is preferable for the relevant therapists to work in the school, the better to forge close links with teachers. Psychologists, both educational and clinical, where they can give a reasonable amount of their time, are also highly desirable members of the team. There are successful instances of speech therapists and psychologists working jointly and interchangeably on language programmes including behaviour modification techniques.

For children with *hearing impairment*, the primary aim is to utilise what residual hearing they may have. It is not proposed in this section to enter the controversy about oral v. non oral methods, and indeed it seems very likely that some system of total communication using both methods may be the preferred one. Certainly it seems, as with aphasic children, that the use of signing does not hamper the development of oral language but may well succeed in improving the child's knowledge of grammatical rules. Whereas work with deaf children has traditionally tended to concentrate on an articulatory approach, intervention now is on a much broader basis. The recognition that melody of speech does much to confer intelligibility has led to a focus of work on this aspect. Then, too, it is acknowledged that ability to articulate clearly is of little value if grammatical form is not understood or used. Much work is therefore concentrated on this aspect also. Work

* See Appendix.

is directed towards multi-sensory stimulation through vision and through tactile feedback. There is a growing number of technical electronic devices which provide visual feedback, thus enabling the child to control and to modify his utterances.

In the United Kingdom, the DHSS,* in partnership with RADAR,† has set up Supraregional Centres for Communication Disorders at which children can be assessed for their ability to use some of the newer electronic appliances that are being developed.

The development of spoken language which, for the majority, comes about with little conscious effort, may represent for those with difficulty a long task demanding application and sustained will. The success of the undertaking is determined by several agencies: first, the child himself, and herein one must adopt a realistic view of his capabilities so that proper goals may be set; secondly, there are the people in immediate contact with the child – parents, teachers, nursery nurses; and finally, there is the speech therapist whose task it is to assess the extent and nature of the language disability, to devise means whereby it may be surmounted and, above all, to encourage and guide both the child and the other members of the team in the carrying out of appropriate techniques, so as to promote a level of language which will enable him to function to the best of his ability in his environment.

PART II   CHILDREN WITH HEARING IMPAIRMENT
By Sheila McDougall and Alan Sherliker

In Part I of this chapter, it was emphasised that hearing is essential to the normal production of speech. It has been found that hearing-impaired babies, even those with profound hearing problems, begin to vocalise like their hearing peers in the first five to six months of life (Northern and Downs, 1976).

*DHSS   Department of Health and Social Security
†RADAR   Royal Association for Disability and Rehabilitation.

They coo, gurgle and even babble, having basic essentials for natural speech development, but speech develops no further because auditory feedback from the sounds they produce and the auditory input from external sounds in the environment (including voices) are impaired. Hearing impairment does not necessarily mean that the child lives in a totally silent world; usually the child hears some sounds, but these are so severely distorted that speech is meaningless and loud sounds may be frightening.

It is therefore essential to find ways of achieving some auditory input and recognition of speech sounds. The ability to recognise and interpret new sounds is a skill which gradually diminishes after the second year of life. It is crucial to identify a hearing loss as early as possible so that the necessary parent counselling and treatment may be started and this skill utilised to the full.

TYPES OF HEARING LOSS

The effects of different types of hearing loss on the child's development of speech are described in Part I of this chapter (p. 145). It is, however, particularly important for those offering specific help for the hearing impairment to differentiate the three types of deafness as the needs of the children and the way of helping will differ.

1)   *Conductive* loss is not associated with any problems in the brain, as the trouble arises within the middle ear, usually due to infection; but it is preventable and treatable and it is therefore doubly important that it should be recognised as early as possible, especially in children who have evidence of impaired brain function. In this context, it is well to remember that, in Down's Syndrome, blockage of the middle ear is particularly likely to happen if the child has frequent colds, and these children need to be under careful surveillance for the possibility of intermittent conductive hearing loss.

2)   A *receptive*, or *sensorineural*, loss is another matter, and is associated with an organic lesion affecting the nerve cells of the inner ear or the nerve cells or pathways within the brain itself. It therefore cannot be corrected, but its extent can be defined and the child, family and teachers enabled to find ways

of helping him to understand language and to develop communication skills.

3) Thirdly, there may be a *mixed type* of loss, partly *conductive* and partly *sensorineural*. This is often difficult to assess as the conductive component will vary from time to time. However it compounds the neural component of the hearing difficulty and needs to be identified and rigorously treated.

CAUSES OF HEARING LOSS

1   *Prenatal*
Genetic or hereditary deafness forms the largest and most significant group, followed by prenatal, non-bacterial infections suffered by the mother in pregnancy, the commonest being rubella (German measles). The developing foetus is particularly vulnerable during the first three months of intra-uterine life and may be damaged not only by viral infections such as rubella or cytomegalovirus, but by drugs taken by the mother. Thalidomide is a well-known example which, in addition to limb deformity, also causes deafness and other handicaps in some children. The less common causes in this group include maternal nutritional deficiencies and endocrine disorders.

2   *Perinatal*
Any factor which results in diminished oxygen supply to the child's brain may result in deafness. Premature babies are particularly vulnerable, both to lack of oxygen and to raised levels of circulating bilirubin released from red cells damaged by maternal antibodies. The bilirubin released by the damaged cells causes jaundice and may, if sufficiently high, damage the nerve cells involved in the conduction of sound to the brain.

3   *Postnatal*
Middle ear infection is the commonest cause of hearing loss in this group. Although not usually severe, its effect on the child acquiring language, or on the child with additional handicaps, can be very significant. Middle ear infection may change a child with a moderate perceptive loss into a child with a severe mixed hearing loss. The mentally handicapped child who is struggling

to acquire language may be robbed of the will to listen, or the loss may occur at a time which is critical to that particular child's speech development. Infections such as meningitis, mumps or measles, and drugs (such as streptomycin in the past) may result in a perceptive hearing loss. A less common cause is injury to the brain following a fractured skull.

EFFECTS OF HEARING LOSS

The effect of a hearing loss upon the acquisition of speech is described in Part I (p. 145). This effect will vary with the age of onset, the severity and type of loss, with the nature of the child and his environment. The earlier the onset and the more profound the hearing loss, the more severe will be the effect on speech and language development.

Other disabilities in the child will add to his difficulties. A physically handicapped child may be unable to compensate for a slight hearing loss by moving nearer to the speaker or even turning his head to the sound source; a blind child is denied the visual clues from the lips, facial expression and body language; a mentally handicapped child, who is also deaf, will have his difficulties in language acquisition compounded; a hyperactive child may be unable to stay still long enough to listen. The amount of language to which the child is exposed and the response to his attempts at vocalisation and speech, along with his ability to compensate for his hearing loss, will affect his success in speech acquisition.

ASSESSMENT

Assessment of a child's hearing must take into account the normal responses to sound at different stages of development and the presence or absence of additional handicaps. The necessary expertise is best provided by a multidisciplinary team with experience in assessing all the factors involved.

1   Assessment of Hearing

The sounds in our environment travel from outside to a small drum (which can be seen at the end of the auditory canal) causing it to vibrate and to set in motion a group of tiny bones in the middle ear, which themselves cause vibrations within the inner ear where the sensitive hair-like nerve endings for sound are situated. These intricate motions are then translated into electrical impulses which go to various parts of the brain.

The majority of speech sounds fall within the range of 250–4,000 Hz, which is commonly referred to as the speech frequency range. On the whole, the vowel sounds in speech are low pitched and loud and give the volume to speech, whereas the consonants tend to be rather softer and higher pitched and give intelligibility. It is therefore important to test a child's responses to low and high pitched sounds. The child with a high frequency hearing loss will respond immediately to the softest voice but may have problems with understanding speech and may himself have defective articulation.

Assessment of a child's hearing includes ensuring that the sound waves can reach the eardrum, that the tiny bones in the middle ear are able to oscillate freely, that the nervous mechanism in the inner ear is working normally and that the brain can make use of the messages it receives.

a) *Screening tests*
Hearing impaired children may appear to be developing normally during their early months; they crawl and walk, they show curiosity (and disobedience!), they handle toys, indicate their wants and respond in ways which may make parents think that they hear normally. As it is known that the first two years are crucial for the development of speech, it is therefore very important that all children should have their hearing tested as early as possible. In the United Kingdom this is normally carried out by health visitors* using distraction screening tests on children aged seven to nine months. (These tests are fully described by Nolan and Tucker (1981) and other authors.)

The tests require the minimum amount of equipment, but the recommended procedures must be scrupulously observed. Tests involving spoken instructions using standardised sets of pictures or toys are used with the older child.

By the age of about three a child will usually co-operate with a conditioning technique and indicate his ability to hear test sounds, including pure tones over the speech frequency range.

These are pass/fail tests and any children who fail after

* Public health nurses.

retesting should be referred for a full audiological assessment. Parents' suspicions should also always be followed up.

b) *Audiological assessment*

To discover the nature and severity of the hearing loss, specialised tests are carried out in an audiological unit which is experienced in testing children. Assessment always involves taking a careful family and medical history, followed by a full clinical examination of the ear and upper respiratory tract before audiological testing is undertaken.

(i) SUBJECTIVE TESTS. These are tests in which the child's response to sounds of varied intensity and frequency are observed. The stimuli used are more varied than those used in the screening test and include, for example, pitch pipes music and warble tones. *Pure tone audiometry* using headphones measures the child's response to pure tones which are recorded in the form of an audiogram (see Fig 12).

Bone conduction audiometry. The stimulus comes from a vibrator placed behind the ear and directly affects the function of the auditory nerve to transmit sounds. If the cause of the child's deafness is in the middle ear, he will respond better to bone conduction audiometry than when wearing earphones.

Speech discrimination may be assessed by playing a tape of phonetically balanced words at a known intensity through earphones to the child, and his ability to repeat all or part of the word is recorded.

(ii) OBJECTIVE TESTS. These are tests which do not require the active co-operation of the child.

A *tympanograph* is used to assess middle ear function. The test takes only a few minutes and the child has only to sit still with a soft plastic plug in his ear. Characteristic graphs are obtained in patients with middle ear dysfunction, eg. secretory otitis media (fluid in the middle ear or 'glue ear'.)

Evoked response audiometry (ERA) The electrical response of the brain or brain stem—BSER* (UK) or ABR† (USA)—to sound stimuli of varying frequency and intensity, may be

* Brain Stem Evoked Response
† Auditory Brain-stem Response

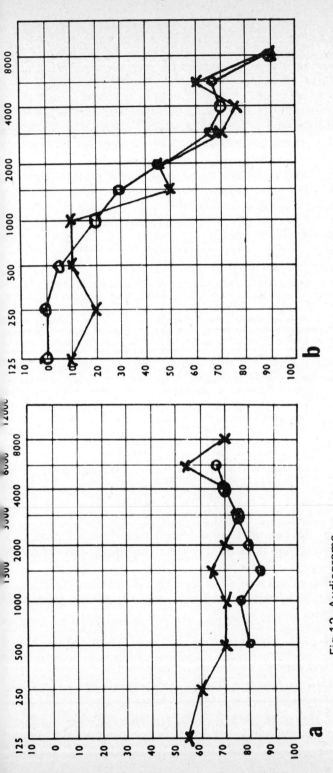

Fig 12. Audiograms

a) Severe hearing loss at all frequencies. Left ear (X) 55 to 70 decibel loss; right ear (O) 70 to 85 decibels. This indicates severe impairment of hearing to every type of sound. b) High tone hearing loss. Low tones are heard within the normal range. The loss of high tones severely limits the hearing of speech sounds and renders speech unintelligible. (Normal hearing produces an audiogram in which the decibel loss readings vary between O and 15.)

measured using three small electrodes on the child's head and analysing and averaging the responses with a computer.

Electro cochleography. This technique involves placing a small electrode through the tympanic membrane on to the base of the cochlea. The procedure is usually carried out under anaesthesia. The computerised responses to test sounds reflect the function of the cochlea and auditory nerve.

These two tests are helpful in assessing the auditory function of a child in whom other methods have failed, or for confirmation of previous test results.

2   Assessment of Other Skills

The multidisciplinary assessment team will normally include an audiology technician on its strength, and it is axiomatic that all children who have delayed or deviant development of speech or language should be referred for a hearing test.

The audiologist, and the teacher of the hearing impaired, will be concerned over the general development of the children for whom they are caring, and it is often helpful to have the advice of a speech therapist as to the way language is developing, and of a psychologist as to the level of the child's cognitive skills.

INTERVENTION

As with all other handicaps, the parents, particularly the mother, are the adults most in contact with the pre-school child, and they have the major role in encouraging development. They will need to provide the background against which the professionals, particularly the peripatetic teacher of the hearing impaired, will help them to learn additional skills in bringing up their child. They will need to acquire additional patience in teaching their child to hear and speak, and to find time to devote to this task.

Most children will be measured, assessed and fitted with the most suitable aid available, and mother and father will need to learn all about it.

1   The Use of Hearing Aids

a)   *Individual choice*

There is no such thing as a universal hearing aid, so that every aid must be carefully chosen for each child, using, wherever possible, the same team who undertook the original assessment, but certainly involving the parents, the home teacher and the audiologist or his technician. There will be certain definite alternatives, such as body-worn *v.* postaural (behind ear); unilateral *v.* bilateral (one or two); and many different types within these alternatives. Readers are referred for further details to Miller (1980), Nolan and Tucker (1981).

b)   *Care of the hearing aid*

This is as important as the choice of aid. A hearing aid that is in good working order is invaluable to a hearing impaired child, but an aid that does not function well is a waste of both time and money. The care and maintenance of the aid are almost bound to fall upon the parents who need to be assured of the whole-hearted and prompt back-up service from the Audiology Unit staff. Instructions for care of the aid should be issued with it and will demand at least daily inspection with some day-to-day maintenance. (Nolan and Tucker (1981) have some useful tips.)

c)   *The use of the hearing aid*

Having selected a suitable hearing aid and learnt how to take care of it, how can the child be persuaded to wear it?

i)   *Getting used to the mould.* This is the first hurdle. The child may not want a plug in his ear (but it will not stop him from hearing!), so it may be best to insert the mould(s) for a short time on their own until he gets used to the feel. It will be necessary for them to be changed from time to time as he grows—a useful rule is a new mould each time a new pair of shoes is required. The mould should always fit well and be comfortable to wear.

ii)   *Getting used to sound.* This will be a strange experience for him, so it is inadvisable to start with the sound as loud as possible; the sound should be switched on 'low' at first and increased only gradually until the child expresses interest and pleasure.

iii)   *Short periods only at first.* Several short periods in a day when the parent can give all her time to the child, preferably during some meaningful occupation, will be more beneficial than constant wear. Remember all sounds are amplified, not only the ones the child needs to hear.

iv)   Contrary to what one would expect, younger children, especially those under one year, adapt more readily than older ones.

d)   *Auditory training*

Once the child has begun to show an acceptance of the aid and an interest in sound, the time has come to start auditory training. There are three inter-related factors involved in this:

i)   *Amplification to listen to everyday sounds.* To adults, the environmental sounds that we hear are taken for granted or even disregarded; to a newly hearing child they may be frightening or mysterious, and often distract him. It is important, therefore, during the early 'listening periods', to introduce the child to the source of the sound—the fridge turning itself on, the telephone ringing, and other pieces of equipment in his environment of which he knows the use, but not the noise it makes; this must be repeated time and again. He must be made aware of the source of every new sound, and the demonstration must always be supported by a verbal commentary. For more detailed suggestions refer to Nolan and Tucker (1981), Sanders (1982) and Boothroyd (1982).

ii)   *Amplification to listen to speech.* This is a most, if not *the* most, important aspect of enabling a child to hear. It is more difficult, and therefore needs more planning and more quiet one-to-one attention. It is probably best to associate these sessions with a verbal commentary related to objects in the environment, followed Sanders' (1982) dictum, 'Early language stimulation must be event related'. Wherever possible, the verbal commentary should follow the child's obvious interest at the moment, should concentrate on the flow of language and should consist of phrases rather than 'labelling' with nouns. Gradually, more abstract ideas may be brought in, using pictures to tell a story. More details from Ross and Giolas (1979), Bess and McConnell (1981), and Sanders (1982).

iii)   *Using amplification to produce and control the child's own speech.* This is the point at which one is looking for the step forward from the understanding to the expression of speech.

At this stage, between 18 months and three years (Yeates, 1980), the speech trainer becomes a useful instrument in the hands of the peripatetic teacher, in which the child can hear his own voice picked up by a microphone, amplified and transmitted through his earphones (Meers, 1976; Ling and Ling, 1978; Yeates, 1980).

2 Total Communication

In deaf children, the early use of amplification and the early introduction of auditory training may enable them to use a completely oral/aural (ie. speaking and being spoken to) method of communication. Other children are greatly helped by one or other of the signing systems (see Appendix) and many learn to lip read, in addition to using a hearing aid and as much speech as they have. (Freeman *et al*, 1981; Yeates, 1980).

Gesture is a most important part of communication and is vital for hearing impaired children, but it is essential that any system relying on sign and gesture for communication should be usable by all (or almost all) the people coming into contact with the child. Therefore the system should be learnt by all members of the family, other relatives, friends and neighbours, the class teacher and other children in the class. It should always be accompanied by its verbal counterparts and the deaf child should be using his aid.

FORMAL EDUCATION

The hearing impaired child may attend an ordinary school, a special school for hearing impaired children or a special unit within an ordinary school. When all information is available with regard to type and degree of deafness, presence or absence of other problems, background of home and leisure opportunities, and local services available, the parents and the team of professionals can come to a mutual decision about the most suitable placement for the child.

If he is to go to an ordinary school, additional help must be brought into service. The peripatetic teacher should be a welcome visitor, but also the school should be encouraged to instal a technical system that will help the child to learn. This may be one of the factors which at the present time may direct the child to a special school with a radio microphone system used with the child's own hearing aid. This system can be used in the home, and it is likely that in the future such a system could be made available in ordinary schools if it would be of benefit to an individual child.

An individual's adaptation to adult life will very much depend on the right educational situation to be provided for the growth of independence and the maturity of mind and character.

References: Speech and Language

BATH, D. (1981). 'Developing the speech therapy service in day nurseries', *British Journal of Disorders of Communication*, **16**, 159–173.

Boehm Test of Basic Concepts (1969). Windsor: NFER; New York: Psychological Corporation.

COOK, V. J. (1979). *Young Children and Language*. London: E. Arnold.

COOPER, J., MOODLEY, M. and REYNELL, J. (1978). *Helping Language Development: A developmental programme for children with early language handicaps*. London: E. Arnold.

CRYSTAL, D. (1982). *Profiling Linguistic Disability*. London: E. Arnold.

FENN, G. (1979). *Word Order Comprehension Test*. Windsor: NFER.

GILLHAM, B. (1979). *The First Words Language Programme*. London: George Allen and Unwin.

GORDON, N. and McKINLAY, I. (1980) (eds). *Helping Clumsy Children*. London and Edinburgh: Churchill Livingstone.

JEFFREE, D. and McCONKEY, R., (1977). 'Involving Parents in language development', *British Journal of Disorders of Communication*, **14**, 3 ff.

MUELLER, H. (1974). 'Speech' in *Handling the Young Cerebral Palsied Child at Home* (pp. 131–138), FINNIE, N. R. (ed). London: Heinemann Medical Books.

REYNELL, J. (1977). *Reynell Developmental Language Scales*. Windsor: NFER.

Further Reading

JEFFREE, D. and McCONKEY, R. (1976). *Let Me Speak*. London: Souvenir Press.

MILLS, A. E. (ed) (1983). *Language Acquisition in the Blind Child – Normal and Deficient*. London: Croom Helm.

NEWSON, J. and NEWSON, E. (1979). *Toys and Playthings: in development and remediation*. Harmondsworth, Middlesex: Penguin.

RIDDICK, B. (1982) *Toys and Play for the Handicapped Child*. London: Croom Helm.

References: Hearing Impairment

BESS, F. and McCONNELL, F. E. (1981). *Audiology, Education and the Hearing Impaired Child*. St. Louis and London: The C.V. Mosby Company.

BOOTHROYD, A. (1982). *Hearing Impairments in Young Children*. Englewood Cliffs, N.J.: Prentice Hall.

FREEMAN, R. D., CARBIN, C. F. and BOESE, R. J. (1981). *Can't Your Child Hear? A guide for those who care about deaf children*. London: Croom Helm; Baltimore: University Park Press.

LING, A. and LING, D. (1978). *Aural Habilitation. The Foundation of Verbal Learning in Hearing Impaired Children*. Washington, DC: A.G. Bell Association for the Deaf.

MEERS, H. (1976). *Helping our Children Talk*. New York: Longman.

MILLER, A. L. (1980). *Hearing Loss, Hearing Aids and Your Child*. Springfield, Illinois: Chas C. Thomas.

NOLAN, M. and TUCKER, I. G. (1981). *The Hearing Impaired Child and the Family*. London: Souvenir Press.

NORTHERN, J. L., and DOWNS, M. P. (1978). *Hearing in Children*, second edition. Baltimore: Williams and Wilkins.

ROSS, M. and GIOLAS, T. G., (eds) (1979). *Auditory Management of Hearing Impaired Children*. Baltimore: University Park Press.

SANDERS, D., (1982). *Aural Rehabilitation: A management model.* Englewood Cliffs, N.J.: Prentice-Hall.

YEATES, S. (1980). *The Development of Hearing.* Lancaster: MTP Press.

8 Specific Learning Difficulties and the Clumsy Child

By Ruth Day and Margaret Radcliffe

PROBLEMS WITH READING, SPELLING AND WRITING

Some children, despite adequate opportunity, show an unexpected difficulty in learning to read and spell, which is quite disproportionate to their general ability. These children have a disorder at one or more points in the processes necessary to decipher and use written language. Reading is a complex process which, at its simplest, involves accurate perception, good short-term sequential memory and the ability to match shapes with previously learned sounds, elicit meaning and produce an accurate sequence of motor actions (speech or writing). See Fig 13.

These activities require very complex integration within the brain, many different parts being linked together by numerous complicated connections, and the whole working through a variety of chemical messengers and minute electrical currents. The immature brain has far greater potential for thought processes than any computer and it is hardly surprising that in some children these intricate functions go awry. In the majority

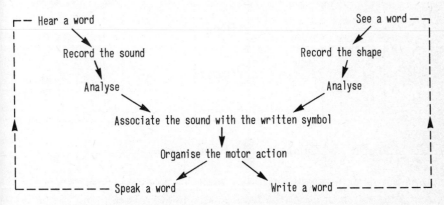

Fig 13. A simple model of the process of reading and writing.

of children who have specific learning difficulties there is no proof, either from the history or from medical examination, of brain damage. Similar learning difficulties do occur in children with definite brain damage. (Boder, 1973; Mattis, French and Rapin, 1975). What is clear is that there is often a family history of similar difficulties.

There are often signs of developmental immaturity, and boys are more commonly affected than girls. This has led to the theory that, in most children, there is a genetic factor which affects the development or rate of maturation of certain parts or systems within the brain. In some people this alone is sufficient for learning problems to occur, but in others additional factors are necessary, eg. mild brain damage which alone would not lead to difficulties (Fig 14a). Other factors, such as intermittent deafness or an unstimulating home background, might similarly compound the genetic tendency (Fig 14b).

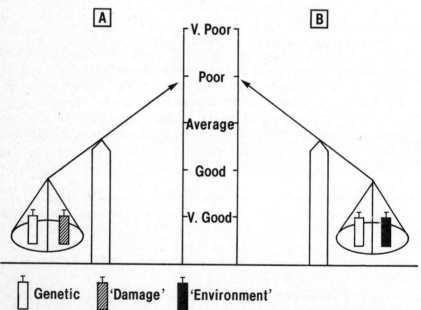

Fig 14. The Multifactorial Cause of Specific Learning Difficulties
A. Combination of inherited factors with mild brain damage.
B. Combination of inherited and environmental factors.

1   Occurrence and Characteristics of Specific Learning Difficulties

Rutter and his colleagues in the Isle of Wight (Rutter *et al*, 1970) studied children with 'specific reading retardation'. They found that four per cent of children were reading 28 months or more below the level predicted on the basis of their age and intellectual ability. Seventy-seven per cent of these children were boys and none of them showed a definite neurological abnormality. They matched the children with 'specific reading retardation' with a group of children who had no such problems. They found no significant increase in mixed dominance, nor an abnormal birth or medical history. It was also shown that 'specific reading retardation' occurred in all social classes and at all levels of ability.

However, certain other characteristics were found to be much more common amongst the four per cent of children who had difficulty in learning to read (Table 2).

Table 2

Factors associated with reading difficulty	Reading Difficulty %	Other Children %
Family history of reading difficulty (1)	33.7	9.2
History of language delay	15.1	4.0
Current articulatory disorder	14.0	7.0
Current language disorder	15.0	6.2
Current poor co-ordination (2)	8.1	1.4
Behaviour abnormality—overactive, (3) fidgety, poor concentration	40.0	20.0

Three times as many of the children with problems had a family history of reading difficulty (1), five times as many were clumsy (2) and twice as many had difficulty with concentration and attention (3). Thus this study demonstrates that learning problems may be preceded by or be associated with other neurodevelopmental problems.

A higher incidence of reading retardation of nine per cent has since been found in an Inner London Education Authority (Berger, 1975). This may reflect the compounding effect of adverse environmental circumstances upon innate difficulty (See Fig 14b).

2 Other Effects of Specific Learning Difficulties

In these children, delay in reading and/or spelling may not appear at first sight to be the basic difficulty. Often, secondary disorders reflect their distress at failing and their inability to elicit sympathetic understanding from parents, teachers and peers. They may develop school refusal, either outright or indirectly in the form of sickness, stomach aches or headaches; they may react to their failure in academic skills by conduct disorders aimed at raising their esteem among their peers; they may show a lack of attention when written material is presented, which may suggest 'not trying' or 'not caring', when in fact the child has come to realise that, however hard he attends, what he sees in books is totally meaningless; he may become fearful, worried or miserable, or show more obvious behaviour disturbance. Emotional and behavioural problems can of course be secondary to problems at home and, if severe, can lead to failure to learn in school. However, when a child has these difficulties, it is very important to check his academic attainments and to look for specific problems, rather than to assume that any learning difficulties are simply due to a disturbed home background, or to not trying, attending or caring. The importance of making a correct assessment is that management in either case is quite different.

3 Assessment

This is a complex task and may sometimes need the services of a multidisciplinary team as described in Chapter 2. In order to give the fullest picture of the child's strengths and weaknesses, the investigation should be wide ranging yet detailed, and related to the child's age and stage of development. The results must be interpreted in the light of the child's developmental history and opportunity to learn.

If a parent, teacher or doctor is suspicious that a child may have a specific learning difficulty, the professionals can extend their own observations in the following way, before asking a psychologist and specialist remedial teacher to confirm the diagnosis and plan management.

a)   The child's attainments in reading and spelling may be measured, using one or more of the standardised tests. The child's reaction to being asked to read or write may be illuminating. He may become acutely anxious, or withdrawn, or may suggest other activities to distract from the task. It should never be forgotten that the cause for refusal may be an acute awareness by the child of his inability to perform the task.

b) Some idea of the child's ability may be obtained by listening to the way he talks and by the sort of questions he is able to answer. Caution is necessary, however, because some children who have difficulty in reading have a primary difficulty with language and will not be fluent in spoken language. If intelligence tests have been carried out, this must also be interpreted with caution as the results may well cover up a scatter of abilities from below average to average or above. This is why a psychologist needs to look carefully at all aspects of the child's intellectual profile.

c) The subskills involved in reading and spelling may be tapped, using such tests as the *Aston Index*. This includes matching shapes (visual perception), copying shapes (visuo-motor), repeating like-sounding words (auditory discrimination), associating sounds with written symbols, and repeating a series of numbers presented orally (sequential memory). Again, caution must be used in interpreting results, as difficulty in one of these areas may be quite compatible with normal reading and spelling.

It must be emphasised again that the above are methods for increasing the level of suspicion that a child may have a specific learning difficulty and indicate the need for a more detailed evaluation by a psychologist.

It is at this stage that it is necessary to consider both medical and educational factors. Any child who has a specific reading or spelling difficulty should have his hearing and vision tested, and some children may need the help of a simple neurological examination from the school doctor or general practitioner. In the majority of children no neurological abnormality will be detected; but some may have 'soft' neurological signs which may merely be evidence of immaturity; in a few, however, more definite neurological signs may indicate the need for further investigation by a neurologist. In yet other children this type of examination may reveal excessive clumsiness which may affect handwriting and other skills and these need to be considered when planning a programme.

4 Outlook

Reading and spelling difficulties may range from mild to very severe. All children are likely to show some improvement when the nature of their difficulty has been explained to them and they have been given appropriate remedial help. However, some children will continue to have very severe, persistent difficulties and these children often make slower progress than those whose reading delay reflects lower intellectual ability.

5 What Can be Done to Help?

The management of these children should consist of three elements:

1) An explanation to the child and his parents of the nature of his difficulties.
2) Specific remedial help with reading and spelling.
3) By-pass techniques to enable the child to acquire knowledge despite his difficulties with written language.

Explaining to the parent and child that he has a specific difficulty with reading and spelling which is innate and which makes it much harder for him to acquire the skill, often produces a dramatic change in the child's morale and the family's well-being. The explanation should include the statement that the child is not stupid but of at least average ability and that it is not that the child is not trying. Indeed, the converse is often true, that the child has been trying harder than his peers but with much less reward. It is very important that everybody dealing with the child accepts that he has got definite, specific difficulties and that he needs positive encouragement rather than ridicule or depreciation. In order to boost his self-esteem and self-confidence he needs to take part in activities in which he can succeed and to receive appropriate commendation for these.

The child needs remedial help geared specifically to *his* difficulties. Each child has an individual pattern of difficulties which need to be recognised when planning remedial help. Clues may be obtained as to what strategies will be helpful for the child by observing carefully how he sets about a task, ie. what he himself has already found helpful.

It is very important for the child's future that he be able to acquire knowledge despite his difficulty with written language. Unfortunately, in our current education system, attainment of knowledge and recognition of knowledge is almost entirely through the written mode. If a child has severe difficulties with reading and spelling he should be enabled to learn by having material read to him either by relatives or on tape and should be able to present his own knowledge either through a scribe or, again, on tape. Concessions may be given in exams to children who have such difficulties. It is important for a child with less severe reading difficulties to recognise that he may misread text books and written exam questions.

It is also important to recognise that many of these children only exhibit their handicap because society demands that they read and spell. Such children should therefore be considered basically normal. Some of them will also have areas of above average ability, eg. in mathematics, artistic and physical skills. It is therefore particularly important to look at each child as an individual and work with his strengths as well as his weaknesses.

TEACHING CHILDREN WITH SPECIFIC LEARNING DIFFICULTIES

The present chapter cannot attempt to summarise the vast amount of literature on reading, spelling and writing difficulties, nor to evaluate the large number of reading and spelling programmes which have been used to alleviate them. The aim, instead, is to say something in terms of general approaches to the problem, and to cite some specific techniques which can be investigated further by teachers or other professionals interested in helping these children.

1   Considerations in Assessing Children with Specific Learning Difficulties

Most young children enter school eager to learn, so that when they meet failure, frustration follows. The child who fails may be bewildered at being unable to acquire skills which his age-mates tackle easily, and his teacher, too, may feel inadequate or guilty. Parents can become anxious and begin to question their own effectiveness. Since help and advice are sought from a number of professionals—psychologist, teacher, neurologist—the study of reading disorders has been carried out in different fields, each profession viewing the child from a different background of training and experience. The criteria for diagnosis, and the label attached to a difficulty may be the subject of controversy, but the clear need for remedial help is agreed by all.

Reading and spelling are complex, learnt skills. Acquiring these skills requires competence in a number of areas: an understanding of language and the ability to analyse it; visual and auditory perception; aspects of memory; and rule formation. A number of factors in the child can affect his success in these skills: his capacity to learn; his level of concentration; his motivation and his ability to direct attention. Given the complex nature of these tasks, it is easy to understand that all children experiencing difficulty with reading and spelling need not be experiencing the same difficulty. Learning is an interactive process. It is a complex mixture of what the learner brings to the situation, and what the situation brings to the learner. The child should be considered, not in the light of preconceived ideas, but as an individual whose own home and school environment and whose own personal development and attitudes are judged in terms of how these affect *his* problem with reading and spelling.

Another important aspect of assessment should be to determine a child's needs not only in terms of learning demands, but also in the light of his social and emotional development. The needs will be different for each child and will also change with time.

The stage of school life, for example, will determine the demands made on a child. The needs of the twelve-year-old boy with poor reading development will be quite different from the seven-year-old with similar difficulties. For the older child, although improvement of basic skills is important, more emphasis might be placed on opportunities to give and receive information and ideas, by means other than the written word. For the seven-year-old, intensive remedial work on basic skills may be the priority in planning help.

2 Planning the Programme

The referral of a child to a specialist teacher may come about in a number of ways. The parents or class teacher may express their concern at the child's apparent lack of progress, or a member of the multidisciplinary assessment team may ask for help. Before embarking on an educational programme, it is always wise to ensure that a child has normal vision and hearing and to ask a speech therapist to explore his language and communication skills. The presence of another disability should not, however, deter efforts to find out the child's own chosen strategies and areas of difficulty.

In planning an educational programme, three major considerations should be borne in mind:

1 The effect of failure on the child's motivation, attitude and feeling of self-worth.
2 The importance of opportunities to allow information and ideas to be given and received without dependence on the printed word.
3 The starting point for a remedial programme aimed at improving basic skills.

Once a scheme has been decided upon, its effectiveness will depend upon
A   the teacher   B   the parents   C   the curriculum

A   The Specialist Teacher's Role, Assessment, Teaching, Evaluation

In planning a programme for a child with specific learning difficulties, the teacher will use any information available from other professionals. Above all, she will use all the basic skills which are part of her normal teaching role but will need to expand these by a knowledge of the specific difficulties which may be encountered.

1   *Assessment of written language skills*

As with any other assessment procedure, this should be a continuous process and should involve monitoring of response to teaching and evaluation of success. It is therefore necessary to determine the child's present level of knowledge, to observe his responses to tasks and to determine what strategies he brings to them. These strategies often give clues as to where his difficulties lie.

a) *Reading.* The process of reading, at one level, involves the ability to decode individual words and to blend sounds together. The teacher must determine whether individual sounds for letters are known, whether the child recognises recurring patterns in words and whether he can synthesise the parts into a whole word which carries meaning. Word recognition tests (eg. Burt, 1974) allow observation when reading single words out of context. The teacher can determine whether guesses are made on the basis of word shape or initial letter clusters. Individual word reading will also tell the teacher whether the child has an extensive vocabulary of words he recognises on sight, or whether he uses a phonic-based decoding strategy.

At another level, reading involves drawing inference and making predictions on the basis of information in the text. It is important, therefore, to observe a child's accuracy when reading a continuous text. This gives information as to the child's use of context clues and whether he has the ability to correct his own errors in the light of information from the text. A standardised test such as the *Neale Analysis of Reading Ability* (1958) gives information as to whether the child's reading and understanding is in line with his age and ability. It also allows analysis of the types of errors made.

Similarly, a procedure like 'Miscue Analysis' (Goodman, 1969) allows the teacher to examine the type of error being made. For example, whether errors are syntactic, semantic or due to difficulty with grapheme-phoneme correspondence. Silent reading for meaning is functionally an important aspect of reading in school. It is useful for the teacher, then, to examine this.

b) *Spelling.* Age-related measures of spelling skills may be obtained using standardised tests (eg. Cotterell, 1970; Schonell and Schonell, 1960). The teacher can glean information from these as to the strategies the child is using, and can learn, from observation, how the child tackles words. For example, whether he articulates the word and bases his spelling on its phonic elements. It is important, too, to consider the words the child spells correctly, as these may provide the starting point in teaching and building 'word-banks'.

Specific information on knowledge of spelling patterns and rules can be further examined on the basis of these errors and correct spellings. A diagnostic evaluation of this type can be found in Margaret Peters' *Diagnostic and Remedial Spelling Manual* (1975). Further information can be gained by examining the child's skill in continuous writing. Three aspects can be usefully assessed: free writing, copying and writing to dictation. As well as providing information about the child's ability to cope with these tasks in the educational setting, these again provide specific information about the child's spelling skill. For example, does the child's free writing indicate use of vocabulary in keeping with the child's level of ability? In other words, does the child use simple vocabulary to avoid spelling errors?

Since continuous writing is a more complex task than writing single words, some words which the child appears to know in one situation may be mis-spelled in another. This provides information for the teacher as to the extent of the child's grasp of particular rules and patterns. The teacher must also be sensitive to the possible breakdown of the child's strategies in different writing situations.

c) *Writing*. During assessment the teacher will have adequate opportunity to observe the child's writing style and to determine whether this is a target area for remediation. Fluency and letter formation are important aspects to consider, as well as observing posture, pencil-hold and lay-out of work on a page.

On the basis of information gained from such observations, a trial period of learning should be initiated. The instructional programme itself then becomes the diagnostic device. That is, the teacher can ascertain by working *with* the child the extent to which he can be taught to use and develop his existing capabilities.

2 *Considerations for teaching*

The teaching methods employed for children with specific learning difficulties are not in themselves new or extraordinary. They are, in the main, variations on existing phonics, whole-word and mixed approaches. However, there are a number of agreed principles which practitioners emphasise as being important.

a) GENERAL PRINCIPLES

(i) *An Individual Approach.* The need for an individual approach was described earlier in considering the number of variables, internal and external, affecting the child's performance. Some teachers interpret 'an individual approach' as one-to-one teaching. It is certainly valuable to maximise instructional time, and this can be effectively carried out in a one-to-one situation. Also, intensive interaction between the teacher and learner has been shown to be beneficial. It allows close supervision, immediate correction of error, and enables the teacher to ensure a high percentage of correct responses. Structured learning requires this close one-to-one interaction.

However, a programme devised on an individual basis need not always be carried out in a one-to-one situation. While there is certainly a need for this kind of contact on occasion, it is sometimes felt to be more beneficial for a child to be part of a group. A child who is anxious about the task may feel under pressure in a one-to-one teaching situation. A small group would be less threatening and would give opportunity for training in good, independent working habits.

(ii) *Advantages of multi-sensory learning.* Multi-sensory learning refers to simultaneous stimulation to all the senses, for example in learning the association of a symbol with its sound. While most children would benefit from learning by simultaneously looking at a symbol, saying its sound and experiencing the motor movement involved in producing both, not all require such intensive instruction to make this kind of association. Children with a record of failure in reading and writing, however, have been found to achieve success with this approach. Hooton (1975) claims that if all three channels of learning and memory are stimulated, a child with a perceptual weakness in one channel will learn to compensate from the start if taught this way.

(iii) *The need for 'over-learning' in a structured, systematic way.* Highly structured programmes have been developed which emphasise careful planning of the sequence of teaching. The aim is to ensure pupil success, to reduce the likelihood of confusion, and gradually to build the child's confidence in his own ability to learn. Regularity and rule-formation are emphasised and 'over-learned' in repeated practice and use.

(iv)   *Teaching from strengths.* Research into the different ways which individual children learn has been stimulated by studies of children with learning difficulties. A number of writers have investigated how difficulties in processing (analysing) sounds and written information affect the learning of reading (Johnson and Myklebust, 1967; Cotterell, 1970). A child is then viewed as having a weakness in one or more areas considered necessary for skilled performance. Emphasis in teaching would be on the 'strong' mode while encouraging development in the area considered deficient.

Not all children fit into these categories and it is important, therefore, to use all the information gained about the child to design an approach to meet his particular needs.

b)   SPECIFIC APPROACHES

Having considered the need for an individual approach, the question now asked is not 'what is *the* best reading and spelling method?' but 'what is the best reading and spelling method for *this* child?' The aim is to match the child's overall pattern of learning strengths and weaknesses with an individual programme.

The methods/programmes most commonly followed by remedial teachers fall into two main categories: the alphabetic-phonic method; and the whole-word method. A few of the most popular approaches for children with these specific difficulties are listed in Table 3.

It is important to avoid over-generalising when describing teaching methods. Although classified as 'phonic' or 'multi-sensory', there are important differences in procedure within these classifications. These must be considered when planning a teaching programme. Each of the methods has its supporters and critics, but most experienced remedial teachers will use ideas from more than one source, tailored to fit the child's learning style. The assessment-teaching-evaluation cycle may

Table 3 Specific Teaching Approaches

ALPHABETIC-PHONIC

1 Alpha–Omega
A structured sequential programme in which sound patterns are gradually associated with their alphabetic equivalents. Language structure is similarly introduced sequentially (Hornsby and Shear)

2 Gillingham–Stillman
A completely multi-sensory approach to phonics. Progression is systematic and sequential.

3 Dyslexia: a Language Training Course for Teachers and Learners (Kathleen Hickey)
Based on Gillingham–Stillman method but produced for British children.

4 The Edith Norrie Letter Case
Letter cards for word and sentence building. Cards are colour coded phonetically.

5 Phonic Cues
Covers all phoneme combinations and spellings in gradual stages. Reading is taught through learning the spelling patterns.

WHOLE-WORD

1 The Fernald Method
Basically a kinaesthetic approach emphasising the word as a whole rather than its constituent phonic elements. Involves visual-auditory and kinaesthetic-tactile link-up.

2 Breakthrough to Literacy
Whole-word, look and say approach. Reading material based on child's own language. Children's 'sentence-builder' allows expression of ideas for children with severe writing difficulty. (McKay et al).

COMPLETE ASSESSMENT-REMEDIATION

1 The Aston Portfolio
Individual assessment provides learning profiles. Techniques appropriate to particular learning stages are provided.

2 Quest
A screening, diagnostic and remediation programme for 7–8 year-olds. Work books provided as part of a remediation programme.

lead the teacher to use one method in the initial stages and incorporate others, as appropriate, as the child's learning develops.

B The Parents' Role

Parents will have provided valuable information to the professionals in the course of assessment and should be included in the discussion of the planned management of their child, so that the best environment can be provided for the child both at home and in school.

It is the parents' natural inclination to want to do as much as possible for their child. For the parents of a child experiencing significant failure at school it is important to have a realistic view of how he can best be helped. Communication is the key, and there are two aspects to consider.

1 *Communication with school*

The teacher and parent should decide together what are reasonable expectations in terms of homework. This may involve setting a time limit on written work or may involve advising parents on the use of scribing or tape recording techniques. If reading is to be practised at home, the teacher and parents should decide together on the method to be employed. Where this involves listening to the child reading, the teacher should give guidance on when and how to intervene if the child has difficulty. The teacher may give the parents advice on paired-reading techniques or on the use of a tape recorder to improve reading fluency.

If parents feel that extra work at home might help their child, this should be decided in collaboration with the teacher so that the child does not become confused.

This collaborative approach will ensure that the child does not become confused by different approaches, that he does not become frustrated by over-emphasising his weaknesses and that he will gain confidence from having his difficulties acknowledged.

2 *Communication with the child*

As adults we can communicate many things to children unintentionally. Our anger, frustration and disappointment at their failure to learn basic skills such as reading and writing are easily communicated by our attitude. It is important to be aware of this and to acknowledge the need for positive communication where possible

Parents should be alert to areas in which their child shows skill and should encourage and develop these. This gives the child an opportunity to feel positive about himself in at least one activity.

There are many ways in which parents can offer practical help to their child. These include: using television, radio, tape-recorders and visits to extend his knowledge; reading him stories to keep alive his interest in books in an enjoyable way; and introducing him to new activities, eg. in sport or music. Praise and encouragement, rather than criticism, will be crucial in developing positive attitudes in the child.

This does not mean that parents should 'pretend' the child does not have these difficulties. It means acknowledging the difficulties, working with the child and school to overcome them as far as possible, and allowing the child to grow and develop in other areas in a natural way.

C The Curriculum

It has been mentioned earlier in this chapter that many children with severe reading and spelling difficulties are denied access to the school curriculum because it is based on the ability to use written language. Many curricular changes are taking place at the moment in both primary and secondary schools, and it seems likely that these will allow more opportunities for children with poor literary skills.

There are some general points which teachers might consider as methods of 'by-passing' the difficulty and offering support and a sense of achievement for the child.

1) Use of scribe, reader, or oral work where possible.

2) Use of a tape recorder; taped stories and novels will serve to maintain the child's interest in literature, to help develop listening skills and to allow access to information and knowledge alongside his peers. The tape recorder can be usefully employed for a number of activities: taping the child's own stories; revising school subject material, and, with a teacher's guidance, improving reading fluency.

3) Extra time might be allowed for written work. Adaptations in the form of work sheets or multiple-choice questions will reduce the amount of written work and enable the teacher to judge the child's level of knowledge in specific subjects.

Again, the concessions appropriate for each individual must be assessed in different situations for different school subjects. Where written work is required, the teacher should make allowances for the child's difficulties and acknowledge that what may be considered a low standard may be the child's best effort.

At the same time, the child requires training in self-correction procedures, methods of planning written work and in techniques for studying subject material. Close liaison between parents and school is essential to allow the child to gain maximum benefit from his school career.

It is also extremely important to emphasise the child's skills in other directions, to encourage them to the full and to give praise for success in these fields.

We have touched on only some of the issues worth consideration in helping children with specific reading and writing difficulties. The aim for the future must be earlier recognition of such difficulties so that corrective teaching can be initiated at an age when optimum responsiveness and effectiveness are likely.

The term 'specific learning difficulty' has deliberately been used throughout. Although much of the literature relevant to these children uses the term 'dyslexia', we have not used this word here because of our concern that it often means different things to different people. This, however, should in no way detract from the value of the literature recommended at the end of the chapter.

THE CLUMSY CHILD (Motor Learning Difficulties)

In any group of children there are a few who stand out as excessively awkward and clumsy. They have difficulty throwing and catching, they may dress and eat messily, they tend to knock things over and their handwriting may be untidy. They frustrate parents and teachers and are often unpopular with their peers. Things are broken, exercise books are a mess and they often rush, giving the added appearance of 'not caring'. For boys, lack of skill at football during their primary school years is a cause of social isolation and the development of a poor self image.

During the first few years of life the child learns a variety of motor skills, both large movements, which involve postural control and adjustment, and finer hand skills. How does he do this? Through experience he develops a schema of self and space so that he can interpret visual information and information from his own muscles and joints. He also practises skills so that they are refined and in some way stored as motor memories. This obviously involves many areas of the brain and these areas need to be well interconnected. With practice the movements become accurate, fast, energy-efficient, subconscious, and imperceptibly and rapidly adjustable to a change in the environment. It is this latter refinement of skills that seems to be deficient in the 'clumsy child'.

Where may the process go wrong?

1   The child may lack experience; he needs to feel the muscle tension, balance and visual sensations resulting from his own actions to learn how to modify his movements to improve his performance. He cannot learn motor skills by verbal instruction or passive manipulation.

2   The child may have poor vision. Visual input is very important for the development of motor skills. The motor development of blind children is significantly delayed. Some children with a severe refractive error which is not corrected until they are four or five years old remain clumsy despite adequate correction of the refractive error.

3   The child may have a mild disorder of motor output, eg. a mild cerebellar ataxia or 'choreiform syndrome'. Some rarer degenerative disorders may also present with clumsiness. These can be recognised by neurological examination.

4   The child may be mentally handicapped and his motor development be commensurate with his mental age even if delayed for his chronological age.

5   The 'clumsy child'. If these four causes are excluded there is still a group of children who are clumsy and they seem to have a disorder of central processing. This may be a disorder of:

a   *Perception* – defined as a difficulty in interpreting sensory input when the peripheral channels are intact. In some children it affects their ability to recognise and match shapes, and in others their awareness of position in space. In yet others the auditory channel is affected.

b   *Motor organisation.* Some children seem to have great difficulty organising a sequence of movements to perform a more complex motor task. This has been called 'dyspraxia'. It may affect such tasks as dressing, feeding, using scissors and speech. A special form of dyspraxia results in a difficulty copying shapes, despite being able to match them.

c   *Control.* When all these groups have been considered, there is still a group of children whose movements are just unrefined and jerky. They often have difficulty with postural control and it would seem as though they may have a difficulty in the rapid fine adjustments that are necessary for any smooth movements.

The above divisions are, to a certain extent, arbitrary and hypothetical; many children have difficulties in more than one area. Some of the children will also have difficulties with reading and spelling and others will have difficulty with attention and be distractable. Although in some children there is a definite history of brain damage, in others there is not, and in their case a developmental disorder of specific areas or connections in the brain is postulated.

As with the children with specific difficulties with reading and spelling, the children may not present with the motor disorder but with a secondary behaviour disturbance.

ASSESSMENT
Before embarking on treatment it is important to assess the individual child's needs and difficulties.

1   Which skills are affected? In some children all areas are affected – gross motor and balance, fine motor and speech. In

others, however, it is only spatial tasks such as throwing and catching. In others, gross motor co-ordination is good but pencil and paper work is poor. Motor learning seems to be fairly specific to the task. Being good at typing does not make you good at playing the piano, and remediation must include practising the deficient skills.

2   Why is the child clumsy? What is the underlying difficulty? Does the child have perceptual, organisational or control problems? This may well affect the main emphasis of the remedial programme.

When administering tests to children or observing them, it is important to be quite clear what processes are involved. For instance, when a child copies a shape with a pencil, this involves motor output as well as visual perception; pure matching tasks are required to measure the latter. How the child performs a task may also give valuable information; for example, when copying a three-brick bridge, the child may give the appearance of just 'not being able to see what is wanted'; or it may be obvious that he knows what is required but his motor control is not good enough. Various areas may be tapped, as shown in Table 4. All these skills improve with age and norms are available for most of them. Probably the most useful formal test of motor co-ordination is the Stott *Test of Motor Impairment* – recently modified by Henderson (1985).

3   What is the underlying neurological disorder? Is there evidence of brain damage, or can the difficulty be considered developmental? If there is any suggestion of the child getting worse it is important that he be seen by a doctor to exclude one of the rare degenerative disorders.

4   Vision should be checked.

5   What is the state of the child's morale? This will affect his attitude to learning. If he is very self-conscious about his clumsiness, initial activities will have to be carefully selected to give success and increase confidence. It is also important to look at the child's needs at the time. If he is an older child he may no longer have any interest in sporting activities and it will be more appropriate to spend time on speed and legibility of handwriting. Does he have difficulties in other areas which

Table 4   Minimum Assessment of a Clumsy Child

a   Skills affected?

Throwing/catching/kicking
Speech
Dressing
Eating
Scissors
Handwriting   Hand used?
Other (important to the child)

b   Underlying difficulty?

Balance	Balance on one leg Hop on spot Heel toe
Spatial and Body Schema	Catch and throw Copy gesture
Visual perception Constructional	Match shapes Copy shapes
Fine motor control	Draw circle between lines Place pegs and build bricks – to compare hands Hand tap, finger tip touch
Memory	Auditory sequential memory (number)

c   Is he improving/getting worse?
d   Vision – to be tested adequately
e   Morale – is he very reluctant to perform?
          – self esteem
f   General ability
    Reading/Spelling
    Attention/Concentration/Impulsivity
g   Current opportunities to practise – at home and school.

may affect management, eg. reading and spelling, attention and concentration?

INTERVENTION

1   *Explanation.* As with the child with reading difficulties, it is important to explain to the parents, the child and the people who deal with him that he has a definite difficulty with co-ordination and is not just being careless or not trying. Motor performance is made worse by anxiety, eg. dropping the best china when being so careful! Fear of being reprimanded for untidyness or poor spelling may reduce the amount the child writes and he may not get credit for what he knows.

2   *Remediation.* The principle of remediation in the clumsy

child must be to enable the child to practise the skills he finds difficult in an environment which is conducive to learning. Initially it may be appropriate for him to have individual sessions, and later it may be helpful for his self-confidence to join in group sessions. Whichever setting is chosen, the atmosphere must be sympathetic and encouraging. Many clumsy children avoid motor activities in order to escape ridicule. When given opportunity to practise, some children will improve quite dramatically.

As well as practising skills, it may be valuable to do extra work on underlying areas of difficulty. During assessment it may be apparent that the child has a poor idea of space, distance and his own body relationships to other objects. Alternatively, he may have shown great difficulty in balancing, ie. postural control. This is an important prerequisite of many skilled actions and may need specific attention.

Any task should be taught through graded activities of increasing difficulty. For example, ball handling skills: initially the child will throw a large, light ball into a large container near at hand and learn to hit a stationary object standing still. He will slowly progress to throwing a smaller ball into a smaller container at a greater distance and hitting a moving object while on the move himself. More complex tasks, such as putting on a jumper or making a pot of tea, may be broken down into their component parts. Vocalising the stages may help some children. The activities must be varied and interesting. Dancing and snooker can supersede more 'boring' exercises.

Very useful information on remedial approaches is given in the book *Helping Clumsy Children* by Gordon and McKinlay. They note that various professionals may be involved, including occupational, speech and physiotherapists, the class or gym teacher and also the parents. It is very important that they create one co-ordinated plan for the child which disrupts his normal education as little as possible.

IN THE CLASSROOM

Handwriting in Clumsy Children
The difficulties for the clumsy child in organising and refining

motor movements will clearly affect his ability to learn to write. At the infant stage, the teaching of pre-writing skills may require to be extended for this child, and when letter formation is taught, he may require much more guidance and practice than his peers.

Clumsy children often lag behind in their handwriting skills, although they may make adequate progress in reading. Although the child has been taught correct letter formations and writing procedures, his difficulty with the task over a prolonged period may lead to the development of idiosyncratic letter formations, so that when 'linking' is taught, his difficulties are compounded.

Good handwriting is important for a number of reasons. The production of clear manuscript provides important feedback to the child, both in terms of what he has written and also in terms of the approval or disapproval with which it is received by others. Writing is important, too, in its relation to spelling. Margaret Peters (1970) says of handwriting, 'It should be swift and effortless . . . The swifter the writing, the better the spelling. This is only to be expected since the child who writes swiftly is accustomed to writing familiar strings of letters together and there is a high probability of certain strings occurring and recurring in English.' Fluent handwriting is also important when ideas are being expressed, so that the flow of thought is not unduly interrupted.

For the clumsy child, then, writing may be a tiring chore which is essentially non-rewarding. He may find it difficult to cope with the amount of written work in everyday classroom activities. Since, through writing, a child develops knowledge of word structure, his spelling is likely to be poor. To add to this, the end product of his efforts is likely to be messy, and the child recognises this fact as much as the teacher. As a result, the child may find ways of 'opting out' of written work, for example, by reducing his output in expressive writing.

There are three areas to be considered when this child is referred for remedial help.

1   Is his writing style so poor that a re-teaching programme is necessary?
2   Should this incorporate a remedial spelling programme?

3   Can changes in classroom organisation be instituted which will reduce the demands on written work?

The teacher must assess the child's level of skill to determine where a remedial programme should begin.

It has already been mentioned that poor writers have often accumulated faulty writing habits over time. Many teachers will recognise the strategy employed by some children who, when starting to write 'd', 'b' or 'p', form an 'o', and continue round and round the 'roundabout' until they decide which road to take to come off. And yet, the starting points for each of these letters should be completely different. There are some children who consistently use the wrong starting point; for example, in the 'o a d g q' group, they may always move from left to right, instead of right to left. This can encourage prolonged production of reversed letters. Even more bizarre formations than these have been noted. The main point is that fluent writing will be difficult to achieve if these are not corrected.

Observation of a child during a writing task is important, as well as examining his written productions. Children with motor difficulties may find it difficult to organise all the constituent elements before beginning. The teacher should, in particular, observe pencil-hold, positioning of the paper, sitting position, posture and balance. The non-writing arm may not be used as it should be, to anchor the paper and balance the child. Some children with poor posture and balance may bear weight inappropriately on the writing arm. The way a child grips the pencil may reduce fluency of fine movements, and the positioning of the writing arm may hinder free movement across the paper.

Checklist of Handwriting Skills

A   The child who is not writing at all should be assessed to determine whether he has the prerequisite skills for writing:

1   Does he understand the vocabulary used in describing the required movements, eg. up/down; back/forward?
2   Can he make the required movements, a) with his arm in the air, b) with his finger on a table/in a sandtray?
3   Can he hold and use a crayon/paint brush/felt pen/

pencil to produce shapes such as circles, triangles, curves, straight lines?

4   Can he combine his shape drawings to make continuous patterns from left to right across the page?

B   The child who has these skills and has begun to write letters or words should be observed to determine whether:

1   Sitting position, balance and pencil hold are appropriate.
2   Left to right movement across the page is established.
3   Letter formations show correct starting and finishing points.
4   Words and letters are suitably spaced.
5   Writing is well aligned.
6   Size of letters is appropriate.
7   Slope is regular.

A very useful handwriting checklist has been produced by Jean Alston for the *Aston Portfolio* (1982). This allows careful examination of sources of difficulty and provides ideas to meet teaching objectives.

Table 4 refers to the minimum assessment of a 'clumsy child'. All these aspects need to be considered in the individual nature of the child's difficulties, which cannot be over-emphasised. When considering a remedial programme, all aspects of the child's development should be considered – his age and stage in school, his good skills as well as his weak points, and the way in which his progress so far has affected his feelings about himself.

PREVENTION
There is no doubt that young children's motor skills are very much affected by the opportunity to practise. It is important to include in nursery and primary education activities which encourage motor control and smooth co-ordinated rhythmic actions, eg. music and movement, gymnastics, ball games.

References

Aston Index (1976). *A Classroom Test for Screening and Diagnosis of Language Difficulties (5–14 year-olds).* Cambridge (England): Learning Development Aids.

BERGER, M., YULE, W. and RUTTER, M. (1975). 'The prevalence of reading retardation', *British Journal of Psychiatry*, **126**, 510–519.

BODER, E. (1973). 'Developmental dyslexia: A diagnostic approach based on three typical reading-spelling patterns', *Developmental Medicine and Child Neurology*, **15**, 663–685.

BURT, C. (1974) *Graded Word Reading Test.* Edinburgh: Scottish Council for Research in Education.

COTTERELL, G. (1970). 'Teaching procedures' in *Assessment and Teaching of Dyslexic Children*, FRANKLIN, A. and NAIDOO, S. (eds). London: ICAA.

COTTERELL, G. *Diagnostic Spelling Tests*, Cambridge (England): Learning Development Aids.

GOODMAN, K. (1969). 'Analysis of oral reading miscues: applied psycholinguistics,' *Reading Research Quarterly*, **5**, 9–30.

HOOTON, M. B. (1975). *The first reading and writing book.* London: Heinemann Educational.

JOHNSON, D. G. and MYKLEBUST, H. R. (1967). *Learning Disabilities.* New York: Grune and Stratton.

MATTIS, S., FRENCH, J. H. and RAPIN, J. (1975). 'Dyslexia in children and young adults. Three independent neuropsychological syndromes', *Developmental Medicine and Child Neurology*, **17**, 150–163.

NEALE, M. D. (1958). *Neale Analysis of Reading Ability.* London: Macmillan.

PETERS, M. (1975) *Diagnostic and Remedial Spelling Manual.* London: Macmillan Education.

RUTTER, M., TIZARD, J. and WHITMORE, K. (1970). *Education, Health and Behaviour.* London: Longman.

SCHONELL, F. J. and SCHONELL, F. E. (1960). 'Schonell spelling test' in *Diagnostic and Attainment Testing*, fourth edition. Edinburgh: Oliver and Boyd.

Specific Teaching Approaches (from Table 3)

Aston Portfolio (1982). *Classroom Techniques and Activities for Creating Individual Teaching and Remedial Programmes in Reading, Writing and Spelling.* Cambridge (England): Learning Development Aids.

FERNALD, G. M. (1943). *Remedial Techniques in Basic School Subjects.* New York: McGraw-Hill.

GILLINGHAM, A. and STILLMAN, B. (1977). *Remedial Training for Children with Specific Difficulty in Reading, Spelling and Penmanship*, seventh edition. Cambridge, Mass: Educators' Publishing Service.

HICKEY, K. (1977). *Dyslexia. A Language Training Course for Teachers and Learners.* (3 Montague Road, London SW19 1TB.) Published by author.

HORNSBY, B. and SHEAR, F. (1976). *Alpha-Omega: The A-Z of Reading, Writing and Spelling.* London: Heinemann Educational.

MacKAY, D., THOMPSON, B. and SCHAUB, P. (1970). *Breakthrough to Literacy.* Teacher's manual. London: Longman, for Schools Council.

NORRIE, E. (1939). *Edith Norrie Letter Case* (Copenhagen). (Available from Helen Arkell Dyslexia Centre, 14, Crondace Road, London, SW6.)

Quest (1984). *A Complete Screening, Diagnostic and Remediation Programme for 7–8 year-olds.* Leeds: E. J. Arnold.

The Clumsy Child (Motor Learning Difficulty)

ALSTON, J. (1982) Handwriting checklist. *The Aston Portfolio.* Cambridge: Learning Development Aids.

BRADLEY, L. (1980a). 'Reading, spelling and writing problems' in *Helping Clumsy Children*, GORDON, N. and McKINLAY, I. (eds). London, Edinburgh and New York: Churchill Livingstone.

PETERS, M. (1970). *Success in Spelling.* Cambridge (England): Institute of Education.

STOTT, D. H., MOYES, F. A. and HENDERSON, S. E. (1972).

A Test of Motor Impairment, revised HENDERSON, S. E. (1985). Windsor: NFER.

General Background Reading

BENTON, A. L. and PEARL, D. (eds) (1978). *Dyslexia: an Appraisal of Current Knowledge.* New York: OUP.

BRADLEY, L. (1980b). *Assessing Reading Difficulties. A Diagnostic and Remedial Approach.* London: Macmillan.

CRITCHLEY, M. and CRITCHLEY, E.A. (1978). *Dyslexia Defined.* London: Heinemann Medical Books.

FARNHAM-DIGGORY, S. (1978). *Learning Disabilities.* London: Fontana/Open Books.

HENDRY, A. (ed) (1982). *Teaching Reading: The Key Issues.* London: Heinemann Educational.

LEVINE, M. B., BROOKS, R. and SHONKOFF, J. P. (1980). *A Pediatric Approach to Learning Disorders.* New York and Chichester: Wiley.

MILES, T. R. (1970). *On Helping the Dyslexic Child*, London: Methuen Educational.

NAIDOO, S. (1972). *Specific Dyslexia.* London: Pitman.

NEWTON, M. and THOMSON, M. (1975). *Dyslexia: a guide for teachers and parents.* London: University of London Press.

REID, J. F. and DONALDSON, H. (eds) (1977). *Reading, Problems and Practices*, second edition revised. London: Ward Lock.

TANSLEY, P. and PANCKHURST, J. (1981). *Children with Specific Learning Difficulties.* WindsorNFER/Nelson. (US distribution Humanities Press Inc.)

9 Mental Handicap

By David Wilson

All who work with mentally handicapped children need to become familiar with the special problems of the child who has a chronic and perhaps permanent disability. Successful support depends as often on the social, educational and home adjustment that can be achieved, as on the purely technical and medical procedures. Parents and family have the major responsibility in caring for and nurturing their children, but the professional should play a direct, as well as a supportive role, in helping the family to meet their responsibilities, identifying and providing those facilities needed for optimal development.

Until a few years ago, mental handicap was defined and classified according to a person's responses to a number of intelligence tests. IQs were quantified and a decision about the person's status was determined by the numerical results obtained. Low intelligence, however it is measured, is still the major criterion in mental handicap, but it is now judged in a variety of ways based upon the person's ability to adapt to his environment. Although the current accepted definition of mental handicap refers to 'a significantly sub-average general intellectual functioning, existing concurrently with deficits in adaptive behaviour, and manifested during the developmental period' (American Association of Mental Deficiency, Grossman, 1973), from the practical point of view, mental handicap can be considered to be a depressed level of functioning and adaptation to social conventions which will require additional help and a protected environment throughout life.

Infants and small children are just beginning to acquire this adaptation, so that unless the child is severely affected or obviously abnormal in development, it is not always easy to be certain at an early stage to what extent independence will be acquired. Some conditions known to be associated with mental handicap, such as Down's Syndrome, can be diagnosed at birth, although the degree of disablement will not become obvious until later. Other children may appear normal at birth and it may be their delay in development, and particularly in acquiring cognitive and perceptual skills, which gives rise to concern.

Cunningham and Mittler (1981) implicate three factors influencing mental handicap. First, the environment which can affect a child's development either adversely or favourably; second, a process of slower maturation; third, specific defects distorting or complicating progress. Delay or distortion may be seen in any of the aspects of development discussed in previous chapters. Mentally handicapped children may or may not show delay in motor development (Chapter 5); in ability to communicate (Chapter 7); and above all in their emotional development and in social adaptive behaviour (Chapter 10). However expressed, mental handicap is a significant cause of lifetime disability, and a complex medical, educational, social and economic problem. This concept underlines the importance of discovering children's difficulties early, assessing their problems in all fields of development and organising a programme for intervention which will be related to the child's individual needs and to the facilities available to help him and to involve his family (Whelan & Speake, 1979).

WHAT CAUSES MENTAL HANDICAP?

Parents' feelings about the impact of a mentally handicapped child are well described in Chapter 3, and the importance of answering their questions is fully emphasised. Mental handicap is often the most difficult of handicaps to understand, as so often it comes 'out of the blue' and is entirely unexpected. It is this surprise and shock which often exacerbates the grief and anger and, sometimes, guilt of parents who ask, 'Why should *this* happen to us?' or, 'What have *we* done to deserve this?' There is no answer to such questions, but there is an increasing knowledge of some of the causative factors, and the advantage of being able to identify a biological cause of the child's condition has already been discussed in Chapter 1. Hopefully, in the future more knowledge will be gained about other causes of mental handicap and ways of preventing it. Often, at the present, we can only realise that the child has suffered a biological accident of some kind which cannot be reversed, the effects of which may be mitigated or exacerbated by the way we handle him. Trust and confidence need to be built up between parents and professionals so that all can cope with the as yet unexplained situation in the best way, to help the child realise his full potential.

In order that we – parents and professionals – learn to help as efficiently as possible, we first have to find out as much as we can about his strengths and weaknesses and then build up a programme to make use of as much as possible of his and our strengths, finding a way around his weaknesses.

ASSESSMENT OF DEVELOPMENTALLY DELAYED CHILDREN
Mental handicap may be suspected in a particular child for a variety of reasons.

1   There may be obvious physical features at birth, as in the case of Down's Syndrome (Cunningham, 1982).

2   The child may have had an extremely difficult delivery or been extremely ill in the neonatal period, therefore putting that child into the 'at risk' group of children.

3   More often, the child may fail to reach developmental 'milestones' within normal periods, and the parent may bring the child to the attention of the health visitor or family doctor.

4   Frequently it is not until the child has fallen behind at school or developed some form of behaviour problem secondary to his difficulties in mainstream education that the teacher may alert parents to the fact that something is wrong.

However suspicion is aroused, it is important that a full and comprehensive assessment of the child's physical and mental development is made. Such an assessment, in the case of suspected mental handicap, requires a widely based observation in depth which should be carried out by a multidisciplinary team of professionals who work together. The full team, as described in Chapter 2, needs to be available, with special emphasis on:

Developmental paediatrician	Occupational therapist
Psychologist	Physiotherapist
Specialist teacher	Psychiatrist
Speech therapist	Social worker

The best geographical site for assessment is a matter of opinion and is discussed in Chapter 2. Most people would agree that the initial approach is best made in the child's home, with gradual introduction into a more structured and formalised educational setting appropriate to that child's age. This home-based service needs back-up from some child development centre, where children can come for a variable period to join in the playgroup, during which time assessment by various professionals can take place, and where ancillary technical facilities are available for necessary diagnostic procedures. There are pros and cons for every method of assessment, and it will need to be worked out, taking into account the area in which the child lives and the local resources available. However, the most important feature is that the team should have the facilities and time to assess children individually, and then be able to meet to pool their findings and to discuss the future management among themselves and with the parents.

Although the mentally handicapped child's needs are likely to be mainly in the fields of educational, social and psychological provision, careful medical investigation in the first instance is necessary to establish, if possible, the reason WHY the child is as he is, and to combine with colleagues in the assessment team to establish HOW his development has been affected and in WHAT ways he can be helped. The process of assessment therefore involves activities in the following main areas:

1 *Medical assessment*
a) General observation begins with a careful case history which should include the history of the pregnancy, delivery and early neonatal development, together with a careful family history, followed by a retrospective developmental history. Careful physical examination, paying attention to height, weight, general physique, head circumference and the presence of any unusual or distinctive physical features.

b) Specific tests – laboratory and other tests – may be necessary to attempt to establish the cause of the condition or to define areas in which disturbed function may require treatment. Where appropriate, estimations of haemoglobin, full blood count, ESR, serum calcium, blood lead, fasting blood glucose, thyroid function test, serological tests for a number of possible prenatal infections, chromatography of blood and urine for a number of common and rare conditions, chromosome analysis, X-ray procedures (including CT* scan where necessary) and electrophysiological investigations (including EEG† and, possibly, evoked responses) may sometimes be required.

c) Specific tests for vision and hearing are always essential – minor impairments may produce disproportionate effects in mentally handicapped children. Severe defects constitute a condition of multiple handicap which will be discussed more fully in Chapter 11.

2 *Developmental and psychological assessment*

An overall impression may be gained in younger children by comparing the child's 'milestones' with those of other children, using known as developmental 'norms'. Simple developmental scales such as the Bayley (Bayley, 1965), the Birmingham scales (Griffiths, 1973; Wood, 1982), the Denver scales (Frankenburg and Dodds, 1967), the Stycar sequences (Sheridan, 1973) and in particular the Ruth Griffiths tests of 1967 and 1970 (which are now undergoing revision), give useful information about various areas of development in younger and retarded children. As a result of this broad-based screen which may reveal a specific profile of delays, it may well be necessary to examine particular areas of development in much more detail. A physiotherapist may need to assess motor disorder, as discussed in Chapter 5; or a much more detailed assessment of language development may be required from a speech therapist, as discussed in Chapter 7.

Having used a broad-based developmental screening test, formalised psychometric testing will then be necessary, in order to delineate the child's areas of difficulty and to monitor

---

* CT scan: Computerised Tomography (a special form of X-ray).
† Electroencephalography (electrical recording of brain waves).

progress. Intelligence is not the result of a single mental process, but includes many factors such as visual and auditory memory, reasoning, verbal expression, manipulative capacity and spatial comprehension. This multifactorial concept is taken account of in the design of psychological tests, but the present practice of measuring so-called Intelligence Quotient (IQ) is probably inadequate. It supplies only averages in composite attainments in some of these mental abilities. Since an IQ test also reflects experience and cultural background of the subject tested, it may conceal more than it reveals. The IQ is not fixed, and it may be modified by a number of factors which are largely environmental. The importance of this concept lies in the fact that various mental abilities do not equally influence social or educational adjustment. However, IQ tests administered by an experienced examiner are probably the most useful index of general intellectual development and progress in an individual child, though are less reliable in the very young. There are many tests, and it is probably better to pool the results of a large number of specific tests than to rely on one single or general test. Examples of these are given in Table 5. Psychometric testing generally involves three stages: first, selection of appropriate tests for a particular child; second, administration and scoring which should be undertaken according to the exact instructions after establishing a good rapport with the child; and lastly, and the most difficult stage, interpretation of the data. It is important, therefore, to use the skills of a professional psychologist who will advise the team regarding the interpretation of the data involved.

3   Social development

Social development, discussed in Chapter 10, refers to the child's level of competence in areas of self care – activities such as feeding, dressing, and toilet training – as well as his communication, and relationship to adults and his peers. A child's ability to relate to strangers and other children will profoundly affect decisions about his placement, and the sort of help that will need to be given to the family. A child who is only mildly handicapped as defined by IQ may have severe behaviour problems when interacting with other children, and because of

Table 5

TEST	AGE RANGE	TESTER	COMMENTS
IQ Tests Wechsler Intelligence Scale for Children	6½–15 years	Trained Psychologist	Profile of abilities from sub tests of verbal and performance. Unsuitable for those with a mental age of less than six years.
Stanford Binet	2½–18 years	Trained Psychologist	Tests weighted towards verbal ability
Merrill-Palmer	1½–6 years	Trained Psychologist	Performance Tests. Useful for lower mental ages.
Developmental Tests Denver Developmental Scale (Frankenburg & Dodds, 1967)	Infancy–6 years	No special training	More useful after four years
Griffiths Mental Development Scale a) 1967 b) 1970	Infancy–8 years	Psychologist or doctor after formal training	Very useful
Social Development Tests Gunzberg (1968) Progress Assessment Chart	Infancy–Maturity	Person involved with care. No special training	Useful visual representation. Useful to monitor progress
Vineland Social Maturity (Doll, 1953)		No special training. Scoring manual available.	Depends greatly on parents' report.

this may require a rather specialised educational placement. Tests of social development, such as the Vineland Social Maturity Scale (Doll, 1953) or the PAC chart (Gunzburg, 1968) may be useful as part of the assessment.

4   *Social work assessment*
The social worker plays a vital part in assessing the family background of a developmentally delayed child. The pro-

fessional needs to get to know the family in their home to discover parental attitudes to child rearing, material standards at home, and general level of family cohesion, so that the part played by environmental factors may be assessed and suitable help provided for individual families.

5 *Psychiatric assessment*

Many parents may need help in accepting the implications of the presence of a handicapped child, and in doing the psychological work that is necessary to come to terms with the situation. The psychiatrist can help in the evaluation of family and marital difficulties that may cause behaviour problems in a handicapped child. Finally the psychiatrist will be able to recognise and treat mental illness in a developmentally delayed child.

From Assessment to Goal Planning and Reassessment

The only point of a time-consuming, accurate and detailed assessment is to start to build up a picture of the child's strengths and weaknesses. His strengths can then be used in devising a programme to teach new skills which will help to minimise the weak areas. It is particularly important that this assessment takes place early; interventions can then be planned so that the child does not 'learn to fail'. Bavin (1974) has made some useful points about guiding principles of teaching new skills which are probably worth reiterating in this text.

> During any teaching period attention to the following principles may be helpful in making your efforts more effective:–
>
> The baby, infant or child must be keen to cooperate, and therefore alert, happy, responsive to you, and interested in the task. Teach when he is most highly motivated, for example feeding is best taught at the beginning of the meal when he is hungry, not at the end when he is satisfied and likely to play about or resist.
>
> The teaching period should be kept short, and ended at once if boredom or protest of any sort begins.
>
> No battling should occur – if it does you will always lose. The session must be fun for both of you.
>
> Demonstrate – wait – encourage – wait – demonstrate, and so on. Give him time to respond, and as soon as he makes any effort encourage him by smiling and talking.

Try to be *positive* – encourage every effort, rather than criticising for clumsiness, messiness, or failure to complete the whole task. Encouragement and praise for every little effort will help him to enjoy learning.

Gradually work backwards from the *end* of the sequence, that is, get him to do the last bit, after you have done the rest. Then get him to do the next-to-last bit, so that he is working into the area which he can already do, and so that he gets the feeling of achievement as if he had done the whole job himself.

If you meet rebellion, or negativism – ignore it, and terminate the session. Remember – the more important a thing is to you, the more likely he is to resist. Why? Because he doesn't like the pressure to conform to your wishes, and because it is so easy to upset you by resisting. *Don't let him enjoy upsetting you.* If he won't eat his meal – calmly take it away (and don't relent – he should get nothing until the next meal, so that it is clear that he upsets himself rather than you). Cruel? Not really – in the long run it is kinder to be firm.

You must have both patience and *time.* Unless the slow, handicapped child has plenty of your calm, unhurried time, he may be unable to respond quickly enough, and may therefore look as if he is not understanding anything. This is particularly true if he is physically handicapped, because his physical responses may be slow, difficult or even impossible. If his limbs are paralysed completely, try to develop another way of knowing whether he understands, such as head nodding for 'yes', or head shaking for 'no'.

Keep on trying if progress is very slow, and look for very small signs of progress. If you give up teaching him, he then has no possibility of learning. If you decide he can't do it, he never will. Remember trying to learn to swim? For months one feels it is impossible, and one can't understand how people do it, then suddenly it comes, and one cannot understand what the problem was.

However much we as parents understand the principles of teaching new skills to our children, we are often cast into moments of doubt and worry about the future: 'Will he ever walk? Will he ever be able to live independently away from home?' This is an extremely natural tendency, but worry tends to be destructive, and it is much more important that parents should concentrate on helping the child now, rather than worrying about the future. Specific programmes need to be used to help individual parents and children, and in order to do this most effectively, it is extremely useful to refer to some developmental check list which is coupled with helpful ideas for teaching the next developmental skill, eg. Portage (Shearer and Shearer, 1972) and *The Next Step on the Ladder* (Simon, 1981).

The Portage Scheme (Cameron, 1982) focuses attention onto the immediate areas of need, and gives helpful guidelines and suggestions about what to teach next. As well as being of great benefit to the child, it is extremely reinforcing for parents as they can see progress, however slow and in however small steps, as their calmer, more co-ordinated approach results in achievement on the developmental check list.

The check list itself is colour coded and divided into five developmental areas: cognitive, self-help, motor, language and socialisation – although there is obviously over-lap between these categories. The model contains an infant stimulation section for young babies, but this can also be extremely useful for children who are very delayed developmentally. Items are arranged in developmental sequence from birth to five years of age, and the check list is used to pinpoint behaviours that the child already exhibits. A fundamental part of the teaching process is breaking-down of any goal into smaller segments, with the general aim of setting teaching targets that will be achievable in a short space of time, regardless of the severity of the handicap. The check list is also designed to provide an ongoing record as the child learns new behaviours.

The card file contains a set of cards to match each item on the check list, and is also colour coded to match the check list. For every item there is a card describing the skill and suggesting materials and ideas to teach the behaviour concerned. It is for the home visitor to translate these ideas into practical teaching programmes, and it may well be that the home visitor and the parent think up ideas of a similar nature to those suggestions on the card to help to teach a new skill.

Hence, with this model of intervention, there is constant assessment and reassessment, usually at weekly intervals. Home visitors in this scheme require special training and also supervision from a suitable professional who may be a physiotherapist, a speech therapist, an occupational therapist, a psychologist, or a paediatrician. In any scheme which involves breaking down a task into its component activities, it is essential that previous assessment should have demonstrated that the child is able to move normally before movements are attempted, to see normally before skills involving eye-hand co-ordination are evoked, and can hear normally before any verbal tasks are attempted. These schemes may be applied at home (Clements *et al*, 1980), in a day nursery (Clements *et al*, 1982) or in nursery school. But they always require a very careful supervision from the appropriate professional, since if a child has another specific difficulty other methods of training may be more appropriate.

Other home intervention programmes, such as the Honeylands Home Visiting (Goddard and Rubissow, 1977) and the Parent Involvement Project (Cunningham and Jeffree, 1975: also Cunningham and Sloper, 1978), rely on therapists and health visitors respectively, backed up, in the former case, by residential and day care hospital facilities in Exeter and, in the latter, by the Hester Adrian Research Centre at Manchester University.

These programmes and others (Pugh, 1981), have largely been developed as a response to local needs and between them offer a variety of approaches which can be adapted and used according to local circumstances.

As the child grows older, District Mental Handicap Teams, as suggested by the National Development Group (1977), often form a very helpful link between the family and the local statutory authorities providing services, particularly when their members have close links with Home Intervention programmes already in use.

From these early beginnings, mentally handicapped children will then be able to go on into the most appropriate educational stream for their known abilities. When they have received a good start in the way of adequate comprehensive assessment and carefully planned programmes of management carried out consistently by parents and professionals working together, they may well continue uninterrupted educational and social progress.

MULTIPLE HANDICAP
As already noted in Chapter 1, children do not always suffer

from a single disability and it is particularly in the group of mentally handicapped children that other disabilities may be present. Sometimes another disability is so severe that this can be seen as the major cause of the child's mental handicap. Whichever disability is seen as the prime cause of the major problem, the basic principles of assessment and programmes of management will be the same as those already described. The assessment will probably need to be more detailed in specific fields and the goals in any teaching task will need to be broken down into smaller steps. The professionals involved may need to be allocated according to the skills which they are able to offer to the family.

The ways of helping children with delayed motor development (Clegg and Griffiths, Chapter 5), impaired vision (Griffiths and John, Chapter 6), difficulties in communication and impaired hearing (Edwards, McDougall and Sherliker, Chapter 7), behaviour problems (Cline and Paddon, Chapter 10), have already been described and the principles enunciated in all these chapters apply equally to mentally handicapped children, although progress may be expected to be slower and more patience will be required from both parents and professionals. The management of seizure disorders in children is mentioned in Chapter 4, but here it is important to emphasise that a balance needs to be struck between adequate control of seizure activity through medication and possible side effects affecting concentration, attention span and behaviour.

Finally, in discussing multiply handicapped children, behaviour disorders and psychiatric problems should be mentioned. In a survey of all the severely mentally handicapped children in Camberwell (Corbett, 1979), it was found that almost half the children suffered from some form of behaviour disorder or psychiatric illness. Behaviour problems are discussed in Chapter 10. Again one should emphasise the importance of a positive approach in always trying to teach new and appropriate behaviours while ignoring undesirable ones. M. C. Jones (1983), in the unit at Beech Tree House, describes ways in which severely disturbed mentally handicapped children can be helped. Occasionally, in disorders such as early infantile autism, (Wing, 1980) and excessive overactivity, tranquilliser-type medications may be useful for a short period of time, to reduce the child's activity level and so improve concentration, so that a consistent behaviourally orientated programme can be instituted.

The outlook for the mentally handicapped child has improved greatly in the last two decades, largely because of a new emphasis on educational, sociological and psychological help to the child and his family. In the early days it is often necessary to emphasise the medical aspects of assessment and diagnosis so that, when paediatric treatment is likely to be needed, it will be readily available. It is not always realised that there are some conditions in which mental handicap can be prevented by specific modifications to the diet (as in phenylketonuria) or by medication to make up for lack of hormones (as in hypothyroidism). It needs to be quite clear that there is no sound evidence that non-specific alterations to diets or administration of vitamins in excess of normal requirements have any effect on the manifestations of mental handicap. Drug control of seizures also has an important part to play, and often the skills of the therapists, occupational, physio and speech, are essential for some children to ensure progress. Health visitors and community nurses also offer a major contribution within the home.

However, the major support thereafter will come from the education, psychological and social services. This support will have to be life-long and must start as soon as the disability is detected. Whilst emphasising the possibility of the child remaining at home in a normal family environment, support needs to be backed up by suitable residential care from time to time, not only at crisis periods, but phased to enable the family, siblings and parents to pursue normal recreational activities and holidays.

During term time (and often in the vacation) the child's school will play the major role in supporting the child and the family. Education for the mentally handicapped has a much wider range than purely academic subjects. The teaching of social skills, including feeding, dressing and toilet training, is often necessary for younger children and must be carried out with consistency between expectations at home and at school. Play, first on their own and then with others, must be introduced and suitable methods of communication, with the help of speech therapists (Edwards, Chapter 7); such schemes as Makaton (see Appendix) were originally introduced to assist communication in mentally handicapped people. Literacy and numeracy can be introduced gradually as individual children become ready, and meanwhile domestic skills such as housework, simple cookery and shopping offer a chance for children to be learning in a useful and satisfying way. All this will form a basis for later experience in living, and a gradual introduction into community life. Because these children are slow learners it is essential to prolong education beyond normal school leaving age.

The needs for residential care will vary considerably from child to child and from family to family, according to the child's disabilities and the family circumstances. Multiply handicapped children require more care and attention than others and it is very important that, for those children, residential care staff should be specially trained to deal with the additional handicap. Where long-term care is requested by parents who feel that they are unable to cope, in their particular situation, with a handicapped child, opportunities for long-term fostering, or even adoption, should be sought. Care at crisis periods, or carefully phased, may be found in foster or residential homes as seems best at the time (Oswin, 1984).

Wherever possible, mentally handicapped young people should have the same opportunities as their normal siblings to leave home for further training and employment, and to live independently with their peers in sheltered or supervised accommodation in the community, enjoying leisure activities, such as music (Wood, 1983), drama (McClintock, 1984) and adventure wherever they are.

References

BAVIN, J. (1974). 'Parents' problems' in *Handling the Young Cerebral Palsied Child at Home* (pp 12–31), FINNIE, N. R. (ed). London: Heinemann Medical Books.

BAYLEY, N. (1965). 'Comparisons of mental and motor test scores for ages 1 through 11 months by sex, birth order and race, geographical location and education of parents', *Child Development*, **36**, 379.

CAMERON, R. J. (ed) (1982). *Working Together: Portage in the U.K.* Windsor: NFER/Nelson.

CLEMENTS, J. C., BIDDER, R. T., GARDNER, S., BRYANT, G. and GRAY, O. P. (1980). 'A home advisory service for preschool children with developmental delays', *Child: care, health and development*, **6**, 25–33.

CLEMENTS, J. C., SMITH, J., SPAIN, B. and WATKEYS, J. (1982). A preliminary investigation in the use of Portage systems in day nursery settings', *Child: care, health and development*, **8**, 123–131.

CORBETT, J. A. (1979). 'Psychiatric morbidity and mental retardation' in *Psychiatric Illness and Mental Handicap.* JAMES, F. E. and SNAITH, R. P. (eds). London: Gaskell Books

CUNNINGHAM, C. (1982). *Down's Syndrome: an Introduction for Parents.* London: Souvenir Press.

CUNNINGHAM, C. and MITTLER, P. (1981). 'Maturation, development and mental handicap' in *Maturation and Development*, CONNOLLY, K. J. and PRECHTL, H. F. R. (eds). London: Heinemann Medical Books; Philadelphia: Lippincott.

CUNNINGHAM, C. and SLOPER, P. (1978). *Helping your Handicapped Baby.* London: Souvenir Press.

DOLL, E. A. (1953). *Measurement of Social Competence.* Minnesota: American Child Guidance Service Inc.

FRANKENBURG, W. K. and DODDS, J. B. (1967). 'The Denver Developmental Screening Test', *Journal of Pediatrics*, **71**, 181–191.

GODDARD, J. and RUBISSOW, J. (1977), 'Meeting the needs of handicapped children and their families. The evolution of Honeylands: A family support unit, Exeter', *Child: care, health and development*, **3**, 261–273.

GRIFFITHS, M. (1973) 'Early detection by developmental screening' in *The Young Retarded Child* (pp 11–19), GRIFFITHS, M. (ed). Edinburgh and London: Churchill Livingstone.

GRIFFITHS, R. (1967). *The Abilities of Babies.* London: University Press.

GRIFFITHS, R. (1970) *The Abilities of Young Children.* London: Child Development Centre.

GROSSMAN, H. J. (ed) (1973). *Manual on Termination and Classification in Mental Retardation*, 1973 Revision. Washington, DC: American Association of Mental Deficiency.

GUNZBERG, H. C. (1968). *Social Competence and Mental Handicap.* London: Baillière, Tindal and Cassell; Baltimore: Williams & Wilkins.

JONES, M. C. (1983). *Behaviour Problems in Handicapped Children: The Beech Tree House Approach.* London: Souvenir Press.

McCLINTOCK, A. B. (1984). *Drama for Mentally Handicapped Children.* London: Souvenir Press.

NATIONAL DEVELOPMENT GROUP (1977). *Mentally Handicapped Children: A Plan for Action.* London: HMSO.

OSWIN, M. (1984). *They Keep Going Away.* Oxford: University Press.

PUGH, G. (ed) (1981). *Parents as Partners.* London: National Children's Bureau.

SHEARER, M. S. and SHEARER, D. E. (1972). 'The Portage Project: a model of early childhood education', *Exceptional Children* **36**, 210–217.

SHERIDAN, M. D. (1973). *Children's Development Progress from Birth to Five Years. The Stycar Sequences.* Windsor: NFER.

SIMON, G. B. (1981). *The Next Step on the Ladder.* Kidderminster: British Institute of Mental Handicap.

WHELAN, E. and SPEAKE, B. (1979). *Learning to Cope.* London: Souvenir Press.

WING, L. (1980). *Autistic Children. A Guide for Parents*, second (revised) edition. London: Constable.

WOOD, B. (1982). *A Pediatric Vade-Mecum*, tenth (revised) edition, INSLEY, J. London: Lloyd Luke.

WOOD, M. (1983). *Music for Mentally Handicapped People.* London: Souvenir Press.

10 Problems in Emotional Development and the Acquisition of Social Skills

By Tony Cline and Tony Paddon

1 INTRODUCTION

Difficult or unusual behaviour can cause the families of severely handicapped children as much worry as the primary handicap itself. Problems may arise because children do not develop social skills at the normal rate or because the children's emotional state appears extremely immature for their age. The social development of handicapped children therefore needs to be understood in the context of what happens to, and what is expected of, normal children.

2 PATTERNS OF DEVELOPMENT IN NORMAL CHILDREN

Young infants depend totally on others for all their needs. Their ability to signal their moods (for example, through smiling or crying or through muscular tension) forms the basis of the earliest social overtures, enabling them to communicate with those who care for them. They appear from the beginning to be engaged in making sense of the world around them and will show a developing awareness of its regularities and complexity. Slowly they come to differentiate among the people whom they see most and to form selective attachments to their parents or particular caregivers. They are more wary of unfamiliar people and more anxious when separated from those they know. But they begin to develop some general attitudes to their environment that will form the basis of their ability to explore it and master the skills it requires, eg. a general sense of trust and a notion of how predictable they can expect it to be.

As they approach the age of two, they begin to assert themselves more, detaching themselves from their parents, demanding the right to use their initiative and do things on their own very much more often. Toddlers become aware of themselves as individual people, noticing what their bodies are like and how they are different from others, learning some of the social implications of sexual identity and, traditionally in our culture, showing clear male or female identification in their play. The mastering of new skills of many kinds is an increasing preoccupation and source of satisfaction. They begin to participate as full members of the family group. They learn to compete and to share with their siblings. The birth of another baby in the family, or the new awareness of the claims of older siblings on their parents, will modify their apparently exclusive sense of possessiveness towards them. They become more aware of some of the social constraints on behaviour and of what others expect of them in a variety of situations. The complex and subtle process of socialisation to their culture steadily advances.

As children enter school, they leave the protective intimacy of home for a wider and initially less predictable period. Their ability to make sense of the unfamiliar is constantly challenged. The normal response after a short time is to show a lively curiosity and an eagerness to explore. Their self-image will be affected by how they feel they cope with these challenges and how they believe others judge their performance. They will be likely to conform to peer group pressures and expectations. At school during middle childhood, close friendships with peers and membership of a larger self-defined group become more important. They need to achieve a modest degree of independence from their parents whom they gradually learn to perceive in more realistic and less idealised terms. But, at this stage, independence is precarious and uncertain, and they need to be able to return readily to their parents' protective control. To the extent that they (the parents) can communicate both trust in children's developing autonomy and loving concern for their continuing vulnerability, the children will be able to move steadily away from their parents' ambit with increasing confidence. They will identify with other people in their world without losing touch with their earliest intense feelings for, and identification with, parental models.

With adolescence, the achievement of full psychological independence is almost complete. For many in our society, this will not yet mean that financial independence is expected, since a large number of occupations require further education or extended training. But normal young people will now feel themselves in a position to define on their own behalf a personal identity, answering questions such as, 'What shall I be like?' 'What shall I believe in?' 'What possibilities lie open to me in the future?' To others they may present as changeable and unpredictable as they try out a number of styles, roles and value systems. Their bodies achieve sexual maturity, so that they are physically able to develop mature heterosexual relationships. In our society this is likely to involve first mixed group functions and then the tentative exploration of individual pairing arrangements. Ultimately a relationship may be achieved that allows the expression of sexual impulses in a context of secure affection, with freedom from anxiety and an intimate and close collaboration over a wide area of personal life. The child will be ready for parenthood.

3 FACTORS AFFECTING EMOTIONAL AND SOCIAL DEVELOPMENT IN SEVERELY HANDICAPPED CHILDREN

a) *Emotional Development*

In other fields, some writers consider it possible to describe physiological function and anatomical pathways within the brain that are specifically related to developing skills, and attention is drawn to these ideas in the appropriate chapters. Emotional reactions are much more complex and are strongly influenced by cognitive factors. No attempt is made in this chapter to discuss this topic in detail.

Children who have suffered brain injury or show general retardation have been found to show increased incidence of emotional disturbance and deviant behaviour (Shaffer, 1976; Chazan, 1964; Rutter *et al*, 1970). The reasons are probably complex; in addition to specific factors described in other chapters, adverse temperamental characteristics, social and family circumstances, immature understanding of social situations, immature command of social skills, and specific behaviour patterns associated with a child's particular syndrome may each contribute, often in combination, to the development of serious difficulties. For example, a child's chronic restlessness may irritate those around him, making it more difficult for them to respond warmly to him, even when they are sympathetic. He, in his turn, may experience intense feelings of rejection as a result, the worse because he cannot fully understand why people react impatiently to him. Severe language retardation may make matters worse because he can neither communicate his own feelings and needs nor comprehend any subtle nuances in the verbal expression of feelings by others. He is likely to be aware, in a powerful though inarticulate way, that he has low status among his siblings and peers, has failed to master a wide range of expected skills and has caused his parents strong feelings of disappointment and guilt. Extremes of moodiness, withdrawal or exhibitionism may be his reaction in his relations with others. The child may sometimes be destructive, or he may kick or bite, hurting himself or others. Some may eventually show feelings of intense misery and anger, and depressive symptoms or uncontrolled and possibly violent behaviour. But most children do not present such extreme reactions; the majority of the severely retarded show an unimpaired ability to give and respond to affection. This can provide the basis for a relationship with their parents and siblings that is deeply rewarding on both sides and enables many practical problems to be overcome.

b) *The Development of Social Skills*
Normal children pick up a great deal from what is going on around them. They notice what others do and enjoy imitating their styles and patterns of behaviour. Retarded children, although enjoying imitation, will often fail to learn the rules and manners of everyday life in this incidental way. They may never achieve a mature understanding of the complex messages that people communicate to each other, not only in language but through gesture and facial expression. Their lack of comprehension of ordinary social norms may become a source of embarrassment to the rest of the family when they, perhaps unknowingly, behave 'badly' in public. When children are physically or mentally unable to care for themselves in ordinary ways, it places a strain on the family, while denying them the simple satisfaction of a modest independence. Dressing and un-

dressing, washing and feeding, are important milestones for the ordinary toddler and may need long and patient teaching for handicapped children, even when they possess the necessary physical skills. It is quicker and often easier for an adult to take over these tasks, and children who find them difficult will possibly be grateful when he does so. But in the long run the continued total dependence of a growing young person is almost bound to be a source of dissatisfaction to all concerned. Achieving bowel and bladder control is a complex task for many ordinary children and may be a particular problem for some of the handicapped. Incontinence presents particular problems of management as children get older.

There are some groups of children who may show distinctive patterns of deviant behaviour. For example, retarded children who have limited mobility are likely to show stereotyped repetitive movements such as body rocking. Those with Down's Syndrome are often said to be relatively friendly and amiable personalities who are rarely aggressive or destructive. It has been claimed that some hydrocephalic children tend to be verbose but talk in a superficial and socially inappropriate way. But, in spite of the distinctive patterns of behaviour sometimes associated with particular syndromes, it is important that every child is perceived and treated as an individual in his own right, with the potential to show great variation in personality development, just as children of normal intelligence do.

One of the best known distinctive groups of children is the 'autistic' group, many of whom (though by no means all) are severely retarded. Early in life, children with the full autistic syndrome show a lack of normal attachment to their parents and a failure to make a normal affectionate bond with them. Later they fail to develop ordinary mutual relationships with their peers. Their pattern of language development is unusual, and they use language very often without the apparent intention to communicate and without evident understanding of the social context. They become involved in stereotyped behaviours and routines, constantly repeating certain actions or showing strong attachments to certain objects, or later showing unusual preoccupations such as with bus or train timetables (Wing, 1980). That general picture is a characteristic one, but is far from universal. Many children show some but not all of these features, and diagnosis is not all straightforward. Even so a fundamental disruption in this social interaction with others clearly differentiates a core group of the children from all others with severe intellectual retardation. By contrast, this emphasises the considerable potential shown by the majority of the severely handicapped, in spite of all the attendant problems, for affectionate and satisfying relationships with others and for the development of meaningful, if limited, social skills. They can and do achieve such goals with realistic help from their families and the professional workers who support and advise them.

4   SUPPORT FOR PARENTS

The organisation of effective professional services to support a handicapped child and his family is a major topic throughout this book. There are many obstacles to effective support, of which perhaps the most important is the difference of perspective that parents and professionals have, and their very different sense of urgency. Parents may sometimes be dissatisfied with what may seem to them an unduly slow rate of progress and what may be felt as a lack of encouragement. As a result they may seek alternative sources of support. Professionals should always be ready to accept a second opinion. It is important that they are sensitive to some parents' need for reassurance that everything possible is being done, and to the wish of many to be actively involved in helping their handicapped child to the utmost of their ability.

A few independent agencies encourage hopes that an energetic commitment of money, time and effort by parents will bring about dramatic change. Novel treatment programmes, such as the Doman Delacato Programme, have many attractions. One problem of such programmes is that they may encourage an excessive focusing of family attention on one child alone in a family. Some programmes involve long hours of treatment and completely distort normal patterns of family and social life. The use of methods associated with evangelism may lead to an impressive conviction among parents converted to such programmes, but in the long term acute disappointment will be suffered if improvements are less than anticipated. This can hinder the normal process of adaptation, whereby parents and siblings develop a realistic and positive perception of what the handicapped child can achieve and of the way family life can be organised to take account of special needs.

5 MANAGEMENT OF CHILDREN'S BEHAVIOUR – BEHAVIOUR MODIFICATION

In recent years, one major advance has been made that can support such processes in the context of ordinary family life: the development of behaviour modification techniques as an approach to promoting the acquisition of social and self-help skills among handicapped persons.

Behaviour modification has been defined variously as 'a discipline of psychotherapy' (Watson, 1979) or 'a set of ways' (Carr, 1980) or 'techniques' concerned with changing observable behaviour. It is an approach based largely on the principles of operant or instrumental conditioning, part of general learning theory, first studied by American behaviourist psychologists, most notably B. F. Skinner in the 1930s. Applied increasingly since then, initially in the USA and more recently also in the United Kingdom, to children and young people with a wide range of behaviour difficulties and varying degrees of handicap or no handicap at all, behaviour modification arguably has a special relevance to children with severe handicaps, because of its explicit concern with observable behaviour (Whelan and Speake, 1979). Its techniques do not depend on the use of language or a knowledge of IQ scores, but on an appreciation of the underlying causes; even diagnostic 'labels' may be helpful in alerting the organisers of the programme to take account of a child's physical disabilities which may make co-operation impossible. With this knowledge, and using the findings of a multidisciplinary assessment process, it will focus on a child's specific behaviour in particular settings, aiming 'to increase the child's behaviour repertoire and to get all behaviour to occur appropriately' (Watson, 1979).

The central principle of behaviour modification – and one long understood by teachers and parents – is that behaviour followed by reward or positive reinforcement, is strengthened and highly likely to occur again. Conversely, behaviour that goes unrewarded, or indeed is punished, tends to weaken and occur again far less frequently, eventually disappearing altogether. Reinforcers may be of various kinds. Social reinforcers, such as praise or approval, clearly have certain inbuilt advantages, and would seem particularly appropriate when used in connection with social learning. Other reinforcers can be edible – or primary – because they are associated with basic needs; secondary, such as tokens or money with a symbolic value that has to be learnt; or articles to be played with or used. What is appropriate will be determined by the child, reflecting not only what he or she likes but what he or she can do. Ultimately, however, it should be something that proves effective for that child at that time. For a few children, frequent changes of reinforcer are required.

Rewards and punishments are, of course, part of everyday life and implicated in everyone's learning, appearing often in a fairly arbitrary fashion and accounting for the acquisition of 'bad' as well as 'good' habits. What is rewarding or punishing for the individual, however, is not always immediately obvious, and many children develop inappropriate behaviour simply because parents, teachers or other adults closely involved in their care are unwittingly rewarding such behaviours, usually by giving the child extra attention whenever it occurs. Precise observation of a severely handicapped child's repertoire of socially unacceptable behaviours is likely to reveal that this is exactly what is happening much of the time. Janet Carr tells how a child's 'excessive crying', which 'tyrannised her family', appeared to be rewarded and maintained by the concerned attention paid to her whenever she cried. The family were advised to ignore or turn away from the child as soon as she began crying and to give her as much attention as possible when she stopped (Carr, 1980). In this necessarily oversimplified example, the principles of extinction, or non-reinforcement, followed by positive reinforcement for desired behaviour, were being applied. In practice, although often accompanied at first by an increase in the undesirable behaviour, this technique can show quick returns for a harassed parent or teacher. It is perhaps worth noting here, although it poses a rather different problem, that some children in very deprived circumstances may become so desperate for attention that even punitive treatment is likely to be rewarding if incidentally it offers personal attention. Children who have destructive habits, or who play with faeces, are sometimes found to receive reinforcement for their behaviour in such a way.

It can thus be seen that behaviour modification is a highly systematic way of arranging matters so that only a child's acceptable behaviour is rewarded. The basic model is a relatively simple one, requiring an assessment of present behaviour in the context of the child's disabilities, the setting of a realistic target and the selection of an appropriate reinforcer. Usually progress towards the target behaviour will need to be broken down into smaller steps, and the successful acquisition of each by the child immediately reinforced, allowing the gradual building up or shaping of the desired behaviour. Much variation is possible, however, in the way a programme can be set up and carried through, depending not only upon the child and the particular behaviour to be worked on, but also on such considerations as where it is to be carried out, the time available for it, the presence or absence of other children and, not least of all, who is to carry out the programme. It is not possible to go into more detail here, and those wishing to pursue the topic will need to read further. Books about behaviour modification abound, but parents in particular will find many of their questions answered in a handbook published by Penguin Books, *Helping your Handicapped Child* by Janet Carr. A sympathetic and comprehensive account of the practicalities of using a behaviour modification approach in the home, this book is based on the author's own experience of working directly with parents. Reassuringly, while in no sense denying the realities of severe handicap in a family, it illustrates with some conviction the hopeful possibility that management of a severely handicapped child need not necessarily require the virtually total sacrifice of parental time and energy, as is demanded by some other schemes. Dr Carr emphasises that some problem behaviours can be dealt with by means of relatively short programmes and that once techniques are assimilated, they can be incorporated into normal daily family routine.

Many psychologists have expressed reservations about the

general applicability of behaviour modification methods, chiefly on the grounds that conditioning theory is inadequate to account for the development of human thinking and language in its most complex forms. However, there is an increasing amount of research evidence and clinical experience to show that the use of such an approach with the severely handicapped is fully justified, at least in purely practical terms, 'because it works' (Carr, 1980). Already it is widely used in hospitals for the mentally handicapped in this country, and less widely but increasingly in clinics in the community and special schools for children with severe learning difficulties. An example is the work described by Jones (1983). A recent report to the Secretary of State for Health and Social Services recommended that behaviour modification should be covered in staff training in all hospitals for the mentally handicapped (Mittler, 1978). So this development undoubtedly represents a major advance in this field, while not excluding other approaches. One thing is clear: severely handicapped children do best when managed by methods which not only offer them encouragement, but organise and clarify adults' expectations of them in a learning environment which is structured and predictable.

6 ADOLESCENCE

This section provides an overview of the types of problem encountered and indicates some sources of support and further information for parents. Broadly speaking, the social and emotional needs of the severely handicapped adolescent are no different in kind from those of normally functioning adolescents. As one parent has it, 'the mentally handicapped are not exempt from the swings of mood, rebellious feelings and depressions which characterise adolescence and which are part of growing up'. (Hannam, 1980). Within this broad group, individual possibilities and family circumstances vary. Behaviour which is seen as a problem in one situation may not be so in another; parents' expectations will differ. In an optimistic (and highly recommended) book written specifically for parents, Whelan and Speake (1979) list some of the problems found most commonly among severely handicapped adolescents, though not restricted to this group: 'threatening others, stubbornness, avoiding others, failing to anticipate the consequences of actions; excessive or inappropriate physical contact; self-injurious behaviour; violent temper'. They work from the premise that most such problems stem from inappropriate or inadequate learning and are therefore essentially failures of education broadly defined. The book describes methods of behaviour modification and also indicates sources of outside support for parents and the family.

The greatest single cause of concern to parents is probably the adolescents' developing sexuality. They may have difficulty understanding their bodily changes and new impulses and show extreme reactions to them. They will often lack the social skills to cope with them acceptably in company. Parents may encounter unexpected problems in teaching a boy that masturbation should only be in private, or helping a girl to deal with menstruation. Fear for girls' pregnancy may also lead them to extreme reactions. The anxieties may be exacerbated because of the ambivalence of society generally towards the sexuality of the handicapped. The achievement of a mature sexual adjustment is undoubtedly more difficult for mentally handicapped adolescents than for others. In the control of socially unacceptable or unhygienic habits, behaviour modification techniques may have a part to play. As with others at this stage of life, there is value in youth group activities that provide a supervised setting in which young people can develop new kinds of relationships with the opposite sex. In some cases, skilled counselling may be required for the parents and for the young person, if it can be offered in a way he or she can use.

Very occasionally, aggressive behaviour, perhaps previously manageable, may become frightening to parents as the child's size and strength increase during adolescence. Even a formerly biddable child may find his ageing parents less awesome as he becomes aware of his own developing physical powers. Containment of extreme forms of difficult, especially violent, behaviour may involve physical restraint or medication as an immediate response, but only a full assessment of possible contributory factors will indicate what will be the most appropriate help in the long term. Some severely handicapped children, particularly those with serious communication problems, may be too disturbed or too dangerous to themselves or others to remain at home.

The first line of support now for parents of severely handicapped adolescents must be the special school. A good school will meet a broad range of children's needs at the levels appropriate for them and maintain a continuing dialogue with parents regarding their progress. Many special schools, either alone or in association with social services departments or voluntary organisations, give children occasional breaks away from the family as a means of improving self-help and other independence skills. These interludes may do much more than offer respite for the family (see Chapter 3). Ultimately, the achievement of the maximum possible independence for each youngster will require a co-operative effort by parents and professionals, that creates an atmosphere of confidence and security for both adults and the young person.

References

*CARR, J. (1980). *Helping Your Handicapped Child.* Harmondsworth, Middlesex and New York: Penguin.

CHAZAN, M. (1964) 'The incidence and nature of maladjustment among children in schools for the educationally subnormal', *British Journal of Educational Psychology*, **34**, 293–304.

HANNAM, C. (1980). *Parents and Mentally Handicapped Children.* Harmondsworth, Middlesex and New York: Penguin.

JONES, M. C. (1983). *Behaviour Problems in Handicapped Children. The Beech Tree House Approach.* London: Souvenir Press.

MITTLER, P. (Chairman) (1978). *Helping Mentally Handicapped People in Hospital.* Report to the Secretary of State by the National Development Group. London: HMSO.

RUTTER, M., TIZARD, J. and WHITMORE, K. (eds) (1970). *Education, Health and Behaviour.* London: Longman.

SHAFFER, D. (1976). 'Brain injury' in *Child Psychiatry.*

*Recommended for further reading

Modern Approaches, RUTTER, M. and HERSOV, L. (eds). Oxford: Blackwell.

SKINNER, B. F. (1938). *The Behaviour of Organisms*. New York: Appleton-Century.

WATSON, L. (1979). *Child Behaviour Modification: a Manual for Teachers, Nurses and Parents*. London: Pergamon International Library.

*WHELAN, E. and SPEAKE, B. (1979). *Learning to Cope*, London: Souvenir Press.

WING, L. (1980). *Autistic Children: A Guide for Parents*, second (revised) edition. London: Constable.

*Recommended for further reading.

11 Multiple Handicap

By Margaret Griffiths

Reference has been made in many chapters to the presence of associated handicaps and their mutual interaction. Emphasis has also been placed on the recognition of these factors, and of the importance of ensuring that a child's disability should wherever possible be prevented from becoming a handicap.

However, 'multiple handicap' is a reality for many children and this chapter attempts to consider the weight of this problem. In working with handicapped children we have to consider a very wide range: from those children who need a limited amount of help in a specific field (such as specific learning difficulty, mild motor disorder, etc.) to enable them to enjoy education, companionship and leisure with their peers and to prevent their disability from becoming a handicap; to those whose multiple severe disabilities preclude them from attaining the usual independence and freedom of adult life but who still have needs for care and affection and a place in the world.

Fig 15 attempts to illustrate the manifold permutations and combinations of interaction that are possible between individual handicaps, and these are summarised below. It can be seen that, although many children will be unaffected by more than one disability, it is theoretically possible for some to experience another six.

1 Visual Impairment associated with:

a) *Hearing.* The combination of these two sensory deprivations is one of the most challenging situations for parents and professionals. Freeman (1975) from her own experience describes many practical aspects of handling and day-to-day activities that can be undertaken. From the professional point of view, very close co-operation between the relevant members of the handicap team is essential; not only audiologists and

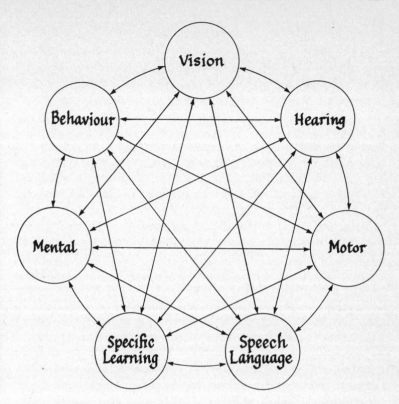

Fig. 15. Diagram of interrelationships in multiple handicap.

ophthalmologists but psychologists and teachers have their part to play. Early intervention and, above all, emotional rapport with the child may help to prevent the very severe behaviour problems that occur in those children whose difficulties are discovered late or who are mentally handicapped. These children usually have considerable residual vision and, although the hearing defect may be profound, some vision may be retained and encouraged to a sufficient degree to enable them to communicate by some form of sign language such as Paget-Gorman (see Appendix).

   b)   *Motor.* This combination makes it even more difficult for a child with the combined handicap to explore the world around. Sykanda and Levitt (1982) consider the significant role of the physiotherapist in supporting parents and teachers in encouraging progress to mobility.

c) *Speech and language.* Recent research (Mills, 1983) suggests that the lack of visual experience may lead to deviance as well as delay in language development, so that some visually handicapped children may need specific help from speech therapy to develop normal language and speech. The speech therapist herself has to exercise considerable ingenuity in encouraging language without visual input.

d) *Specific learning difficulties.* Use of the printed word is not possible for totally blind children who usually show no difficulty in cognitive and conceptual activities when using Braille. Partially-sighted children do not necessarily have more difficulty with the enlarged printed word than do their peers.

e) *Mental handicap.* Surveys in the United Kingdom (DES, 1972: Griffiths, 1979; Jamieson *et al*, 1977; Zinkin, 1979) suggest that 28 to 35 per cent of visually handicapped children have severe intellectual retardation. These children need very careful long-term assessment in a suitable environment (usually their home, with regular attendance at a suitable playgroup) where they receive support from a professional with experience of visual handicap who can help and supervise progress in communication, mobility, cognitive and social skills. It is often very difficult to determine to what extent the visual handicap is contributing to the general retardation. It is particularly important that minor degrees of visual impairment should be detected and corrected wherever possible.

f) *Behaviour.* The usual problems of self determination in ordinary small children are just as characteristic of visually handicapped children and are explained in some detail in Chapter 6. More severe behaviour disturbance may occur as a result of frustration if the visual problem is not adequately dealt with, but may also occur in spite of adequate help, especially in the presence of mental handicap, and in these children behaviour modification schemes as described in Chapter 10 may be needed.

2 Hearing Impairment associated with:

a) *Motor.* The most common association here is in children who have cerebral palsy. Fortunately, the high tone deafness previously associated with athetosis, due to rhesus incompatibility, is very rare now that the condition can be prevented. However, hearing impairment may be difficult to detect and assess in very severely physically handicapped children and recourse to some of the objective methods of testing, described in Chapter 7, may be necessary.

b) *Speech and language.* It is almost inevitable that children with hearing impairment will have difficulties in these fields. The subject is fully covered in Chapter 7.

c) *Specific learning difficulties.* With skilled help from hearing aids, auditory training, a good visual input and adequate social experience, the occurrence of reading, writing and spelling difficulties at the child's cognitive and conceptual level is no different from that of his hearing peers.

d) *Mental handicap.* Mental handicap of itself usually leads to delay in the acquisition of communication skills. In contrast to the 'normal' hearing-impaired child who is able to define objects by use (Yeates, 1980), the mentally retarded child shows delay in this parameter also, but even so may in addition have a hearing loss which needs assessment and management in the same way as the normal child. Any child with delay in acquisition of speech and language should have a thorough audiological assessment at a special centre. In the presence of more than one handicap, parents more than ever need the help of a multidisciplinary team, and together they will have to sort out the priorities for each individual child and family.

e) *Behaviour.* In a child with hearing impairment who has no other disabilities and is receiving adequate support from the statutory services, behaviour problems do not differ from the general incidence in ordinary children. The presence of other disabilities, particularly mental handicap, or delay in diagnosis of deafness, may lead to or be associated with the kind of severe behavioural disturbance discussed in Chapter 10.

f) *Vision.* See paragraph 1a).

3. Motor Disability associated with:

a) *Speech and language.* Cerebral palsy may lead to difficulties in both comprehension and expression of language. Comprehension may partly be affected by limited experience. Expression may occasionally be limited by the lack of ability in processing thoughts. There are typical patterns of dysarthria varying with the motor pathways that are affected (Mueller, 1974).

b) *Specific learning difficulties.* Abercrombie (1964) and Wedell (1961 and 1973) have demonstrated both visuomotor and perceptual problems in children with spastic types of cerebral palsy, and it is important that these difficulties should be kept in mind when children with cerebral palsy are admitted to ordinary schools. Delay in learning may be attributed to mental or physical handicap, and the child should always be carefully assessed along the lines described in Chapter 8.

The difficulties of clumsy children are considered in detail in Chapter 8 (Wedell, 1980). All these children have problems both in understanding symbols and in using their hands to write. Cerebral palsied children may also have additional difficulties in scanning the paper.

c) *Mental handicap.* Mental handicap occurs in children with a wide range of motor disorders. Some children with very minor cerebral palsy may have severe mental retardation, often associated with epilepsy; others have such a severe disability of movement (including speech), that they may only be able to communicate by eye movements, to show pleasure by a smile, and unhappiness by tears. So that it is often only after a long period of observation and intervention that the child's intellectual status can be defined. A similar problem may arise in children suffering from hydrocephalus. The response of these children to physiotherapy can be very slow, and co-operation from parents and teachers can do most, under the guidance of a physiotherapist (Presland, 1982).

d) *Behaviour.* As children grow up and acquire control of movement, speech and social skills, they are able to translate these into ways of annoying their parents and others through temper tantrums, aggression, unacceptable language and so on. Expression of their feelings is not so easy for children with motor problems, and they are more likely to turn in upon themselves and to show more negative behaviour in apathy, listlessness and lack of interest. It is important for parents and other caregivers to recognise that children with severe physical problems need a great deal of encouragement even to cope with the simple activities of daily living. Professionals need to ensure that the activities they devise are rewarding for parents and child.

   e)   *Vision*. See 1 b).

   f)   *Hearing*. See 2 a).

4. Speech and Language Disorders associated with:

   a) *Specific learning difficulties*. Fig 13 (p. 169) outlines the pathways for production of both spoken and written language, and reading and writing difficulties are often known to be associated with deviant speech patterns or clumsiness. Children who are known to have been dysphasic always need to be carefully observed at the start of reading, so that any specific difficulties can be easily identified.

   b) *Mental handicap*. Very often, the earliest indication of mental handicap in a child who has apparently shown normal development up to the age of one year is a delay in developing understanding of language and verbal communication. Parents of Down's Syndrome children are often misled in the early years to have an over-optimistic estimate of their child's potential, since, if he has been given adequate help, he may show near normal motor and social skills and his delay in acquiring language is therefore disappointing. Other children who do not have easily recognisable physical configuration may not appear to have any problems until their retardation is shown in their speech and language. These children are very often helped by the use of a sign language (provided it is always accompanied by verbalisation) such as Makaton (see Appendix). Their parents usually need the guidance of a speech therapist, and may also receive help from a home intervention programme such as Portage (see Appendix). Parents can usually be reassured that the child will make steady but slow progress.

   c) *Behaviour*. Some of the more severe speech and language disorders, such as dyspraxia, may be associated with withdrawn and obsessive types of behaviour and may present a very similar picture to 'autism', which itself is almost invariably associated with severe communication problems, whether spoken, gesture or affectionate, including eye-to-eye contact.

   d) *Vision*. See 1 c).

   e) *Hearing*. See 2 b).

   f) *Motor*. See 3 a).

5   Specific Learning Difficulties associated with:

a)   *Mental Handicap.* Mentally handicapped children have global learning difficulties so that most will eventually learn to read and write at their own pace, although a few may show some of the deviance discussed in Chapter 8. The description of specific learning difficulties given there is applied to those children whose cognitive and conceptual ability enables them to keep up or even to excel, in other educational spheres.

b)   *Behaviour.* As mentioned in Chapter 8, severe educational problems may lead to school phobia or even truancy, so that when children manifest this type of behaviour it is always wise to enquire into possible difficulties at school (Rutter and Yule, 1970).

c)   *Vision.* See 1 d).

d)   *Hearing.* See 2 c).

e)   *Motor.* See 3 b).

f)   *Speech and language.* See 4 a).

6   Mental Handicap associated with other Disabilities

The terms mental and multiple handicap are often thought to be synonymous. The previous paragraphs in this chapter will have shown that this is not invariably the case but when mental handicap is present it often has a profound effect upon the child's ability to cope with a sensory or physical disability.

'Special care' is a term used in the mental handicap field to indicate that extra resources in staff and equipment are likely to be needed for children who, in addition, are sensorily or physically disabled or who have severe behaviour problems. These are all very different situations and the children have very different needs. Staff need to be extraordinarily expert in their own disciplines and able readily to co-operate both with colleagues in other specialities and with the parents, in order to be able to accept a slow rate of progress in an often back-breaking task. Kiernan (1977) suggests an approach to a curriculum for some of these children, building upon their individual interests and abilities, and Jones (1983) describes a residential programme for severely disturbed children. Presland (1982) has a plea for more physiotherapists to come forward to help children who are mentally and physically handicapped and advocates a classroom approach, even in their absence.

The emphasis must be, firstly, on careful assessment of all their difficulties, followed by a willingness to tackle the other disabilities or handicaps, and a readiness to build on each child's strengths.

7   Behaviour Problems associated with other Disabilities

Chapter 10 is largely concerned with the behaviour of severely mentally handicapped children, and gives a full account of the problems that children and their parents face, and of ways in which they can be helped.

The difficult behaviour occurring in some children with visual, auditory, motor, communication or learning disability is dealt with in the appropriate chapters and also in the other paragraphs of this chapter. Emphasis is put upon early identification of impairments, comprehensive assessment of the child's difficulties and treatment/intervention, both with the parents at home and the teacher at school, that is as thorough and effective as possible. When these procedures fail to alleviate or reverse the behaviour, psychological or psychiatric measures may be necessary, as discussed in Chapters 9 and 10.

References

ABERCROMBIE, M. L. J. (1964). *Perceptual and Visuomotor Disorders in Cerebral Palsy.* London: Heinemann Medical Books.

DEPARTMENT OF EDUCATION and SCIENCE (1972). *The Education of the Visually Handicapped.* London: HMSO.

FREEMAN, P. (1975). *Understanding the Deaf/Blind Child.* London: Heinemann Medical Books.

GRIFFITHS, M. I. (1979). 'Associated disorders in children with severe visual handicap' in *Visual Handicap in Children* (pp 76–91), SMITH, V. and KEEN, J. (eds). London: Heinemann Medical Books; Philadelphia: Lippincott.

JAMIESON, M., PARLETT, M. and POCKLINGTON, K. (1977). *Towards Integration. A study of blind and partially sighted children in ordinary schools.* Windsor: NFER.

234 WORKING TOGETHER WITH HANDICAPPED CHILDREN

JONES, M. C. (1983). *Behaviour Problems in Handicapped Children. The Beech Tree House Approach.* London: Souvenir Press.

KIERNAN, C. (1977). 'Towards a curriculum for the profoundly retarded, multiply handicapped child', *Child: care, health and development*, 3, 229–239.

MILLS, A. E. (ed) (1983). *Language Acquisition in the Blind Child – Normal and Deficient.* London: Croom Helm.

MUELLER, H. (1974). 'Speech' in *Handling the Young Cerebral Palsied Child at Home* (pp 131–138), FINNIE, N. R. (ed). London: Heinemann Medical Books.

PRESLAND, J. L. (1982). *Paths to Mobility in Special Care.* Kidderminster: British Institute of Mental Handicap.

RUTTER, M. and YULE, W. (1970). 'Reading retardation and antisocial behaviour – the nature of the association' in *Education, Health and Behaviour* (pp 232–239), RUTTER, M., GRAHAM, P. and YULE, W. (eds). London: Longman.

SYKANDA, A. M. and LEVITT, S. (1982). 'The physiotherapist in the developmental management of the visually impaired child', *Child: care, health and development.* 8, 261–270.

WEDELL, K. (1961). 'Follow-up study of perceptual ability in children with hemiplegia' in *Hemiplegic Cerebral Palsy in Children and Adults.* London: Spastics Society.

WEDELL, K. (1973). *Learning and Perceptuo-motor Disabilities in Children.* London, New York and Sydney: Wiley.

WEDELL, K. (1980). 'Growing points in understanding and assessing perceptuo-motor problems' in *Helping Clumsy Children*, GORDON, N. and McKINLAY, I. (eds). Edinburgh, London and New York: Churchill Livingstone.

YEATES, S. (1980). *The Development of Hearing.* Lancaster: MTP Press.

ZINKIN, P. (1979). 'The effect of visual handicap on early development' in *Visual Handicap in Children* (pp 132–138), SMITH, V. and KEEN, J. (eds). London: Heinemann Medical Books; Philadelphia: Lippincott.

Appendix

1 COMMUNICATION SYSTEMS

Human communication relies largely on spoken or written language, the former often being reinforced through facial expression, gesture and bodily movements. Previous chapters in this book have made it clear that a child's ability to use language for communication may be affected in a number of different ways. In some children, intervention to help the primary disability may lead to the acquisition of intelligible speech; other children, however, with similar disabilities, may need to learn initially to communicate by other means, in order to supplement their inadequate production of spoken or written language.

A number of systems of non-oral communication are presently available, and these need to be used in the best way to suit individual children and individual circumstances. Each system differs considerably from the others in its application to various conditions, although all have the common objective of making it easier for the child to understand language and to use speech wherever possible.

The decision as to which system should be used can be difficult and in this certain criteria need to be observed.

(i)   The professional working with the child, the family and the school must be thoroughly trained in one, or sometimes more, of the systems available.

(ii)   The choice of system must take account of environmental factors as, although the initial involvement from the professional will be with child, parents and possibly the immediate family, eventually communication will be necessary in a much wider context. Schools may need to concentrate on a single system.

Further research and monitoring of the results of all the

systems are needed, and in the United Kingdom a Group has been set up to do this.

Reference

The Co-ordinating Group for Communication Systems (1982). 'Code of research practice – non-speech systems of communication', *Child: care, health and development*, **8**, 51–55.

a) Bliss Symbol Communications System (Blissymbolics)

A system of symbols based on meaning rather than words which needs neither a knowledge of the alphabet, nor adequate hand function. It uses symbols rather than pictures, as by this means a wider range of information (both concrete and abstract) is made available. It can be used by all children who can see the symbols and who can indicate by eyes, finger, hand, pointer or electronic means the one they wish to use. The appropriate word accompanies the symbol and is vocalised by the helper and by the child. The major use is for children who have limited ability in the production of speech and in hand function (eg. children with cerebral palsy), but it also has application for children with other causes of speech and language delay.

References

ARCHER, L. A. (1977). 'Blissymbolics – a non-verbal communication system', *Journal of Speech and Hearing Disorders*, **42**, 568–579.

BAILEY, P. A. and HAMMOND, J. M. (1976). 'An experiment in Blissymbolics', *Special Education: Forward Trends*, **3**, 21–22.

McDONALD, E. T. (1980). *Teaching and using Blissymbolics*. Toronto: Blissymbolics Communication Institute.

OWRAM, L. (1982). *Introducing Blissymbolics – A Guide for Parents and Friends of Symbol Users*. Toronto: Blissymbolics Communication Institute.

SILVERMAN, F. H. (1979) *Communication for the Speechless*. Englewood Cliffs, NJ: Prentice Hall.

VAN DER LEIDEN, GREGG, C. (1978). *Non-vocal Communication Resource Book*. Baltimore: University Park Press.

WARWICK, ANNE. *Blissymbolics for Pre-School Children.* Ottawa: Crippled Children Treatment Centre.

Blissymbolics Communication and Resource Centre, South Glamorgan Institute of Higher Education, Western Avenue, Llandaff, Cardiff CF5 2YB.

b) British Sign Language (BSL)

A communication system for hearing impaired adults and children, based on finger spelling with additional signs involving gestures of the head, body and arms. It must always be used as part of total communication which includes the use of hearing aid, lip-reading and voice. Younger children can learn the larger signs and add the greater detail possible with finger spelling as they grow older; thus the system is of special value to school leavers.

References

CORMAT, P. T. (1971). *Ten Graded Exercises in Manual Communication for Learners.* Published by author, available from Royal National Institute for the Deaf.

JONES, H. and WILLIS, L. (1972). *Talking Hands: an Introduction to Communicating with People who are Deaf.* London: Stanley Paul.

The Royal National Institute for the Deaf, 105, Gower Street, London WC1E 6AH.

This is a strictly British system although it applies to the English Language. The American Sign Language (ASL) differs in some attributes and is described by Freeman *et al* (1981).

Reference

FREEMAN, R. D., CARBIN, C. F. and BOESE, R. J. (1981). *Can't Your Child Hear?* Baltimore: University Park Press; London: Croom Helm.

c) Cued Speech

A manual signing system for hearing impaired adults and children to be used as an adjunct to lip reading and speech in the context of total communication. The listener needs to watch the combination of lip shape with hand shape and position (eight shapes representing consonants and four positions representing vowels). Hearing persons with normal speech use the hand cues for their side of the conversation. This system has the advantage that it cannot be used without speech (the hearing impaired person also uses his hearing aid). Young children can learn it, but it is too difficult for children of below average intelligence.

Reference

CORNETT, O. (1967). 'Cued Speech', *American Annals of the Deaf*, **112**, 3–13.

The National Centre for Cued Speech, London House, 68, Upper Richmond Road, Putney, London SW15 2RP.

d) Makaton

This is a vocabulary of signs which affords a language programme mainly for hearing children (although many of the signs have been selected from the British Sign Language) who are handicapped mentally or physically or have other communication difficulties. Speech is always used with the signs, which are adapted to common usage and presented in grades of increasing complexity so that children and their parents can learn a little at a time. Specialist training is needed for the professional working with the child and those in his environment. Teachers need to keep ahead of the children in their class.

The Makaton Vocabulary Development Project, 31, Firwood Drive, Camberley, Surrey, GU15 3QD.

e) Paget Gorman Signed Speech (PGSS)

This system was introduced originally for hearing impaired children, with the objective of teaching grammatical language. More than any other manual communication system it lays great emphasis on this aspect. However, it can also be used in a simpler version to convey meaning without grammatical accuracy. When suitably adapted, it can therefore be used for communication in children whose language may be expected to be disordered or limited, as in mental handicap, and has proved very helpful to children with combined impairment of vision and hearing (deaf/blind children). As with all other systems, it is always accompanied by speech.

Reference

Rowe, R. (1981). 'Paget Gorman Signed Speech', *Special Education: Forward Trends*, **8**, 25–27.

Paget Gorman Society, 3, Gypsy Lane, Headington, Oxford OX3 7PT.

2 EARLY INTERVENTION PROGRAMMES

Two major principles are maintained in almost every chapter. Firstly, that help should be offered to a family as soon as it seems possible that a child has a developmental problem and, secondly, that the parents and family should be supported from the outset.

There is, however, still a great deal of confusion as to the kind of assistance that is needed, who should deliver it and where it should take place. This will come as no surprise, as the diversity of handicaps that need to be considered has become manifest in the earlier chapters.

However, it seems reasonable to assume that for very small children the home should be the starting point, and to agree that the person delivering the help should be one who has been trained to understand the child's problem and who has the confidence of the parents.

Reader (1984) undertook a review of pre-school intervention programmes. He differentiates between programmes for disadvantaged and for handicapped children, finding that the former have been evaluated more thoroughly than the latter programmes which concern us. It is certainly the case that more and more early intervention programmes are being provided by health and education authorities, very often jointly and in such cases more effectively. Pugh (1981) reports on a number of these, and it will be helpful to refer to three schemes which are mentioned several times in earlier chapters.

References

PUGH, G. (1981). *Parents as Partners.* London: National Children's Bureau.
READER, L. (1984). 'Preschool intervention programmes', *Child: care, health and development*, **10**, 237–251.

a) The Honeylands Project, Exeter

This project depends upon a hospital-based unit, sited separately from the hospital, and dealing only with children. It offers the following facilities:

(i)   a multidisciplinary team for assessment and support;

(ii)   a home visiting service from appropriate professionals (including parents) (Carlyle, 1980);

(iii)   a playgroup which can be used regularly or intermittently;

(iv)   residential short-stay facilities on a regular basis or for emergencies or holidays on request (non-handicapped siblings can also be accommodated).

Green and Evans (1984) have recently reviewed the need and effectiveness of such a service. They found that children over two years of age who needed the facilities outside the home had a variety of problems, ranging from developmental behaviour disturbances, which all settled before the children were of school age, to severely handicapped, heavily dependent or very over-active children who had frequent needs for short-term residential care. This programme therefore supports its home intervention services with both day and residential care, available to but not needed by all. The strength of such a centre lies in the fact that it is able to offer help to the families of children with all kinds of handicap, and it affords a flexibility which cannot be attained in a more limited context.

References

CARLYLE, J. (1980). 'A paediatric home therapy programme for developmental progress in severely handicapped infants', *Child: care, health and development*, **6**, 339–350.
GREEN, J. M. and EVANS, R. K. (1984). 'Honeylands' role in the preschool years. II Patterns of use; III Factors in-

hibiting use', *Child: care, health and development,* **10**, 81–98.

b)   The Portage Project

This home intervention programme, devised in Wisconsin (Shearer and Shearer, 1972) has been adapted for British use (Revill and Blunden, 1980; Cameron, 1982) and its use is spreading in this country. A description of the way in which the programme is administered is given in Chapter 9. The South Glamorgan Home Advisory Service was one of the first to adapt Portage to British use and has been a focus for training both professionals from a wide area and health visitors and parents in its own locality, in home teaching methods (Clements *et al*, 1979). One of its functions has been to evaluate the results, and from their reports insight has been gained into its value. Barna *et al* (1980) found that the monthly rate of developmental gains by children in the programme was greatest in the children whose delay was due to environmental deprivation, was good in children with Down's Syndrome and non-specific developmental delay but was disappointing in children with cerebral palsy and visual handicap. A later survey (Bidder *et al*, 1983) showed that teaching by activity charts or target setting was more effective than by suggestion, but that progress in the group of children whose developmental delay was due to cerebral palsy and visual handicap was significantly slower on all methods. They suggest that, in addition, modelling and practice are important, and these are the methods advocated in Chapters 5 and 6 to help cerebral palsied and visually handicapped children.

References

BARNA, S., BIDDER, R. T., GRAY, O. P., CLEMENTS, J. and GARDNER, S. (1980). 'The progress of developmentally delayed pre-school children in a home training scheme', *Child: care, health and development*, **6**, 157–164.

BIDDER, R., HEWITT, K. E. and GRAY, O. P. (1983). 'Evaluation of teaching methods in a home-based training scheme for developmentally delayed pre-school children', *Child: care, health and development*, **9**, 1–12.

CAMERON, R. J. (ed) (1982). *Working Together. Portage in the U.K.* Windsor: NFER/Nelson.

CLEMENTS, J. C., BIDDER, R. T., GARDNER, S., BRYANT, G. and GRAY, O. P. (1980). 'A home advisory service for pre-school children with developmental delays', *Child: care, health and development*, **6**, 25–33.

REVILL, S. and BLUNDEN, R. (1980). *A Manual for Implementing a Home Training Service for Developmentally Handicapped Preschool Children.* Windsor: NFER/Nelson.

SHEARER, M. S. and SHEARER, D. E. (1972). 'The Portage Project: a model for early childhood education', *Exceptional Children*, **36**, 210–217.

c) Health Visitor Home Visiting Project (Hester Adrian Research Centre, Manchester)

The Hester Adrian Research Centre at Manchester University has for some years been interested in the provision and study of schemes for parental involvement in helping their children (Cunningham, 1975; Cunningham and Jeffree, 1975). One of their projects has been the setting up of Health Visitor Home Visiting for Down's Syndrome children (Pugh, 1981). In the field of developmental delay, Down's children stand out as those children who can be diagnosed at birth, whose parents urgently need support at that time, and for whom home intervention can be planned at the earliest possible moment. As a result of their experiences in helping Down's Syndrome children, Cunningham and Sloper (1978) have been able to publish a detailed description of how parents can help Down's Syndrome children and other mentally handicapped children as soon as they are recognised.

References

CUNNINGHAM, C. (1975). 'Parents as therapists and educators' in *Behaviour Modification with the Severely Retarded, Study Group 8* (pp 175–193), KIERNAN, C. and WOODWARD, F. (eds). Amsterdam: Associated Scientific Publishers.

CUNNINGHAM, C and JEFFREE, D. M. (1975). 'The organisation and structure of workshops for parents of mentally handicapped children', *Bulletin of the British Psychological Society*, **28**, 405–411.

CUNNINGHAM, C. and SLOPER, P. (1978). *Helping Your Handicapped Baby.* London: Souvenir Press.

PUGH, G. (ed) (1981). *Parents as Partners*, pp 64–69. London: National Children's Bureau.

Summary

These three successful pre-school intervention programmes illustrate various facets of services which may be provided by professional and/or statutory organisations. It is impossible to enumerate many of the voluntary schemes which spring up in various parts of the country in response to local needs, sometimes backed by national voluntary societies. The ideal service to families would seem to be a flexible combination of all that may be available, based upon a local Centre. This might be a Health Authority Child Development Centre, an Education Authority Family Centre or a Voluntary Opportunity Group from which health, education, social and voluntary services all contribute their expertise as appropriate to individual children and families.

3 NATIONAL ORGANISATIONS CONCERNED WITH HANDICAP

Association for all Speech Impaired Children, 347 Central Market, Smithfield, London EC1A 0NH. Tel. 01 236 3632/6487.

Association for Brain Damaged Children, Clifton House, 3 St Pauls Road, Foleshill, Coventry CV6 5DE. Tel. 0203 665450.

Association for Spina Bifida and Hydrocephalus, 22 Upper Woburn Place, London WC1U 0EP. Tel. 01 388 1382.

Association of Paediatric Chartered Physiotherapists, c/o Chartered Society of Physiotherapy, 14 Bedford Row, London WC1R 4ED. Tel. 01 242 1941.

Association of Crossroad Care Attendant Schemes, 94 Coton Road, Rugby, Warwickshire CV21 4LN.

Association of Parents of Vaccine-Damaged Children, 2 Church Street, Shipston-on-Stour, Warwicks, CV36 4AP. Tel. 0608 61595.

Association to Combat Huntingdon's Chorea, Borough House, 34a Station Rd, Hinckley, Leics. Tel 0455 615558.

British Diabetic Association, 10 Queen Ann Street, London W1M 0BD. Tel. 01 323 1531.

British Dyslexia Association, Church Lane, Peppard, Oxfordshire RG9 5JN. Tel. 049 17 699.

British Epilepsy Association, Crowthorne House, New Wokingham Road, Crowthorne, Berks. Tel. 0344 77 3122.

British Sports Association for the Disabled, Stoke Mandeville Sports Stadium, Harvey Road, Aylesbury, Bucks HP21 8PP. Tel 0296 84848.

Brittle Bone Society, 112 City Road, Dundee DD2 2PW. Tel. 0382 67603.

Centre for Studies on Integration in Education, 16 Fitzroy Square, London W1. Tel. 01 387 9571.

Chest and Heart Association, Tavistock House North, Tavistock Square, London WC1 9JE. Tel. 01 387 3012.

College of Speech Therapists, Harold Poster House, 6 Lechmere Road, London NW2. Tel. 01 459 8521.

Cystic Fibrosis Research Trust, 5 Blyth Road, Bromley, Kent BR1 3RS. Tel. 01 464 7211.

DHSS (Department of Health and Social Security), Alexander Fleming House, Elephant & Castle, London SE1 6BY. Tel. 01 407 5522.

Dial U.K. HQ: Victoria Buildings, 117 High Street, Clay Cross, Derbyshire. Tel. 0246 864498. *(Nationwide telephone information and advice services.)*

Disability Alliance, 25 Denmark Street, London WC2. Tel. 01 240 0806. (*Publish Disability Rights Handbook*.)

Disabled Living Foundation, 380 Harrow Road, London W9 2HU. Tel. 01 289 6111.

Downs Childrens Association, 4 Oxford Street, London W1N 9FL. Tel. 01 580 0511/2.

Family Fund, P.O. Box 50, York YO1 1UY. Tel: 0904 21115.

Friedrich's Ataxia Group, Burleigh Lodge, Knowle Lane, Cranleigh, Surrey. Tel. 0483 272741.

Haemophilia Society, 16 Trinity Street, London SE1 1DE. Tel. 01 407 1010.

Handicapped Adventure Playground Association, Fulham Palace, Bishops Avenue, London SW6 6EA. Tel. 01 731 2753.

Hyperactive Children's Support Group, 59 Meadowside, Angmering, Littlehampton, West Sussex.

Invalid Children's Aid Association, 126 Buckingham Palace Rd, London SW1. Tel. 01 730 9891.

Lady Hoare Trust for Physically Disabled Children, 7 North Street, Midhurst, W. Sussex. Tel. 073 081 3696.

Leukaemia Society, 45 Craigmoor Avenue, Queen's Park, Bournemouth. Tel. 0202 37459.

Mobility Allowance Unit, DHSS, Norcross, Blackpool, Lancs.

Motability, The Adelphi, John Adam Street, London WC2N 6AZ. Tel. 01 839 5191.

Multiple Sclerosis Society, 25 Effie Road, London SW6 1EE. Tel. 01 381 4022.

Muscular Dystrophy Group of Great Britain, Nattrass House, 35 Macaulay Road, London SW4 0QP. Tel. 01 720 8055.

National Association for Deaf/Blind and Rubella Handicapped, 311 Grays Inn Rd, London WC1X 8PT. Tel. 01 278 1000.

National Association for the Education of the Partially Sighted, East Anglian School, Church Road, Gorleston-on-Sea, Great Yarmouth. Tel. 0493 62399.

National Association for the Welfare of Children in Hospital, Argyle House, 29–31 Euston Road, London NW1 2SD. Tel. 01 833 2041.

National Autistic Society, 276 Willesden Lane, London NW2 5RB. Tel. 01 451 3844.

National Bureau for Handicapped Students, 40 Brunswick Square, London WC1N 1AZ. Tel. 01 278 3459.

National Council for Special Education, 1 Wood St, Stratford on Avon, Warwicks CV37 6JE. Tel. 0789 20 5332.

National Deaf Children's Society, 45 Hereford Road, London W2. Tel 01 229 9272.

National Eczema Society, Mary Ward House, 5–7 Tavistock Place, London WC1. Tel. 01 388 4097.

National Physically Handicapped and Able Bodied, Tavistock House North, Tavistock Square, London WC1H 9HJ. Tel. 01 388 1963.

National Portage and Home Teaching Association, R. J. Cameron, Winchester Portage Service, Silver Hill, Winchester SO23 8AF. (*Work with parents of young handicapped children.*)

National Society of Phenylketonuria and Allied Disorders, 26 Towngate Grove, Mirfield, West Yorkshire. Tel. 0924 492873.

Network, Bedford House, 35 Emerald Street, London WC1. Tel. 01 504 3001. (Advice Service).

Play Matters/Toy Libraries Association, Seabrook House, Wyllyotts Manor, Darkes Lane, Potters Bar, Herts EN6 2HL. Tel 0707 44571.

Pre-School Playgroups Association, Alford House, Aveline Street, London SE11 5DJ. Tel. 01 582 8871.

Royal Association for Disability and Rehabilitation (RADAR), 23–25 Mortimer Street, London W1N 8AB. Tel. 01 637 5400.

Royal National Institute for the Blind, 224 Great Portland Street, London W1N 6AV. Tel. 01 388 1266.

Royal National Institute for the Deaf, 105 Gower Street, London WC1E 6AH. Tel. 01 387 8033.

Royal Society for Mentally Handicapped Children and Adults (MENCAP), 117–123 Golden Lane, London EC1Y 0RF. Tel. 01 253 9433.

Scottish Information Services for the Disabled, Claremont House, 18/19 Claremont Crescent, Edinburgh EH7 4QD. Tel. 031 556 3882.

Scottish Society for the Mentally Handicapped, 13 Elmbank Street, Glasgow G2 4PB. Tel. 041 226 4541.

Spastics Society, 12 Park Crescent, London W1N 4EQ. Tel. 01 636 5020.

Spinal Injuries Association, Yeoman House, 76 St James Lane, London N10 3DF. Tel. 01 444 2121.

Index